FOOTPRINTS HEAVENWARD:

OR,

UNIVERSALISM

THE MORE EXCELLENT WAY.

BY REV. M. J. STEERE.

"I have for a long time been thinking that a few years only will suffice to sweep away the popular theology upon that subject [endless punishment],—that all our common schools are but so many volcanoes underneath it,—that it must be abandoned, or we must go back to the age of unthinking barbarism." — LEBBEUS BROOKS.

"The thinking portion of the church are the doubting portion, in refer ence to endless punishment." — IBID.

BOSTON:
PUBLISHED BY JAMES M. USHER,
37 Cornhill,
1861.

INTRODUCTION.

Practical Questions — Object of this Volume and Origin of it — Love, the way to Heaven — That way obstructed — Church must clear it — Church's slow progress, and when it will be swifter — Demand of Christian Civilization — Tides of Popularity changing — Conservatives alarmed — Discussion Discouraged — Proofs demanded — Discussion will come and is safe.

What is the condition of the dead? With what emotions should they be contemplated? With what feelings should we go to join them? These are eminently practical questions, in which interest is every day becoming more intense. And this, not simply in view of the fresh graves of yesterday, but of all the desolations of mortality which have made the earth one vast grave-yard, in which human dust is disturbed by every furrow of the plow!

The ancient question, "If a man die shall he live," is put beyond Christian controversy by that Scripture which saith, "There shall be a resurrection both of the just and the unjust." But what of this certified resurrection life?

Is it a blessing, or a curse? The view has long prevailed that it is a blessing to *some* and a curse to others. The view is now prevailing that it is a blessing to *all.* And it is to awaken attention to the relative value of these views, that this volume is published.

It is the outgrowth of an experience somewhat peculiar, and may therefore at least add to the variety of Christian literature. The material of which it is composed had been for some time accumulating as the result of private meditations along the way of religious enquiry. Such as it is, it is committed in humble trust to the wise providence of Him who smiles upon every effort to clear Love's way to his Throne.

And to that throne Love is the only way,—that Love, of which, obedience is the outflow. Hence Jesus makes all the Law and the prophets hang upon Love, while his chief apostle urges that all the obedience that lacks Love, "profiteth nothing."

But Love is neither blind nor coercible. And because it must act in reference to the quality of its object, none should grumble at its seeming obstinacy. To ask Love for what seems unlovable, is to ask a simple impossibility; and this, equally, whether the object be earthy or heavenly, a creature or the creator. Well, therefore, did an English statesman both, the way to God is obstructed, only in different degrees. And, therefore, in preparing "the way of the Lord," the Church has yet much to do, even in her own sanctuary. Not till musty accumulations of traditionary rubbish have been removed from its threshold, shall her Lord so enter it that she shall see his full glory and cry out as never before, "*My Lord and my God!*" For not till then shall Love's way to Heaven be *clear* before her face.

The progress of the Church towards her prophetic goal has, for a long time, been so discouragingly slow, that a miraculous breaking in of the Lord God, has been anticipated, to send it forward.* But in view of the much by which her course has been retarded, I see not how it could have been more rapid. Nor so long as these obstructions remain, do I see how her progress can be accelerated. But only let the degrading eclipse of tradition pass away from the Bible and its light blaze forth, pure from the Father, and then shall the every day progress of the Church sufficiently forestall her glorious consummation. Nor shall good men then be tempted to rest in their redemptive work, waiting for Jehovah to come and do it all up at once and suddenly.

It is useless for Theology to ignore Christian civilization. For, think as men will, talk as men may, that civilization has

* Concord of Ages, p. 5, etc.

say, "If you would have me love my country, give me a country that is lovable."

As then, Love is the way to heaven, that way must be seriously obstructed by any seeming imperfections in its heavenly object. Nor is it pleasing to him who ordained the law of Love, that we should attempt to disregard such imperfections. For he knows that for us to do so, were to vitiate the fountain of our own affections, and become less "worthy to be called his children." So true is it, that whatever clouds the divine character, darkens the human pathway! So true is it, that the character of the creature is more or less elevated and depressed with the elevation and depression of the character of the God he adores! And hence, so *sad* is it for the soul to contemplate a Deity who fails to meet its ideal of moral excellence! — all of which is illustrated by the Spanish inquisition, as an outgrowth of Spanish theology, and by the flames in which Servetus perished, as an outgrowth of *old* Calvinism.

And thus it appears that the way to God and heaven, not only may be, but *is* obstructed. Nor this alone where the Pagan cloud hangs, but also where the Christian sun shines. So that, if the heathen sit where the "*true light*" reaches them scarcely at all, the Christian is often found where it reaches him, only as "the Sun through mist." To now reached a point where it cannot *rest* in a Divine Father who plunges his tender offspring from the very threshold of their existence into endless woe. Permeated by the spirit of the Gospel from which it sprang, that civilization now asks and *will* ask, for a God to whom it can commit its dead for *keeping*, rather than for *tormenting*—for a God in whose image man is made! In the contemplation of any other God, it sees Heaven's way seriously blocked up, and, in attempting to pursue it, may well cry out, "all is dark! dark! dark! and I cannot disguise it." *

Deeply and sadly impressed with considerations like the above, the Author throws the following letters before the public, satisfied, if the principles they advocate shall prove as valuable to the reader as they have to the writer.

The doctrine of endless punishment has been popular from the middle ages downward;—so popular that the people have in time past consented to have their attention to whatever opposed it, put under complete interdict. But not so now. Buttressed by reason and Revelation, an opposing doctrine is risen up "like a strong man to run a race," and the people *will* think about it. That doctrine is Universalism; and, conquering a reluctant respect, its spirit is spreading in every direction. Indeed, the people are coming to

* p. 77.

like it. And hence, in part, the unparalleled popularity of the Ward Beechers and the Chapins. And hence, the many chaplains of liberal faith, now called to solace with love ministries the battle fields, on which lies staked beneath the eye of Heaven, all that is dear to an American citizen. And hence, too,——but the following letters will tell the rest.

And what is the result? Why, conservatives are of course alarmed.* They would stay the evil they deplore. And *how*, but by suppressing discussion? Not, indeed, by suppressing *ex parte* discussion, or, perhaps, even set public discussion; but that varied, private discussion, which admits the possibility of popular error, and implies a general reading, thinking, inquiring, conversing, arguing among the people. Hence many a good pastor will treat his flock to a sermon on Universalism, and then be greatly alarmed to learn that a work of Balfour, Ballou, Whittemore, Guild, Cobb, Rogers or Thayer, is circulating freely among them. So dangerous do many still deem a Bible let loose! So is the right of private discussion, by not a few, still regarded much as the right of "private judgment" was in old papal times.

But discussion of the faith advocated in this volume is necessary, and must prevail. Such is the verdict of awaking Christian thought. Already are the tables turning, and

* p. 263.

hereafter shall "orthodoxy" be holden strictly responsible, for its every dreadful assertion and implication concerning the dead; — and this, equally, whether stumbling among the bones of old battle-fields, meditating in grave-yards, or standing up in funerals. The people are discovering that the question of human destiny has two sides, and would hear both. Let them hear them. For though the discussion be all the more vehement for having been so long repressed; yet, if conducted fairly, it can hurt neither the "oil nor the wine." And it is in this calm faith that the author commits his book to the public, praying that it may serve the cause of "our Lord and Saviour Jesus Christ."

M. J. S.

HAVERHILL, MASS., AUG. 20, 1861.

P. S. The note at the bottom of page 21, has reference only to the first part of the letter. Bro. T. was an able and useful man, "full of the Holy Ghost," known only to be loved, moving only to be felt, and dying only to ascend to the Father. His friendship was liberal, loving, lasting!

The illustration on pages 174-5, is the substance of one I remember to have read in a work entitled "*Pro and Con*,"—an excellent work, which I am happy to recommend, but have not at hand. A note to this effect was appended to the text, but failed to appear there.

This work, swelling far beyond the author's expectation, the Appendix, originally designed, is omitted, with other prepared matter which must "*bide its time.*"

CONTENTS.

FIRST SERIES.

LETTER I—Love and Union.......................... 15
" II—Honesty and Agitation.......................... 21
" III—Abuse of Creeds.......................... 32
" IV—Change of Opinion *vs.* Persistence in....... 40
" V—Universalism Misunderstood................ 48
" VI—Error, Jewish and Christian.............. 54
" VII—Is Your Faith Satisfactory................ 59
" VIII—Great Minds in Trouble—Barnes........... 71
" IX—Great Minds in Trouble—Edward Beecher. 84
" X—Great Minds in Trouble—C. F. Hudson..... 90
" XI—Safety.......................... 97
" XII—Universalism Practically Defined..........108
" XIII—Destiny—When Absurdities Alarming.......124
" XIV—First Absurdity—Man Created for Endless Misery..........129
" XV—Second Absurdity—The Devil 136
" XVI—Third Absurdity—Infants Saved, Adults Lost..........142
" XVII—Fourth Absurdity—Child of "Five Points"..156
" XVIII—Fifth Absurdity—Men Fix Each Others' Doom..........169

LETTER XIX—Sixth Absurdity—Endless Revenge..........178

" XX—Seventh Absurdity—The People and the Preacher..........186

" XXI—Eighth Absurdity—Heathen Lost..........197

" XXII—Obliviousness to Consequences..........210

" XXIII—A Point Between Two Moments..........221

" XXIV—The Difference Between Mens' Hearts.....230

" XXV—The Argument from Temporal Suffering....240

" XXVI—The Three Standpoints—Bigotry, Conservatism and Progress..........251

SECOND SERIES.

LETTER I—The Bible and its Meaning..........273

" II—Pentateuch *vs.* Endless Punishment..........279

" III—Joshua—Psalms..........292

" IV—Proverbs—Malachi..........301

" V—New Testament Examined..........317

" VI—Orthodoxy Approaching Universalism......377

" VII—Reaction..........398

LETTERS.

LETTER I.

LOVE AND UNION.

Variety in Unity needed in the Church—Cudworth—Love the basis of Union—Dwellers in God and in Ism—Union Sectional—Diversity seeks Unity—Centripetal thought-currents—Men wonder at one another, but no matter if they dwell in Love—Going inside—No Pandora's Box to be feared—Where harm is—The two Shipmasters—Unmoor thy craft.

DEAR BROTHER,—

When we joyously tread the cool forest in the heat of summer, how interesting the thought, that no conceivable search among its countless leaves, were adequate to the discovery of two, exactly alike. Yet, is their unity of aspect unbroken, while they seem sweetly to enjoy the common breeze of heaven, and harmoniously to murmur their Maker's praise together. So wonderful and beneficent is the law of variety in the natural world. Why should it be less so in the moral? And why then should it be remarkable that you and I differ in opinion, seeing that we come within its ample sweep. Certainly our difference will be the less regretted, provided we put on fervent charity, practically to illustrate, in the moral world also, this beneficent law of variety in unity; — a thing which is more needed in the present age, than all the sharp "*points*," on which so many souls hang impaled!

> "In faith and hope the world will disagree,
> But all mankind's concern is charity."

"To see brethren dwell together in unity," is always "good and pleasant." But at no other time *so* good and *so* pleasant, as when it exists in spite of wide disparities of belief. Then is religion decked in her best robe, exalted above all that is earthly, and set off against a back ground of heavenly sky. And hence, though we do not thank God that we differ, I think we may thank him that our differences may be turned to so good an account; that they afford us opportunity to illustrate the supremacy of Love. And as Cudworth said before the British House of Commons, "let us express this sweet harmonious affection in these jarring times; that so, if possible, we may tune the world into better music. Especially in matters of religion let us strive with all meekness to instruct and convince one another. Let us endeavor to promote the gospel of peace, the dove-like gospel, with the dove-like spirit." And how do these words of the old prelate come down to us, bearing still the charm of his heart; as if the words of love, like love itself, were imperishable. Love is, indeed, "the sweet harmony of souls." Its fervent words are precious, and he who drops them upon the currents of the world, is its benefactor. So also is he who takes them up and hands them down to posterity. Love is the essence of the universe. "God is Love; and he that dwelleth in Love, dwelleth in God and God in him." Those therefore who "dwell in God," must, as they dwell in love, dwell harmoniously together. In spite of all, there *must* be union between them; and because union, communion.

Not so, those who dwell in *ism* merely. With them union is sectional. They know no spirit more Catholic than that which makes fellowship between men of the same faith. And this is the calamity of the ages. Its spirit finds various development; then, in whips, chains, and faggots; now, in reproach, shame and casting "out of the synagogue." Happy will it be, when all the members of the church, whatever their favorite *isms*, shall no longer dwell in them, but only in God; then, and not till then, will she present the pleasing and sublime spectacle of "brethren dwelling together in unity."

But it is true, after all, that in theology diversity seeks unity. Though the Christian world, in days of ignorance so stumble along its mazy ways, as to provoke the smile or taunt of skepticism and infidelity, still let no one despair; for there is a divine spirit brooding upon the chaos of conflicting opinions, and a law of tendency pervading it, which shall at length reduce it to order. In the moral world, all things are, upon the whole, centripetal to a perfect truth, and shall at length reach it; all men, though after many irregular wanderings, shall, at length, find the clue to the concentric labyrinth in which it is hidden. Towards that truth, the great currents of human thought are ever tending. Like a river seeking the sea, they may have many windings among mountains, and eddyings among rocks; like Israel in the desert, they may move very circuitously. But their general course is the same; and he who boldly commits himself to them, though sometime strangely carried backwards, and furiously dashed about, shall at length reach the haven of quiet, — the central rest of truth — loving spirits. And, thence arrived, I think, brother, that even we shall agree at last. And what if we shall then find that our present conflicts of opinion, incidental to the infancy of our being, were, under the great Providence, but the excitements of mind necessary to our Christian growth!

"I am a wonder unto many." So exclaimed the Psalmist. But in that, he was hardly peculiar. For who is there much known, or having much character, that is not wondered at by more or less of his neighbors,— not to say by "strangers and foreigners,"— for what they deem his singularities? Where can you find two persons so alike, that the one is not, in some respects, a wonder to the other, that there is not a mutual wondering between them? So it is between you and me. You wonder that I am a Universalist, and I wonder that you are not one, even as I wonder that I was not one earlier. But no matter, so long as we dwell in love. For as we have seen they who dwell in love dwell in God, and are united by a spiritual bond which no wonderment can sever. But my heart grows warm, and I fear I am detaining you too long upon the threshold. Let us go inside; nor fear to lift curtains, open doors, and pull drawers.

We are not heathen, treading the enchanted grounds of mythology, that we should fear a Pandora's Box; but we are Christians, treading the terra firma of theology, where no hidden mystery can be dangerous to the discoverer. Harm, never in the way of sincere truth-seekers, delights to infest the mouldy seats and musty lounges of those, who, too indolent or too timid to advance, try to content themselves with their present attainment, or even with their hereditary theological possession. These two classes of persons are like two ship-masters; the one of whom, through dread of labor or fear of storms, or lack of hope, never weighs anchor, or unfurls a sail, till his good ship rots away in the haven upon which she was launched, and in sight of the blocks upon which she was constructed; while the other, no sooner finds his ship afloat, than his canvas is spread and he is "far, far, at sea," navigating all waters, and freighting himself for his home-bound voyage, with the various riches of every clime. And "which of the twain does the will of his Master?" "Which of two thinkest thou" the benefactor of his race? The latter? Then unmoor thy craft, weigh anchor from the haven of thy peculiar Westminster, and do likewise. So shalt thou also do the will of God, and be a benefactor of men.

Yours truly.

LETTER II.

HONESTY AND AGITATION.

Kind words acknowledged,—No compromise with duty,—Rebellious plea,—To "Worms,"—Old friendships remembered, and to be renewed.—" Honesty the best policy,"—Honesty of Paul,—Pulpit temptation,—Godliness and Honesty,—Truth and Search,—Why the Author a wonder,—More Character, more Danger,—Jesus the wonder, — Paul,— Reformers,— The Church stagnant,— Daring heretics,—Uses of agitation,—Agitation often unwelcome,—Not to be feared,—Tempestous round about Jehovah,—Why the author is sad.

DEAR BROTHER,—

I thank you for your very kind allusion to my past labors and associations.* They affect me tenderly, I appreciate the catholic charity which they breathe. It is, to my soul, like a soft gale from Paradise. It blesses me with emotion. For *I*, too, have not forgotten the past; and deeply do I sympathize with you in your regrets that we cannot still be united in our labors. Nay more. For it seems to me, that your regrets in this matter, cannot be deep like mine. I have not sought my own pleasure, but

* This letter was originally written in reference to remarks of an excellent minister now in heaven—Rev. E. M. Tappan. See also appendix B.

consented to the disruption of my long cherished denominational ties, only when the sternest necessity laid its hand on my conscience. And what else could I then do? Would you have had me compromise my honesty? Had I not in my covenant vows, sworn faithfulness to the God of truth?—promised to "follow the Lamb whithersoever he goeth?"—and all this at whatever expense of sacrifice and self denial? What then could I do when I found myself in error, but abandon it?—when I discovered a new truth, but embrace it? Would you have had me done otherwise?—and that, under the plea of my old friends and associations,—the greatness of the sacrifice required? Vain plea! A pious fraud upon the truth! The spawn of a secret infidelity! Rebellious plea against God, such as ever returns to curse the inventor! My heart would have rebuked it, and one thought of Christ crucified, silenced it! I could not have put it in! You would not have had me; for I am persuaded that you, too, have found "that it is neither safe nor expedient to act against conscience;"—that truth, with its consequences, though it carry us to "*Worms*," is better than error with *its* consequences, though it seemingly carry us to the skies. At any rate, we must take it, consequences and all· So did the Master and so must his disciple, as the primary condition of discipleship. No matter though it sadden and practically alienate a multitude of friends,—friends with whom he had lived and labored long, on terms of the sweetest Christian amity, and with whom it were the strong desire of his heart to live and labor till death. All these tender considerations must go for nothing, when weighed against duty. Though backed by all these, and more, what is the creature that he should "reply against God!"

You see, brother, what was my dilemma. Would you have chosen the other horn of it,—the earthy one? I am persuaded not. For we have both heard the Master say, "he that loveth father or mother more than me is not worthy of me; and he that taketh not up his cross daily and followeth after me is not worthy of me." We both regard conscience as the gray lock of the human soul,—God's monitor in the human breast. To us both, therefore, the only true discretion lies in submission to Heaven!

The old friendships of which you speak—ah, I remember them well.—they are my treasures still! Not one of them is renounced. Not a heart that throbbed in them, unloved. Those friendships are not dead, but only visibly suspended. Their light is not quenched, but only eclipsed;—and that, but temporarily,—at longest, only till our "dust shall return to the earth as it was." And so long we can afford to wait, confident that then it shall be relumed, to be dimmed or eclipsed no more, forever. And then, we think there will be no more wondering that either man or angel should believe in the universal and inalienable Fatherhood of God, and brotherhood of his offspring. Then, in the retrospect from eternity, how will man's earthly state seem well expressed by the line,

> "His time, a moment, and a point his space."

How trifling will then seem the trials which we now suffer to annoy us,—and then, how will the soul better understand its God, not only as the "I AM," but as the "ALL IN ALL!"

For the present, however, we must be content for a season to differ. We are yet in this earthy world, where objects, seen from its various stand-points, through the dim windows of the flesh, affect us variously. As we have said, however, we need not despair, for the great law of unity is working. Already we agree in many things; and among the rest that "honesty is the best policy."

> "Honesty, even by itself, though making many adversaries,
> Whom prudence might have set aside, or charity have softened,
> Evermore will prosper at the last, and bring a man great honor."

But this "best policy" is not always easily followed. So the tradesman sometimes finds it. So the theologian. And so also the preacher. The word of God, like dollars, may be handled deceitfully. It was so handled in Paul's time, but not by Paul. "For "says he," we are not as many, which corrupt the word of God; but as of sincerity, but as of God, in the sight of God, speak we in Christ." And again he says, we "have renounced the hidden things of dishonesty, not walking in craftiness, nor handling the word of God deceitfully." Satan delights to assault the pulpit. And if, in this age, it is freer from dishonesty than the mart, it is not because it is less open to temptation. In the pulpit as elsewhere, no man is honest without an effort all engrossing; while, even in spite of such effort, the soul will sometimes consciously tremble towards some uncertain issue. So mighty is the spirit of "eye service," to control those who are, like clergymen, dependant both for themselves and families, upon the continued smiles of their neighbors; and who are placed, like them, in circumstances calculated to inflame their ambition.

But though strict honesty, is ever the creature of much watchfulness and effort, yet is its path the only safe one. I am sure, you would not have a friend swerve from it, even to shun the brand of heresy. Too well do you know that honesty,

"Evermore will prosper at the last."

Too well do you appreciate that old apostlic

couplet, "godliness and honesty," one and inseparable; its members, each, necessarily, involving the other; the two, constituting a twin light, the elements of which no prismatic theology can separate; each vital to man's spiritual life; — each "profitable to all things;" so that error holden in righteousness, is better than "truth" holden "in unrighteousness." For it is not for man's possession of the truth, but for his love of it, that Heaven gives him credit; — so that the search without the truth, is often better than the truth without the search; — a little truth, searched out, better for the substance of the soul, than much truth received by inheritance. And this, I think, is a consideration, which should make you less sad about your old friend, however gross the error, into which you deem him to have fallen.

But I presume that the more sincere you regard me, the more you wonder at me. Had my avowal of Universalism been preceded by an *evident* "fall from grace," all would have been as natural, as an election sermon said it was, that "when Satan entered paradise, damnation should follow."

Moreover, such credit do I give you for broad benevolence, that, as it were to you less wonderful, so, I think, it were to you less sad, had what you deem my fall into error, been preceded by such a fall from grace. For then you could have found solace in saying, "the disguise of his hypocricy is so thin that he can impose upon nobody. He lacks character to do much mischief. And though it is sad to think that he is going down to endless pain, sadder, indeed, it were, had he a weight of reputation by which to sink others down with him; or by which others should *be* carried down, while he, under cover of ignorance, or something else, should, "so as by fire, escape into heaven." And in this, you would be consistent with yourself. It is right to wish that influence weak, which seems only bad; but we must be careful not to mistake the quality of influence, as the Pharisees mistook that of the Son of God. Things may be strange and yet true.

The most singular and wonderful fact in history, is the mission of the Son of God to earth. No other ever so disturbed and agitated the religious world. The disciples heard indeed, strange things that day when he who was, emphatically, the "Prince of Peace," said unto them, "suppose ye that I am come to give peace on earth, I tell you nay; but rather division." Wonderful paradox! But then Jesus was "*the wonderful.*" And while I would not disparage great Christian reformers, by mentioning my name in their neighborhood, I may say that they have ever been rare characters, standing oddly out from their generation, at whom the *established* religion of their age has wondered,— strange persons, upon whom good men of the church have looked down with sadness, and over whose heresy, many a tear has been piously shed. But the world has moved on, and their honesty has prospered at the last. Haman is hanged, and Mordecai brought to honor!

Why, brother, the world goes very much by wonders. Every now and then, as you well know, the church stagnates under the bondage of stereotyped creeds; and as it stagnates, so it corrupts. Its turbid waters lying heavily, breed infectious disease. So it was in Luther's time. So in Wesley's. And so on a larger or smaller scale has it been, at intervals, ever since the Christian era. And who is it, that, from time to time, has been the honored instrument of breaking up this stagnation and consequent corruption? Who but some daring spirit, that, regardless of every thing but his own deep convictions, has startled the church by dashing some rock of heresy into the sea of apathy, in which its religious life has lain, water-logged! Who but some "thinker let loose,"— some independent questioner of the religion he was reared in?

Look at the outward world. There all things are purified and conserved by wonderful agitation. The winds have a mission, so have the tides. And even the sweep of the hurricane, and the tread of the earthquake, are in fulfilment of a merciful purpose! Thus it is in the world of matter. Shall it be otherwise in the world of mind? I tell you, nay. For there, also, agitation goes before purification. The gospel is but the essence of agitation. Its Author must be crucified before glorified. And Saul must feel himself as in a shower of earthquakes mingled with fire, before he will question his hereditary religion or withdraw his persecuting hand! And so it ever *is*, that some wonderful agitation is made the harbinger of some wonderful good.

We have spoken of apathy. Of all apathy, theological apathy seems most profound. So it was found in Jesus' time. Nothing could stir it up, short of electric currents, sent through it, direct from the throne of God. And so it often is. And so it would ever be, but for the agitation of which the timid stand in awe. Let him who will, tie up the winds, fetter the tides, and then sit down to welcome the consequent death. But let no man lay an interdict upon the winds of thought or the tides of mind. "For these things have an end,"—a glorious end. Nor are cross winds and whirlwinds, and tidal inundations, exceptions. All are necessary, and all, therefore, should be welcome; though they overturn old temples, shatter old altars and scatter the fondest sectarian hopes as the chaff of the summer threshing floor. Yet are they often unwelcome, and never more so than to a sectarian age. Nor can they be very welcome to this. For this age, though not a little liberalized, is still sufficiently pharisaical to deprecate the innovation of awakening religious thought.

You will perceive, that I am here merely illustrating a principle; — a principle equally involved in the ordinary and extraordinary cases of theological agitation; from the earthquake of the Reformation, all the way down to the slight tremor which may, possibly, to some mind, result from these unpretending letters; — a principle, which, I pray you always to bear in mind, nor fear that truth and religion can suffer under the agitation of free enquiry. Let us leave that fear to the Romanist. For truth always feels humiliated, when its holders are afraid to have it freely grapple with error. It dreads agitation no more than Lebanon dreads the mountain tempest which expurgates its shaggy top of withered foliage and dead limbs. Jehovah's moral pathway is ever marked by agitation — revolution. When he moves, it is often "tempestuous round about him," but never destructive of good. Though the sea "roar and be troubled," Jehovah is there to assure the hearts of his children, with his, "Fear not for I am with thee, be not dismayed, for I am thy God."

Enough on this subject; perhaps you will say too

much. But when I see the many who hold the truth, (as they suppose) as if they thought contact with error would smash it, I am sad. For I say, either they doubt whether they have the truth, or else, confident of having it, they have no faith in it. If the former is the case, they ought to court discussion—agitation. If the latter, they surely need not shun it. For the agitation of free discussion is, to the truth, what fire is to gold, or the polishing wheel to steel. Otherwise the gospel, that great fountain of deepest agitation, though planned in heaven, were an ill-devised expedient for saving the world.

Yours truly.

LETTER III.

ABUSE OF CREEDS.

Creeds should be shed when outgrown—When dangerous—Farcical confession of—Good for life—Cause of "dead orthodoxy"—Why worn patiently—An accidental property—Resisted at peril—Persecution not outward—Fear to examine—Are you afraid?—Self-conviction.

DEAR BROTHER,—

In my last letter, I incidentally spoke of the bondage of creeds. Against creeds, however, we have nothing to say, provided the church will shed them as fast as she outgrows them. They have their legitimate uses. It is their misuse that is mischievous. Tradition was well enough in the Jewish church, till it began to "make the commandments of God of none effect." So are creeds well enough in the Christian church, till they begin to trench upon the Scriptures, assume their authority, and fetter free enquiry. But when this occurs, as you know it often does, then are they to be deprecated as a tyranny. Then their imposition upon the young mind, as it crosses the threshold of the church, is an *imposition indeed;*—the Chinese shoe, applied to the immortal mind. How many poor souls are wearing it to day, God only knows!

Creeds, written or unwritten, are, perhaps, well enough, till their blind devotees become afraid of them, or of the power that is entrenched behind them; that is, till they clothe them with an awful sacredness with which they dread to meddle, or till they see, behind them, an ecclesiastical power which they dare not offend. But when this is the case, and when they become mental labor-saving machines, superseding the necessity of old plodding methods of reaching truth,—when men reason by saying, not, "For thus it is written in the prophets," but thus it is written in the *creed;* not, "thus saith the Lord," but thus saith the *church*, then are creeds of the very essence of evil,—dumb idols, fit only for the iconoclast.

And this truth is not without its application. For what multitudes of even Protestant Christians of to day, test their theology by their creed, whether written or oral, rather than their creed by the Scriptures. Witness the farce of children and young people, and even ignorant old people, confessing a system of faith at the baptismal fount. Have these persons thoroughly examined the Scriptures, that they should know all about "trinity" and "unity," "perseverance" and "depravity," "heaven" and "hell,"—doctrines about which profound theologians have stumbled and differed for ages! Surely, we may well wonder at them, as did the Jews when they asked concerning Jesus, "How knoweth this man letters, having never learned?" while in our case, unlike theirs, nothing of miracle is apparent, that our wonder should be allayed. But these confessors have read a creed, or heard it from the pulpit, assumed its truth, and are, therefore, ready prayerfully to subscribe to it! Whereas had they chanced to have fallen in with a different one, very likely they could have assumed and subscribed that as freely. Why, brother, you know how all this is, and need only look at it to be impressed with its absurdity. Had John Wesley been blessed with a hundred sons, who questions but they would have nearly all been Methodists? and that the complexion of most persons' credal theology depends on the circumstances under which they were born, bred, or converted? Again, I say, you know how all this is; and that a creed, once subscribed, is thenceforth sacred to the subscriber. Once taken, however ignorantly, it is ordinarily, thenceforth, good for life.

When creeds become popular, nothing else is *so* popular. They are then spoken against, only at a great peril. And as their holders, though somewhat suspicious of them, dare not *speak* against them, so they are not likely to *think* much against them. Hence the worst form of conservatism prevails. The people become only nominal believers, that is, only less than disbelievers. And so the church, filling up with persons who have no radical faith in its doctrines, and too timid or apathetic to call them in question, becomes but an aggregation of "dead orthodoxy,"—a thing which an able orthodox clergyman declares to be "the worst form of infidelity;" thus do creeds become fetters. And it would be quite remarkable how patiently they are worn, only that, early imposed, and so silken as the gown of the churchman, their uncomfortableness is not appreciated by the wearer, who, regarding them as *of course* necessary, contents himself with thinking the length of their chain.

The religious bondage of Roman Catholics is proverbial. I am afraid you would start if I should intimate that a bondage scarcely less fearful,—and tried by its light perhaps more so,—prevails extensively among Protestants. But is it not so? Have not the masses even of New England Protestants, descendants of the Pilgrims and of Roger Williams, taken their faith, and are they not now holding it, without any thing worthy to be called an examination. To be sure, there are honorable exceptions. But are they not exceptions merely? *Look and see!*

Now a faith, thus received without a reason, and

holden from fashion, fear or habit, can have nothing radical in it; — though hugged ever so tenaciously, it is no part of a person's self, but a purely accidental property, originated and controlled by circumstances; as the ancient theology of the Roman people was controlled by the theology of the Roman Throne; as, in Macedonia, when the kings neck was wry, the people all carried their heads on one side.

Furthermore, when the people have, from father to son, fallen into the habit of blind faith, and, consequently, all heads are elevated or depressed to the fashionable dead level, ill fares it with him who straightens himself above it, and by the free expression of a free thought, exposes the established faith to popular investigation. So, when Jesus uttered thoughts, unfashionable in his age, and which fell like hammers upon the stereotype plates of effete Judaism, the leading religionists took alarm, sounded it, and the cry was heard, "*Crucify him! Crucify him!*" Let the "*robber*" live; but the *Innovator* die! So, also, when Paul, led by a divine hand from the feet of Gamaliel to the feet of Christ, was in the very act of narrating his wonderful experience, these same religionists,— the orthodoxy of their time,— hear not his words, but drown them with the outcry, "away with this fellow from the earth; it is not fit that he should live."

To be sure the present age has not much of *outward* persecution. It is, in some sense, too intensely spiritual for that. The Pharisees do not now cry for blood. Calvin does not now burn Servetus in literal fire. Racks are not now made of wood and iron. But is the spiritual connection between halters and heresy forgotten? We complain not of our own fare. But you know, brother, that under many circumstances, where orthodoxy is in possession, he who, standing in the midst of it speaks a word against it, does it at his peril. "They feared the Jews, for the Jews had already agreed that, if any man did confess that he was Christ, he should be put out of the synagogue." "Thou wast altogether born in sin, and dost thou teach us?" "And they cast him out."

Nor is this all; for when, as we have before intimated, men become afraid to deny their creed, so do they become afraid to examine it, lest they should feel called upon to deny it. This may seem strange, but so it is, as I think multitudes of experiences can testify; and this, especially, in relation to the doctrine of endless punishment. Perhaps you are not the person that I mean, but you will not be offended at my asking, whether even *you* have not sometimes been strangely deterred from a full examination of the grounds and consequences of certain ugly points in your faith, by a vague presentiment that it would be likely to bring them under uncomfortable suspicion? and whether you are not, in spite of yourself, annoyed with doubts about your fellow beings sinking into *endless* pain, under the Great Father's eye? and whether these troublesome doubts are not emboldened from year to year, and ever successfully demanding some more liberal construction of the terms of your creed, so that your creed to-day means very differently from what it did years ago? It may not be so. But I think I understand you, "being myself also flesh and blood." And, if you *are* the person that I mean, you are obliged to keep a sharp look-out against reasoning too impartially and too far, lest the doubts which now, perhaps, come and go as shadows, should become permanent and harden into absolute disbelief. But, whether you are the man that I mean or not, you will agree with me in what has been substantially said,—that in an age of fashionable theology, the want of courage to think independently, or, which is the same thing, the fear of offending against the faith in which men have been educated, is among the worst fetters of the Christian mind. And the man who breaks them from his soul, is ofttimes what the comet was to the ancients—a "blazing scimetar," rushing wildly—the very devil let loose! But it is now pretty well understood, that the seemingly lawless comet, burning athwart the planetary orbits, is, after all, an orderly body, and quite necessary to the harmony of the spheres. And so will it yet be found that men who think outside the zodiac of scholastic theology, and athwart its prescribed circles are quite orderly, and necessary to the harmony of the moral universe.

And now, brother as I close this letter, let me hope that you will "think on these things." Nor, do I doubt, that if your mind shall be thoroughly aroused to them, however easily you may parry the force of these fraternal letters, your own head and heart will become a storehouse of arguments, before which you shall quail, and, without shame, surrender. For it is no shame to surrender to one's self, even as no man is truly convicted till he convicts himself.

Yours truly,

LETTER IV.

CHANGE OF OPINION *versus* PERSISTENCE IN.

Change, causes of—As, constitutional weakness—Ambition—"Filthy lucre"—Inflexible devotion to truth—Change may argue *stability*. *Persistence*, causes of—As thoughtlessness, obstinacy, cowardice, or the love of truth—Illustrated by an incident—Theology crystallized in the nursery—Caution against being dwarfed.

DEAR BROTHER,—

If what we have already said is true, it must necessarily generate in the public mind a strong prejudice against change of theological views; while, as the natural counterpart of such prejudice, we should expect to see men pride themselves in their theological immutability. And so are the facts. Many Christians glory in a theology like "the laws of the Medes and Persians," abhor change, and require that whosoever proposes change in the church, shall do it with the rope round his neck. Whereas, there is neither honor nor shame, either in *change* of theological views, or *persistence* in them, only, as that change is considered in relation to its causes. The former may result from constitutional instability. There are some pretty good men, who naturally lack the ability long to do or believe the same thing. Their desire for change is ever becoming father to the thought that demands it. They are rather weak than criminal, and should be judged charitably. It is enough, perhaps, that we say to them as the dying patriarch to his "first born;" "Unstable as water thou shalt not excel."

But, further, change of views may result from vanity, pride, ambition, or an eye to the loaves and fishes. It is then pure sin,—its subject a pure sinner, to be dealt with accordingly. And, further still, such change may result from the best of considerations,—considerations deeply seated in a trained and vigorous reason, and an active and healthy conscience; considerations, involving the dearest interests of the soul, and its vital relations to its God; considerations, high as the heavens, and which may not be put aside without the sacrifice of "Godliness and Honesty;" that Godliness, without "which no man shall see the Lord," and that honesty, without which the man in the pulpit were better in the felon's cell. And, surely, nobody will demur at change, proceeding from such causes, save those who are too thoughtless to appreciate them. For it then may argue for its subject, not merely integrity, but stability, also; that higher stability of virtue and divine trust, which stoops beneath no burden, but, unawed by frowns and unflattered by smiles, stands, firmly balanced upon its own centre of gravity, and looks " steadfastly up into Heaven."

God " sees not as man sees." Stability in *his* sight,—stability in prosecuting a high religious purpose,—may be quite another thing from stability in the sight of men. And when the one or the other must be sacrificed, the true heart will not hesitate which to retain. It sees no desirable stability, but in the truth, no uprightness, but in " walking with God ; " in a steady progressive conformity to patterns, " shown in the holy mount." Such a heart says, with that old apostolic innovator, " let God be true," and acts accordingly, whether Felix tremble, or Festus rail, or Agrippa grow penitent. And, in this world of increasing light, such a heart is no more fickle than is the germ, in refusing to stay pent up in the darkness of the bud, or the sun, in refusing to stay in the same sign of the zodiac. It only goes on to perfection.

Change in religious opinion, then, considered in its moral quality, is to be judged by its causes ; and so judged, may be degrading, and may be ennobling ; nor can which be *guessed* out, but must rather be judged carefully in the premises. And the same is substantially true of *persistence in the same* opinion, a quality in which the Catholic Irishman excels the Protestant American, and the Mahometan Arab, excels both. For the sake of vividness, let us illustrate by reference to an incident :

A Christian minister has offended, by publicly avowing his disbelief in the doctrine of endless misery. His brethren are in ecclesiastical council upon his case. The offence is by many deemed grave, and by none more so than by one who rises, and, among other things, says, "I have found no occasion to change my views for more than forty years, and the old broom sweeps pretty clean yet." But as he stands there, with the "old broom" in his hand, in the presence of the offender, who may say which of the twain has shown the greater fidelity to truth, and thereby the better served his God? The former has indeed been unchangeable. But, perhaps he has been so only because he has been thoughtless. For the thoughtless Christian will no more turn away from a bad creed, than will the thoughtless sinner, from a bad way. Regarding his creed as necessarily true, and of course, whatever opposes it, as necessarily false, or, at best, under a show of discussion, only magnifying arguments against it, such a person finds no *occasion* to change. Nor is it any glory to him that he dies in the faith he was born with, or upon which he early stumbled. If it be a good one, it only argues for him a lucky nativity, or a lucky youthful accident. Now, if you choose, you may call such a person stable, but I call him simply stupid. And so stupid is he, that if his creed is bad, he never will find it out, or discover the truth it conceals; as the stupid Mexicans never could discover the treasures of California.

But, further, this stability of forty years unchangeableness, may be but the stability of dogged obstinacy,—an obstinacy which will neither bend before the truth, nor advance with it,—an obstinacy which, engrafted upon Methuselah at twenty-one, would, in the spite of all contingencies of increasing light and knowledge in the world, and even though he live through a half dozen dispensations, have clearly forestalled his exact theological *status*, at nine hundred and sixty-nine. Now, if men choose to dignify this obstinacy—in which, by the way, the religionists of our Saviour's time superabounded—as Christian stability, let it go so. There is not much in a name. But lacking, as it does, the childlike element of Christian teachableness, it lies quite outside the pale of the Christian virtues. And there we leave it, "old broom," in hand.

And, still further, this forty years of unchangableness may result from vanity, ambition, love of lucre, or, all in one, from moral cowardice. The subject of it may retain the old broom, merely because he dare not throw it away. Suspecting breakers upon either hand, he may be sailing, ever, upon the same tack, without the least regard for the compass of truth in the ship's binnacle. He may continue a Jew, for fear of being cast out of the synagogue.

Not having sufficiently considered that one soul, with God on his side, is a majority against the universe, he may persist in a suspicious faith, rather than be left isolated and out in the cold. You may call *this*, stability, if you please. But it is not Pauline. It is not Christian. It is human. It is cowardice, and its subject a coward. Nothing, knows he of the grandeur of moral heroism and self-sacrifice, as illustrated in the life of the Crucified. Ignorant is he of that spiritual enlargement, which the faithful feel, and of the grand and soul-inspiring views of being, duty, and destiny, which eternity is ever opening up to the eye of those, who, teachably, "follow the Lamb whithersoever he goeth,"

But there is a bright side to everything. This forty years unchangeableness may argue, or at least be consistent with, a commendable stability, in a progressive Christian mind. And so it is when the subject of it is studious, truth-loving, and self-sacrificing. And so we then give him credit, but must say that he was very fortunate to be born into, or so early to fall into, such theological perfection. Such fortunates must be like "angel's visits." For the Bible is a pretty large book, in which, as Peter says, are some things hard to be understood. So, also, is its counterpart, the book of Nature. The teachings of both are quite profound. That a person should be born to so exact knowledge of them, were not only quite remarkable, but would overthrow the prevalent notion of no innate ideas,—thus creating a necessity for change somewhere; and that a person should attain to so perfect understanding of the great doctrines of Scripture, to say nothing of Nature, by a reading—not to say study—so cursory and imperfect as the youth of most of these men of forty years' unchangeableness afforded—not to say, as often might be safely said, by almost no reading at all—were, indeed, truly wonderful. They must indeed have been very rapid learners, and blessed with a wonderful discrimination for immature minds. For, how else should they have learned so much in so short a time, and in the general sweeping in of theological knowledge, learned nothing which maturer years should require them to unlearn, as if the net, broadly cast, should bring to shore no fishes, fit only to be cast away.

And now, from the preceding general remarks, what is the conclusion? It is this; that neither change of religious opinions, nor persistence in them is, of itself, censurable. Which of the two is the more liable to be so. I leave you, brother, to judge. And if you take into account all the elements of the case, and, not least, the fact that most of the theological opinion now rife in the church, was crystallized for its subjects, in the nursery or in early childhood, so that children, almost invariably follow the doctrines of their fathers, or those prevalent in the community in which they are reared; I cannot doubt what your verdict will be. The former may argue a soul intent on progress, flexile before truth and conscience. The latter may argue a soul careless of progress, dead to live issue, stiff-necked and inflexible. The former, may argue the Bible Christian, the latter, the Bible Pharisee. The former, Paul at the feet of Jesus, the latter, Saul at the feet of Gamaliel. And if the former argue but a "living dog," the latter, only a "dead lion."

But, however all this may be, I trust you, brother, are above the moral cowardice that durst not see, know, and do its whole duty to truth and to God; whether it be to abandon an old position, or to adopt a new one. Said an able man, "there is but one word greater than the word *progress*, and that is the name of Deity." Brother, let us appreciate both these words, nor once think that we have "attained, or are already perfect," seeing that we find ourselves "occupying a little spot of ground, surrounded by an immense unknown expansion." Let us be careful, lest, with all our capacity for "growth in grace," by refusing wholesome truth, the proper nourishment of the soul, we shrivel into mere Rabbinical Pharisees, and become wretched monuments of the shame of dwarfing what, under a more independent culture, might have been developed into a noble Christian manhood.

Yours truly.

LETTER V.

UNIVERSALISM MISUNDERSTOOD.

Catholic lady — Her case not peculiar — Sanctuaries shunned—Universalism misdefined — Antipathy against it subsiding — Best hated when least understood — Ignorance of it, not confined to the laity — Instance of — Why ignorant of it — Conference room and pulpit — The more intelligent preach less against it, and less as though they believed in endless punsihment, and why? — Partialism wanes with the increase of light.

Dear Brother,—

As I resume my pen, I am reminded of a Roman Catholic lady, at a time resident within the limits of my parish, and whom I vainly invited to attend upon my ministry. Protestantism was, to her, the very Beelzebub of heresies. Immovable as a rock, she was resolved, as she said, to "*continue in the religion she was reared* in." So I left her, saying to myself, *poor woman!* And I have no doubt, if she still lives, that she is a Catholic still, and that she will glory in dying in her "holy mother church."

Cases like the above are striking, rather than peculiar. For multitudes of Protestants are, to-day, no less blindly judging doctrines not their own; and equally bound up in the peculiar faith upon which they chanced first to open their eyes, or which they received with their small clothes; and, with no ear for anything else, they will doubtless die in "the religion they were reared in." Many are, even now, judging Universalism, as ignorantly as the lady referred to, judged Protestantism, and shunning its sanctuary, as she shunned the sanctuary of Protestantism. We do not thus write to blame them. We take it they are sincere, as that lady was. They know not what they do. Early wrapped in a prejudice, through which only the fewest rays can struggle, and never hearing Universalism preached, but only preached against, how should they know! How can they but be as ignorant of it, as that boy was of his lesson, who pronounced the word *frigate* with *a* and *i* long, and guessed it meant some kind of a four-footed animal. And so, in their ignorance, like the good lady, they turn an angel from the door in the traveller they unwittingly despise.

The above remarks, are, of course, subject to honorable exceptions. And we are happy to know that such exceptions are becoming more and more numerous, as pharisaical antipathy to Universalism subsides with the increase of light upon religious subjects. And especially happy are we, that the prospect is that they will continue to multiply, till they shall cease to be exceptions, and become the law. But that happy day is not yet. Nor can it come, till the people gather independence, self-reliance, and moral courage, to look beyond those watchmen who advise them to know of Universalism, only through its enemies,— that beyond that, ignorance is bliss; —just as though Universalism was *best* hated by being *least understood.* And so, no doubt, it is. But this were a strange thing, to be affirmed of error. Error pales under fair investigation. Whereas, I think it is generally understood to be a recommendation of a thing, that it improves upon acquaintance. But according to the counsel of many spiritual guides, the reverse would seem to be true with regard to Universalism. *Because* it improves upon acquaintance, the people are advised that they can become acquainted with it only at their peril. And, brother, I think this should be a startling consideration to those who have been accustomed to regard it as a dangerous heresy; — that it should raise in their minds the enquiry, whether they or the heretics are the more heretical; whether heresy, in *this* age, does not sit in the place of true Orthodoxy, as in our Saviour's time the Scribes and Pharisees sat in Moses' seat, casting away the pentateuch and unrolling tradition for law.

But the ignorance of which we speak, is by no means confined to the laity of the dominant sects. Many of their clergy, and especially as a general rule, those who have most to say against our faith, are ignorant also. Early assured that it is "a refuge of lies," and that "the serpent was its first preacher," they have felt no call impartially to examine it, and so "continue in the religion they were reared in." Why, said one of my good old clerical friends, as he took my arm a few months since, "Universalism cannot be true," because nature itself teaches that there is a difference between right and wrong; "—just as though our faith did not recognize that difference. How many are *so* ignorant I will not say. But I will say that many are so ignorant of it that, when,— and as we think without any design of caricature — they attempt to define it for the benefit of their people, they define something as unlike it, as the "he goat" of Daniel, to the "Lamb" of the Apocalypse! And why should they not be ignorant of it. Its authors, they have never read, or read only with the spirit of exparte criticism. And, as to the Bible, they have some few figurative texts, which they think condemn it, while they are perfectly sure that it is full of disproof of the scandalous heresy. And woe to him who affirms the contrary. You may think the above remarks extravagant. But I think there is nothing in them overdrawn, if considered in relation to the many opponents of our faith, whether lay or clerical, who are *hot* against it. Those of our opponents to whom they do not apply, will generally be found those who are the more intelligent, and who look upon us with the less disfavor. Why, brother, you know how this is, and that you will hear more said against Universalism, and in vindication, or rather *assertion* of endless punishment, in one *ignorant* conference room, than in many *intelligent* pulpits. And I think you might know that among the more intelligent of the Orthodox clergy, are not a few who would have no objection to a free fellowship with Universalists, but for the consciences of their less intelligent parishioners. At any rate, certain it is, that the more intelligent among the preachers of endless punishment, preach it the less as though they believe it. And I think it is equally obvious that the studious and progressive among them, preach it less and less, and with less and less earnestness, as they advance in years, and their minds mature with culture, while by equal ratio the asperity of their words against our faith is softened, and their number diminished. Whether it is because, gradually coming to a more just conception of endless misery, and the Bible teaching about it, they find it harder to believe, or whether, coming to a better knowledge of Universalism, they find it to improve upon acquaintance, I leave you to judge. But the fact is certainly very significant. And what does it signify but that Partialism is to fade away into Universalism, in just about the inverse ratio by which light increases?

Please suspend any rash judgment upon this letter till, in a future one, I state definitely what Universalism is.

Yours truly,

LETTER VI.

ERROR, JEWISH AND CHRISTIAN.

Man an Errorist—The Jew's great Error in spite of his Scriptures, amazing, seeing that he was not skeptical of them—The veil upon him—Corresponding error of the Christian—Origen—The Church comes out of the middle ages, how—A Caution.

DEAR BROTHER,—

When we consider man, theologically, and in the light of history, he seems little better than a mere errorist. Thus considered, one might suppose him, not only *liable* to err, but even *bent* on erring, wilfully, and in spite of light. Look at the ancient people of God,—the Jews. Though familiar with the Old Testament Scriptures, and notwithstanding those Scriptures are full of promises to the Gentiles, still were they certain that their own nation was to monopolize all the blessings of Messiah's reign. What was it to them, that their Scriptures said, "In that day there shall be a root of Jesse which shall stand for an ensign to the people; to it shall the *Gentiles* seek; and his rest shall be glorious." What though their Scriptures say of Messiah, "He shall bring forth judgment to the

Gentiles;" and what though they make the Father say to the Son, "I give thee for a covenant to the people, for a light to the Gentiles;" and what though they make the Prophet say to the church under Immanuel, "And the *Gentiles* shall come to thy light, and kings to the brightness of thy rising," and, again, "the *Gentiles* shall see thy righteousness and all kings thy glory;" and what though those ancient writings say that "*all flesh* shall see the salvation of God;" what was all this to the Jew! What was it to *him*, that the promises of his Scriptures to the *Gentiles*, were plain, full, and cumulative? In spite of them all, and "in erring reasons spite," he was perfectly certain that his hoped for Messiah should have no blessing for the poor Gentile. Dives should be perpetually pampered, and poor Lazarus, with his dog-licked sores, must lie perpetually at his gate.

Now that the Jews, and, especially, the Rabbinical Jews should have set up and established a faith, so plainly and directly against their Scriptures, is, indeed, amazing. We certainly should say that it implied that they *disbelieved* their Scriptures, did we not know that they, not only believed them, but clung to them with a tenacity, almost without a parallel. They guarded their text even to its minutest "jot and tittle," with the most faithful and laborious assiduity. In reference to it, they knew nothing of skepticism. They believed it *all*, and conscientiously accepted its teaching. And yet, while, as we have seen, it so clearly and fully taught, that Messiah should bring a blessing for the *Gentiles*, they fully believed the contrary. So was their mind "blinded,"— such was "the veil" upon it, "in the reading of Moses" "and the prophets."

And what was that veil, which concealed from the Jew the chief glory of his Scriptures, — as the temple's veil concealed from the people, the most holy place, — but the narrow prejudice, the original product of selfishness and ignorance, which he unconsciously cherished.

But those very Jews, after all, were more human than Jewish. Nor should we wonder too much at the palpableness of their errors, seeing that we are human also, and liable to be "in the same condemnation;" so that, while "we are astonished, that they should have been so blinded to the sublime import of the *Old* Testament, we do well to inquire whether we are any less blinded to the sublimer import of the *New* — whether we are not intent on a mote in their eye, while a beam is in our own. And if an exclusive spirit, gendered by prejudice, so wrought in the very body-disciples of Christ, that, in spite of his *positive command*, they hesitated to preach the *Gospel* to the Gentiles, till God spoke to them by the vision of a "sheet let down from

Heaven," it is hardly surprising, that Christians of this later day, should, through some similar prejudice, narrowly mistake the comprehensiveness of the Gospel plan! And, especially, seeing that the popular theology of our day, has come down to us, out of darker ages than ever brooded upon the Jewish mind; and seeing that, long before those ages, in the comparative infancy of Christianity, we know that Universalism prevailed. Origen, the illustrious Christian father, and the first real scholar in the church, was a staunch advocate and defender of it, nor have we the least intimation that it was then regarded as heresy. But the church gradually entered the cloud of the middle ages, and after traversing vast regions of darkness, historically unexplored, she at length appears again, with her head full of error and her hands full of blood, fierce to set up and pull down dogmas, through councils, backed by the sword.

The above consideration requires careful attention. For as it is much easier to see the mote in our brother's eye, than the beam in our own, so, also, it is easier to see the faults of other denominations and ages, than the greater faults of our own. We see the folly of the ancient people of God. We wonder that they, in spite of *their* Scriptures, should have believed that Jews only were to be blest by Messiah. They were prejudiced. But may not our folly equal theirs, while, in the face of our Scriptures, we believe not only that almost all the Jews are lost, but that only a small fraction of the swarming Gentiles up to the present time, are saved. May we not also be prejudiced. And as we think of ancient theological folly, may we not well say with the wise man, "that which has been is now"? And among believers of the present day, are there any more intensely Jewish in their prejudices than the many who, making the scope of salvation, embrace only the relative handful of the elect, are blind to all the beauties of a more liberal faith, and deaf to all the appeals of reason and Scripture in its behalf? Are there not many to-day who say, "we see," whose minds are, after all, so darkened by prejudice, that only the fewest rays of true light can struggle into them? So it seems to me. But these are matters of which I here affirm nothing. I only throw them out that you may weigh them. May you weigh them well.

Yours truly.

LETTER VII.

IS YOUR FAITH SATISFACTORY?

Are you *quite* satisfied?—Descent to Woe—Nominal Faith—The sweet babe—Antediluvians and Post-diluvians—Neighbors dismissed to woe!—Earnest Question—God's image—Relief—Illustration from the "Pemberton Calamity"—Description of it—Eternal Prison House—Ideal of a better Faith—Return to the Ruins—*Fire!*—All over!—Application—Everywhere men descend out of sight—Stolen Relief—Midnight Mourning—Why questions deemed delicate—Faith for Funerals—Temporal evils explicable—They have an Afterwards—Not so endless evil—Mystery—Whence comes the notion of endless misery—Practical conception of it—Walk in the fields—The *heart* rebels—Jehovah only as the publicans, and worse—Earth a stepping stone to woe—Quotation from Pope—From Thomson—Strange dissatisfaction—What is radical in all religion—Caution.

DEAR BROTHER, —

My imagination may do you injustice; but I seem to hear you saying with yourself, "Much of what he writes is, perhaps, well enough; and, it *is true*, as he says, that most of our theology is either hereditary or taken on trust. The Jews were greatly mistaken, many others have been,—I *may* be, — but what then? If he thinks his faith is better,—

very well,—let him have it. But as for me, why should I trouble myself about it, seeing that I am satisfied with my own."

But, brother, are you sure that you are satisfied with your own faith? Does not its contemplation sometimes make you shiver, as if nearing the cold mists of skepticism? From the strained effort to believe, against your heart, so much as your faith requires, do you not, now and then, find yourself reacting towards believing nothing, and perplexed with expedients for relief?—modified definitions and palliative constructions? At any rate, are you sure that you are quite satisfied with your faith, in view of endless misery to which it makes so many of your fellow beings descend?—misery to which it exposes you, yourself, every hour, and your escape from which, it makes ever as doubtful as is your fitness for heaven?

You will perceive, brother, that I am not here setting you down with the merely nominal believer, whose faith, however awful, is a mere Sunday suit, and sets as lightly upon him as fleecy clouds upon either! I am rather assuming that you really accept your creed with all its dismal consequences. And so, I press still the question, are you satisfied with it. When a child is born to you, (or to somebody else) are you satisfied to feel that the sweet little stranger, upon whose brow the fond mother parts the springing locks, so lovingly, and whose infant prattle thrills to the very centre of your own manly heart, is exposed to *endless* woe, and probably shall suffer it, unless it die early; and this, too, at the hand of the "Everlasting Father" who brought it into being? Are you? And does your punitive faith satisfy you, as "memory like a tomb searcher," runs through all the past, and down through your dark world of woe, among antediluvians and postdiluvians, long lost and lost forever? Does it? And are you satisfied with it, as from time to time it dismisses one and another of your neighbors and friends, from their families and fire-sides, to your woe-land of eternity? Are you?

I am not here asking whether your creed is true. I am only trying to put you upon examination of it, by earnestly asking whether it satisfies you — whether it satisfies your most Christian bosom, as it heaves with the charity towards all men, which Christianity bids us cherish; or whether as you contemplate its logical consequences, you are not sometimes tempted to say, "If it is true, then I am not made in the Father's image? — then there is no Father in Heaven?" And, furthermore, whether, however well you deem yourself satisfied with your faith, it would not, on reflection, be inexpressible relief to know that all the dead are mercifully cared for?

Our city (Lawrence, Mass.,) has recently been visited by a calamity, awful and appalling, almost beyond a parallel. "In a moment, in the twinkling of an eye," at the breaking of certain pillars, one of its large factories fell completely down, burying some six or seven hundred persons beneath its ruins! It was on a winter afternoon. And, as the slow hours passed, the sun went down, the stars appeared, and the night advanced, what agony was there! — agony of fathers and mothers, sons and daughters, husbands and wives, hanging tearfully and tearlessly, over that chaotic mass of roofing, flooring, brick, mortar and machinery, moaning piteously for the dear ones, buried, dead or alive, within it! And, as in the slow process of disentombment, a father saw his son, a mother her daughter, a brother his sister, a husband his wife, brought forth, uninjured, among the mangled and the dead, how did his heart leap for joy, and there, in the presence of the wild congregation, and under the "cold light of stars, what thanksgiving then went up to Heaven!

And now, brother, would not your heart leap for joy also, and would not your thanksgiving be moved, if out the eternal prison-house to which your creed consigns so many of your dead, you could see them all emerging, under the light of the everlasting Father's smile? And thus, however well satisfied you are with your present faith, have you not the ideal of an infinitely better one?

But to return to the ruins. At midnight the cry of "*fire!!*" is heard upon them. "*Where?*" "*Here!*" The "brakes" are plied; but all in vain! The fire sweeps through the chaos, suffocating and consuming numbers who were on the very threshold of rescue! All was over! Nor did the vast concourse hardly know whether, more to sorrow that all life was extinct, or to joy that all suffering was ended.

Now, brother, had you been in the midst of that scene, as I was, would your faith have *there* satisfied you? *Could* you have then been satisfied with it, while it made endless woe, seize the "souls of most of those poor perishing operatives,* the moment the fire or some other element of the calamity seized their vital breath,—while it made all the horrors of that dreadful night, but the agency of their *transfer* to *hopeless* despair; so that, sad as we felt while they were imploring our aid, sadder should we have felt when they were silent. For then, according to your faith, they were in deeper misery, whence aid is not implored, because thence hope flies forever.

But why speak of *special* calamity. The way of death is everywhere, and everywhere are men

*The victims were mostly Roman Catholics, not unlike those ordinarily found in such establishments.

descending it out of sight. And as your eye follows them to the verge of darkness, are you not often obliged to confess that your faith dissatisfies you, and to try to feel as though you did not believe it,— that is, holding one faith are you not obliged to flatter yourself with hopes afforded by another, or else be too sad for earth, with its breeze and flower? And yet do you say that it satisfies you?

Moreover, when at some midnight hour, you are wakeful with mourning for dear ones whom the great Father has, by the terms of your creed, consigned to everlasting pain, do you not find it hard to sing with the Psalmist, "My soul shall be satisfied with marrow and fatness, and my mouth shall praise thee with joyful lips, when I remember thee upon my bed and meditate on thee in the night-watches." These may seem delicate questions. You may, perhaps, doubt their propriety. But they involve only the *very simplest* practical application of your penal faith. And therein I apprehend lies the objection to this plain questioning. But, surely a radical doctrine that will not bear application, — which cannot be carried into funeral circles and mourning midnights, but must rather be forgotten, in the very hour when consolation is most needed, or the sad one be sadder still, is certainly very questionable and were better altogether unknown. For a known doctrine *so* dreadful, is not easily forgotten at will. To every *real believer* in it, it is sure to be kept in remembrance by its very terribleness. And do you say you are satisfied with it?

Perhaps you will refer to temporal evils, and reason from them to eternal evils. But you will perceive that the permission of temporal evils to finite beings, destined to immortal progress, admits of explanation. To all these there is an afterwards of opportunity for the sufferer's reformation, when, as disciplinary process, they *may* yield the peaceable fruits of righteousness to all who are exercised thereby. But who shall explain the evil of *endless* misery. Who shall explain why the wages of so short a sin, by so feeble a sinner, placed by the infinite goodness, under the wretched circumstances of earth, should be so long a death! A death which admits of no "afterwards," but which is all pain, pain, pauseless, everlasting pain! Surely, such a death, under the eye and law of the Christian's God, is fearfully and overwhelmingly inexplicable. Jehovah's foot, forever upon a writhing worm! — are you satisfied with your faith's contemplation of it? Or do you sometimes feel that you could love the Father better if you had evidence that his punishments were more paternal?

I know, brother, how you are accustomed to quiet your troublesome heart, under these disturbing considerations. But, I beseech you, pause and carefully consider, whether the credal terrors before which you flee into mystery, are anything more than the gloomy creations of human theology scholastically distilled from heathen mythology, in the alembic of darkness.

And so far as mystery is concerned, let it be here said, that if there is any thing of which the human mind can have a distinct practical conception, it is of a misery that never ends. And of the moral quality of no act, do I conceive that man can have a clearer conception, than of that of an infinite God creating intelligent beings in full view of their endless misery, and of course keeping them alive in it forever — forever refusing to them the coveted boon of absolute death. Philosophise over these propositions as you will, they will remain in their strength. And if you seemingly overturn them, I think they will still remain in your consciousness. Why, then, talk of mystery? Our conception of endless death and its infliction, is as clear as our conception of endless life, and its bestowment!

But, further still, and on another tack; as you walk over this fair world, listen to the melody of birds, and the murmur of waterfalls, witness the descent of silver showers, and joy in the genial beams of the morning, as they glance across the dewy meads and gloriously transfigure the silver lake; and as you think that all these are but the universal smile of the Living Father, who "makes his sun to rise on the evil and on the good, and sends his rain on the just and on the unjust," and whose very thunders are yielding up a benevolent purpose, under the keen eye of science,— do you not, sometimes, have serious misgivings whether, this Living Father has, actually, ordained endless damnation for the creatures of his power — creatures whom he absolutely foreknew,— for man of whom he is "mindful," and the son of man whom "he visits" — for creatures whom he loves, and whom, in the beginning, he was under no obligation to create, other than the self-imposed obligation of his own benevolent nature? Do you not then find something in your best heart, rebelling against the notion that, in the future world, the mercies of God are to be "clean gone forever;" — that, in that world, He is to be found like the *publicans* in this, loving *only* those that love him, and shutting up all the rest, by statute or common law, in the darkness of despair forever! So that the angels, in reference to Jehovah's acts, might well ask, "do not even the publicans so," while the saints might well reply, "Nay, the publicans do not so. If so partial in their love, they are not so terrible in their hate;" and all the lost might say, *amen!*

Ah, my brother, as you thus read nature's elder

Scripture, do you not suspect that you have misinterpreted her younger? and whether it is not a mistake that, from Eternity, it was pre-arranged in God's foreknowledge that earth should be but a stepping stone, by which multitudes of immortals should pass from the shades of nothingness to the more dimal shades of everlasting despair? In a word, do you not then suspect whether the God of your creed is not quite another, from him who "vital breathes" around, — him whose benignity

"Warms in the sun, refreshes in the breeze,
Glows in the stars, and blossoms in the trees,
Lives through all life, extends through all extent,
Spreads undivided, operates unspent?"

You have, doubtless, admired the closing strain of Thomson's inimitable hymn, — fit appendix to his "Seasons:"

"Should fate command me to the farthest verge
Of the green earth; to distant, barbarous climes;
Rivers unknown to song; where first the sun
Gilds Indian mountains, or his setting beam
Flames on the Atlantic isles; 'tis nought to me,
Since God is ever present, ever felt,
In the void waste, as in the city full,
And where He vital breathes, there must be joy!
When e'en at last the solemn hour shall come,
And wing my mystic flight to future worlds;
I cheerfully will obey. There, with new powers,
Will rising wonders sing. I cannot go
Where universal love smiles not around,
Sustaining all yon orbs, with all their suns,

From seeming evil, still educing good,
And better thence again, and better still,
In infinite progression. But I lose
Myself in Him, in light ineffable!
Come then expressive silence, muse His praise."

On the margin of the leaf, in my library, containing this poetry, an orthodox friend once wrote, "*May this be my sentiment.*" And, brother, are you not saying, "*may it be mine?*" But as you admire it,—the natural outgush of the free soul, so honorable to God, and comforting to man,—do you not feel a strange sort of dissatisfaction with the portion of your creed, which it so radically violates? As you think of penal sorrow, whose endlessness necessarily admits of no "afterwards," in which "good," may be "educed," from it,—of sorrow, eternized by the judgment fiat of Jehovah, or, which is the same thing, by a law of sin which he himself ordained, do you not feel a very troublesome distrust of the faith into which you have been baptized? "Finally," brother, "whatsoever things are true, whatsoever things are honest, whatsoever things are just, whatsoever things are pure, whatsoever things are lovely and of good report; if there be any virtue, and if there be any praise, think on these things." Deeply do I feel how worthy they are of your attention,—how essential to your Christian perfection and usefulness. Though intended only as suggestive of enquiry, they deeply involve what is radical and controlling in all religions,—*the character of God!* You will not put them aside lightly. An angel may be in the wayfarer! a son of God in the Nazarene!

Yours truly.

LETTER VIII.

GREAT MINDS IN TROUBLE—BARNES.

Great minds most troubled with ugly dogmas—Sad case—Quotation from Barnes' commentary—Quotation from his published sermons—The contrast between the two—His anguish—Cause of it, particulars noted—Reasoners for endless punishment rebuked—Barnes' difficulties not only "real," but vitally practical—Their removal leaves but Universalism—Beauty of the plan of salvation, unseen—Plan of damnation, rather—Strength of the language of Barnes' confession—General restlessness among the intelligent clergy—Intances.

Postscript.— Stuart's difficulty — Experiences suppresed — Quotation from Edward Beecher, with comment—Quotation from Channing—Foster—Bad for a child to lose its father, yet is there something worse—Relief of indifference.

DEAR BROTHER,—

It is by no means peculiar to weak and uneducated holders of your creed, to find very serious trouble with it. Not with the reason and affection of such persons does it make its chief havoc, but the contrary. This I will now attempt to show, by certain references, preparatory to which, I here introduce the following sad occurrence.

"Oh, if I could believe as you do, I should be one

of the happiest men on earth." So said a Christian lawyer, a few months ago, to one of his legal brethren, who vainly tried to raise him from a state of deep melancholy, by presenting him with a more cheerful faith. He was, by the common verdict of his fellow citizens, and of his church, an excellent and devout Christian, and yet he was wretched; for he not only *believed* in endless misery, but his creed was, to him, as it should be to every holder, like a *living reality*. Its contemplation overwhelmed him, reason reeled under the weight of it,

"And frantic driven,
He dreamed himself in hell and woke in heaven."

He died a suicide, and yet his memory was justly blessed. And, indeed, was it not to his *credit*, that his mind broke down? What mind, not stiffened up by the most rigid theological stoicism, but must break down before the open full contemplation of the multitudes of fellow-beings actually in endless woe or descending into it. O, there is no estimating the strength of that mind and heart, that can, intelligently sustain the weight of its pressure. To sustain it merely nominally, as many do, (that is to say, not to sustain it at all), is indeed a small thing. And yet, if we take Christian consistency into the account, not very small, either, in the eyes of Him, to whom such consistency is a jewel, though it lie in the coffin of a suicide, and Christian inconsistency, but rottenness, though it stalk an angel.

I will delay you no further upon this illustration of the workings of your creed. But, occurring as it did, in my own immediate neighborhood, it deeply impressed my mind. I know not whether it will yours. Give it what weight you please.

We now come more directly to our present task, which is, to establish the proposition at the head of this letter. And our first witness shall be a man whose ripeness as a scholar, and profoundness as a theologian, are beyond question, and whose excellent commentaries are widely circulated;—I mean the Rev. Albert Barnes. Nor is he here referred to, to impeach his integrity, but rather, incidentally, to endorse it. And if, under cross-examination, he appear inconsistent, it will not compromise his character, but only show the struggle of a good heart with an impracticable creed. His case, though often before the public, we never have seen examined with the fulness it deserves.

And that we may the better accomplish our design in referring to so worthy a man, let us first ponder the following excellent extract from his commentary:

"The effect of religion, or, of the influence of the Holy Spirit, is to open the eyes, to show the sinner his condition and his danger, and to lead him *to look* on Him whom he had pierced. Yet, at first he sees indistinctly. He does not soon learn to distinguish objects. When converted, he is in a new world. Light is shed on every object, and he sees the Scriptures, the Saviour, and the works of creations, the sun and stars and hills and vales, in a new light. He sees the beauty of the plan of salvation, and wonders that he has not seen it before. Yet he sees at first indistinctly. It is only by repeated applications to the Source of light, that he sees all things clearly. At first religion may appear full of mysteries. Doctrines and facts appear on every hand, that he cannot comprehend. His mind is still perplexed, and he may doubt whether he has ever seen aught or ever been renewed. Yet let him not despair. Light in due time, will be shed on these obscure and mysterious truths. Faithful and repeated application to the Father of Lights, in prayer, and in searching the Scriptures, and in the ordinances of religion, will dissipate all these doubts, and he will see all things clearly, and the universe will be filled with one broad flood of light."*

These are true words,—excellent words,—"apples of gold in pictures of silver;" well calculated to guard the young Christian, perplexed with difficulties, against faint-heartedness and despair. None who *rightly* studies the sacred Scriptures, and keeps his conscience clean, but shall find them true. But

Com. vol. I., p. 180.

did their author find them true in his own experience? Let the following quotation from his practical sermons testify. And, brother, let us ponder its testimony:—

"That the immortal mind should be allowed to jeopard its infinite welfare, and that trifles should be allowed to draw it away from God, and virtue, and heaven, that any should suffer forever,—lingering on in hopeless despair, and rolling amidst infinite torments without the possibility of alleviation, and without end; that since God can save men, and will save a part, he has not proposed to save *all;* that, on the supposition that the atonement is ample, and that the blood of Christ can cleanse from all and every sin, it is not, in fact, applied to all; that, in a word, a God who claims to be worthy of the confidence of the universe, and to be a being of infinite benevolence, should make such a world as this, full of sinners and sufferers; and that when an atonement has been made, He did not save *all* the race, and put an end to sin and woe forever.

"These and kindred difficulties, meet the mind when we think on this great subject; and they meet us when we endeavor to urge our fellow-sinners to be reconciled to God, and to put confidence in Him. On this ground they hesitate. These are *real,* not imaginary difficulties. They are probably felt by every mind that has ever reflected on the subject; and they are unexplained, unmitigated, unremoved. I confess, for one, that I feel them, and feel them more sensibly and powerfully, the more I look at them and the longer I live. I do not understand these facts; and I make no advances towards understanding them. I do not know that I have a ray of light upon this subject which I had not, when the subject first flashed across my soul. I have read, to some extent, what wise and good men have written. I have looked at their theories and explanations. I have endeavored to weigh their arguments; for my whole soul pants for light and relief on these questions. But I get neither; and in the distress and anguish of my own spirit, I confess that I see no light whatever. I see not one ray to disclose to me the reason why sin came into the world; why the earth is strewed with the dying and the dead; why man must suffer to all eternity.

"I have never seen a particle of light thrown on these subjects, that has given a moment's ease to my tortured mind; nor have I an explanation to offer, or a thought to suggest, that would be of relief to you. I trust other men — as they profess to do — understand this matter better than I do, and that they have not the anguish of spirit which I have; but I confess, when I look on a world of sinners and of sufferers; upon death-beds and grave-yards; upon the world of woe, filled with hosts to suffer forever; when I see my friends, my parents, my family, my people, my fellow citizens; when I look upon a whole race, all involved in this sin and danger, and when I see the great mass of them wholly unconcerned, and when I feel that God only can save them and that he does not,—I am struck dumb. All is dark, dark, dark, and I cannot disguise it."

Such and so melancholy, are the words of Barnes, as an experienced *Christian preacher*. And singularly and sadly do they contrast with the cheerful words, just previously quoted from Barnes, as a *Commentator*;—the former, closing up in a "*flood of light*," the latter, in *three-fold* "*darkness*." In the former, he assures the young Christian, perplexed with "*mysteries*" and "*doctrinal facts*," that "if he is faithful, he will yet see all things clearly, and the universe will be filled with one broad flood of light." In the latter, he confesses that, to him, no light comes, and — what is important as showing that his difficulties are, as he says, "*real, not imaginary*,"—that darkness deepens with the increase of years and knowledge. As a Commentator, he speaks of "beauty in the plan of salvation." As an experienced Christian, he speaks of that plan, as a cause of "distress," "anguish," dumbness, darkness, to his "tortured mind." And all this he feels the more sensibly and powerfully, the longer he looks upon them, and the longer he lives. The inconsistency here involved is, indeed, strange; but, as we have before intimated, no stranger than often occurs between the head and heart of a *good* man, holding a *bad* creed.

But let us note particularly the cause of our Author's "anguish," as by himself set forth. It is that "any should suffer forever;"—it is that, "since God" * * * "the God who claims the confidence of the Universe" * * * "*can* save men, and *will* save a part, he has not purposed to save *all*." It is that "the blood of Christ" * * * is not in fact applied to all." This is the cause of his "anguish of spirit." Because of this, all is *so* "dark," and all this might be safely paraphrased about thus:—*When I consider that the Divine Government is not administered upon the principles of Universalism, "I am struck dumb! All is dark, dark, dark, and I cannot disguise it!"*

And all this, coming from so high and unexceptionable a source,—the sincere outgush of such a heart,—how does it rebuke all the attempts of scholastic theology, to *prove* the *reasonableness* of endless misery, or the *unreasonableness* of Universalism. For, whatever else may be involved in the complaint of our author, his notion of endless misery is the chief; so that were that removed, and the doctrine of the final holiness of all men put in its stead, other causes of complaint would be little thought of, or thought of only as spots upon the sun's disc, which do not seriously intercept its beams. The real difficulty lies in *that ugly doctrine*, and as he says, "it *is* real, *not* imaginary." Otherwise it could not increase with the increase of light, as he says it does.

Notice, too, how eminently *practical* are the difficulties which Barnes found in grappling with this theological hydra. They were no mere entanglements in metaphysical subtleties, — valueless abstractions! They were *practical!* This, our author frankly confesses. Nor does he speak for himself alone. For, says he, "they meet *us* when we endeavor to urge our fellow sinners to be reconciled to God, and put confidence in him. On this ground they hesitate." Mark the words, "*on this ground they hesitate!*" For O, how eminently practical is that dogma which stands right in the ministers way, when he would "persuade men" to be "reconciled to God,"— that dogma which makes them *then* "hesitate." Certainly, any theological system, in which such a dogma inheres, were rendered more efficient by its removal. For one difficulty, at least, were then out of the way. And yet, you have only just to remove from Orthodoxy *that* difficulty — the very one which makes sinners hesitate,— and it becomes *Universalism!*

There is, indeed, "beauty," as Barnes says, "in the plan of Salvation,"—beauty which fills with overwhelming joy, the person who contemplates it from the stand point of the Fatherhood. But Barnes could see that beauty, only as he lost sight of his penal creed. For in view of that creed, the whole creation and government of God, in its relations to responsible humanity, were, rather, upon a plan of *damnation*. Do not start at this remark, brother, till you have well considered whether it is not strictly true. For in the eye of that creed, what is the mass of responsible humanity, but one vast, everlasting Sahara, relieved only by here and there a little oasis. Certainly, by that creed, many more of the accountable children of earth, are lost than saved. Why, then, not *call* it a place of *damnation*, making its *name* correspond with its *leading feature!* And why wonder that an intelligent believer in it, should be sad, especially when a heart of true Christian sympathy, throbs his breast!

Furthermore; we shall not have seen all, unless we note the *strength* and *significance* of our author's confessions. "*I confess for one,*"—"*I cannot disguise it!*" "*I trust other men*" * * * "*have not the anguish of spirit that I have,*" &c. These phrases are almost infinitely expressive. They are such as come out, only when the lips part from necessity,—when the struggling emotions of the heart, like the seething elements of earthquake, will have way! They suggest, how many there may be, who, with less moral courage than Barnes, are like him chafed and galled and choked with the ligaments of their creed. In them, we see the deep theological restlessness of the age,—a restlessness well expressed by an able Orthodox clergyman, recently ascended to the Father, who, in a note to the author, on learning that he had become settled in the liberal faith, said, "*I am thankful if one poor soul has found rest!*" and, also, by another of the author's old clerical friends, who said, "I find relief from the horror of endless punishment by thinking that the wicked will be annihilated;" and by another of the same who said, "future punishment is no matter of faith;" and still another, who said "no *text* in the Bible teaches it," and "I cannot say that all who die in sin must lie forever outside of heaven;"—a restlessness, every where apparent among the thinking portion of the dominant sects, but seldom so freely and intensely *expressed*, as in the extract just under review. And however it may be with you brother, can it be that Barnes was satisfied with a creed so distressing.

Yours truly.

P. S. But Barnes did not walk this dark path-way alone. I think we have a right to infer that Moses

Stuart had not a little similar experience. For after supposing that saints in heaven would be made reconciled to seeing "those dear as their own life perish at last," he says "how this will or can be done, we may never know in the present world; nay, we may have" many a *distressing* hour, while enquiring how it can be done, unless our very nature itself is wholly changed."

And who may say how "many a distressing hour" the learned Professor might have himself experienced on this account. For, in the language of Dr. Edward Beecher, "it is an experience which men are not disposed to make public:" just as any other experience is, which militates against the popular creed. It is only when *sorely* pressed, that such minority experiences find expression. Few, therefore, speak out like Barnes and Foster. "How many," says the Beecher above quoted, "ever pass, in fact, into this dark valley, I have no means of determining. But," he adds, "I knew one man of eminent piety, and distinguished as a clergyman, who had had trials of great severity from tendencies to such views." It were easy to imagine who that "one man" was, and to see in him foreshadowed, the Theological confusion of one of the noblest, and most philanthropic families that ever honored the earth. Channing says, "we can endure any errors but those which subvert or unsettle our conviction of God's paternal goodness. Urge not upon us a system which makes existence a curse, and wraps the universe in gloom." But such views are often urged upon the minds of thinking men, by the almost resistless force of education, circumstances, and established modes of reasoning out of the Scriptures. And then it is, that the Father's glory is eclipsed and "the universe wrapped in gloom,"—or, as Foster says, "occupied with a lurid and dreadful shade; and this the rather, the more the soul progresses in Christian spirituality,—the more it is raised above the world,—the more thorough it is brought into sympathy with infinite love. Sad it is, for a child to lose its father. But infinitely more sad, is it, when the fatherly is lost out of the father. For then the very word, *father*, becomes a source of unmeasured anguish. And it is but poor relief that is found in the vain effort to believe the father good, while his conduct is but a rational exponent of absolute badness. That very effort does but tear and exhaust the soul, every moment in danger of reacting into absolute skepticism. Oh, the "*distressing hours,*" relieved only by relapses into indifference, as the tired slave is relieved by relapses into the sleep of his cabin! Our next witness shall be Dr. Edward Beecher.

Yours truly.

LETTER IX.

GREAT MINDS IN TROUBLE — EDWARD BEECHER.

Beecher and his works—His dilemma—Must do one of three things —His discovery and relief—How great the pressure, darkness, wretchedness, hallucination, to which *such* a discovery is relief— A similar dilemma awaits all educated like B. as light advances— How many, involved like him, fall off into infidelity !

Dear Brother, —

In my last letter I referred to Dr. Edward Beecher, incidentally. I wish now to refer to him, particularly, as further establishing the proposition, that it is by no means peculiar to weak and uneducated minds, to find serious difficulties with your creed.

Born of a noble stock, reared beneath a noble family tree, educated in the school of orthodoxy, he is an able minister of Christ. A wide observer, a profound thinker, a vigorous reasoner, and, withal, pious and independent, his equals are, doubtless, relatively few. He is now best known as the author of the "Conflict of Ages," that root-breaking book, which is, to the fallow ground of Augustinian theology like a mighty breaking up plow, drawn through forests by giants. His "*Papal Conspiracy Exposed*" would have given him a name. So also would his "*Concord of Ages.*" But he is very much stauncher in his "*Conflict,*" than in his "*Concord,*" as Milton, in his "Paradise lost," than in his "Paradise regained." It is not, however, with his works that we now have to do. We refer to them, only to indicate the mould of the man.

The education of Beecher was, as we have seen, orthodox. He believed in depravity, he believed in endless misery, he believed in a God of infinite goodness. But here belief clashed with belief. That a good Father should punish forever his sinning children of earth, seemed to him absolutely unreconcilable with his own moral intentions,— with the principles of "honor and right," which he was deeply conscious, God's own finger had written, before all Scriptures, authoritatively upon his heart. Hence, his dilemma. And thus he describes it. "For a time, the system of this world, rose before my mind, in the same manner, (as far as I can judge), as it did before the minds of Channing and Foster. I can, therefore, more fully appreciate their expression of their trials and emotions. But I was entirely unable to find relief as they did. The depravity of man, neither Christian experience, the Bible, nor history, would permit me to deny. Nor did reason or Scripture afford me any satisfactory grounds whatsoever, for anticipating the restoration of the lost to holiness in a future state. Hence, for a time, all was dark as night." * So here, again, as in the confession of Barnes, darkness is the word. Marvellous is it, how orthodoxy and darkness go hand in hand, in the experience of thinkers so profound and independent! Must there not be a mistake somewhere? And this, the rather, because this peculiar affinity becomes the stronger and more prevalent, as Christendom becomes more enlightened.

But to return. "For a time," Beecher found all, "dark as night." And then it was that he looked for light and behold darkness, "for righteousness" on the part of God, "and behold a cry!" What shall he do? He must either change his opinion concerning the penal Scriptures, or deny his consciousness, or find some hitherto unknown method of reconciling the two. One of these three things he must do, or lose his confidence, either in the Scriptures or in God, and so fall off into despair. The *first* of these, his education and habit of thought forbids. The *second*, he finds as impossible as to deny his eyes. The third only remains, and that must be attempted. It is attempted, and the attempt is rewarded with a supposed discovery which,

* Conflict, p. 189.

to his mind, answers for success—a discovery which reconciles with *his* reason and conscience, the notion of endless misery as the sequel of the dying sinner's earthy state. And what is that discovery which relieves him? It is this,—that this world is but a last and forlorn hope, for all who come to breathe its vital air;—that the human race is but the refuse of a pre-existent mass of beings, sent down from a former state; a state in which their probation, unlike the probation of earth, had been so favorable and so long, that man's sense of "honor and right," approves the verdict of Jehovah, which, after *this* trial, condemns the unholy to endless woe! This is the discovery. And on making it, our author says, "it was as if when I had been groping in some vast cathedral, in the gloom of midnight, vainly striving to comprehend its parts and relations, suddenly, before the vast arched window of the nave, a glorious sun had suddenly burst forth, filling the whole structure with its radiance, and showing in perfect harmony the proportions and beauties of its parts."*

So Beecher found relief, and, in keeping with our design in introducing his case, several things may here be said, and,

First, who can estimate the pressure of difficulty, upon such a mind as his, necessary to drive it, in pursuit of relief, through all the avenues of fact,

*Conflict, p. 191

away back into the cloud-land of pre-existence. Surely his supposed discovery would seem but an invention, whose alternative was despair,—whose mother was the most terrible necessity. And,

Second, what must have been that midnight of mind, to which a few conjectural rays, gleaming faintly through clouds and darkness, from a land of imagination, should seem as the bursting forth of a glorious sun, before the nave window of a midnight cathedral. And,

Third, what must be that theological wretchedness, to which it is such abundant relief, to discover that this world, with all its garniture, instead of being a primary state, bears only a purgatorial relation to a former one, while unlike the purgatory of the papist, the masses of human beings who enter it, generally, make their exit from it, more miserable than when they entered, and to be more miserable forever. And,

Fourth. All this but shows of what fearful hallucination, the God-like mind is susceptible, under the distressing obscuration of a false theology. And,

Fifth. If Beecher could not find relief as "Foster and Channing" did, it is, surely, no wonder that Barnes could not find relief as Beecher did. The experiences of both go to establish the proposition with which we set out,—that it is by no means peculiar to weak and uneducated minds, to find serious difficulties with the hitherto popular penal creed. And,

Sixth, This case strongly suggests, whether the time does not hasten, when the eyes of all sincere Christians will be so open, that, in obedience to the absolute law of consciousness, as Beecher defines it, they will feel obliged, either to abandon the doctrine of endless punishment, as untaught in the Scriptures, or abandon the Scriptures themselves, or find, also, some strange, fanciful or mysterious solution of their difficulty.

At any rate, I hope, brother, that you will consider well why it is, that strong, educated, honest, earnest, independent and progressive minds, should find such occasion to *struggle* with difficulties, in what has been long and widely accepted, as the most reasonable of creeds. Beecher appears to have made the discovery of pre-existence as the alternative of abandoning the Scriptures. This is plainly gathered from his book. How many, involved in the same difficulty with him, and failing to penetrate beyond the mysterious bourn of his newly discovered region, and, through the force of education, like him unable to find relief as did "Foster and Channing," fall off, and shall fall off into skepticism, God only knows! Evidently the number of such is already "legion." Would that we could hope that it would never be greater.

Yours truly.

LETTER X.

GREAT MINDS IN TROUBLE — C. F. HUDSON.

Mr. H's book—His dilemma and relief—Quotation from his book—Praying against truth—Sad adjustment—*Terrible* dilemma—Wicked of no account—Conquer your prejudice!—Wicked of some account here, and in the resurrection—Why not after it?—Why their slumbers broken—Wrong time to perish!—Clinging to the Father—Gloomy prospects—Babel of confusion—Confusion increases—When it will subside.

DEAR BROTHER,—

Permit me, in this letter, to refer to one other person, the Rev. C. F. Hudson, as further illustrating the trial which thinkers experience with the doctrine of endless misery. Mr. H., formerly an Orthodox clergyman, having repudiated that doctrine as unreasonable and unscriptural, is now well known as the author of the very scholarly and elaborate work, entitled, "*The Doctrine of a Future Life.*" In that work, he disproves endless misery, and attempts to prove "annihilation." Involved in theological difficulty equally with Barnes, Foster and Beecher, he neither suffers on with the one, nor finds relief as do either of the other two. He loses *his* burden neither in future existence, nor in *pre-*

existence; but, in NON-EXISTENCE! Speaking of eternal misery, or as he expresses it, "the eternal evil that remains," he says, "Temper it as he [the Christian] will, it still challenges many doubts. Christian theology has labored for generations past, to find the maximum of reason, and the minimum of doubt. This has been the Conflict of Ages. And the conflict could not be confined to the schools. Filling the minds of all classes of men, and producing the various forms of false theology we have noted, it has borne most heavily upon the engineer of the doctrines of salvation,— the preacher of the gospel. It pursues him in every effort to maintain a theodicy. It pursues him in his resort to mystery, and in his appeal to man's innate sense of duty.* It meets him at the bedside of the dying and in the funeral of the dead. Whether he feels it or not, it haunts him every where, baffling his skill or marring his labor, in all his efforts to persuade men."— p. 407.

"But," he adds, "dispense with the doctrine as unauthorized, and how soon it appears needless. Let the wicked be regarded as if no account, and, as having no part in the world to come, and the powers of that world find their natural adjustment."

The truth of the major portion of the above quo-

* We have already heard Barnes say of the difficulties of endless misery, "They meet us when we urge our fellow sinners to be reconciled to God and put confidence in him. *On this ground they hesitate.*" How practical the difficulties!

tation, what thinking preacher of endless punishment has not felt,—what observing one, has not seen! How many, like one the author knows, have been obliged to pray against what they have deemed a satanic temptation to abandon that doctrine—but really, against the waking of their own consciousness, reason and affection.

But, says our author, "let the wicked be regarded as of no account, and as having no part in the world to come, and the powers of that world find their natural adjustment." And just by so regarding them, he finds his own theological system, adjusted to his great satisfaction. And though this adjustment may, to many minds, seem quite unnatural, still the contemplation of the annihilation of the wicked is satisfactory, compared with that of their endless woe.

But it is not, after all, a miserable relief we gain, by thus regarding the wicked as of no account in the future world! And must not that be a most terrible orthodox dilemma, from which the soul *rejoices*, to find deliverance by the dark and gloomy way, every where bestrown with the annihilated shades of our fellow beings, "bone of our bone, and flesh of our flesh," and *soul of our soul!* What must be that sorrow, to which it is joy to sit down in a family sepulchre to be reached by worse than no *resurrection.*

"Let the wicked be regarded as of no account in the world to come." Ah, yes, conquer your prejudices in favor of humanity, sever all the ties that bind you to your race, rend the delicate net-work of the Christian virtues, chiefly interwoven with love to all, insolate yourself from all but the pure and holy, if you chance to belong to that class, and regard all the rest as "of no account," and *then*, you are relieved — then your faith has found "its natural adjustment"! Sad relief! The relief of the body by amputation of the heart! But the Bible does not say, if thy benevolent heart offend against thy *creed*, "pluck *it* out and cast *it* from thee!" In reference to such an adjustment, we can but say, in the language of Mr. H. about endless evil, "Temper it as he will, it still challenges many doubts."

But the wicked *are* of some account in this world. And it is well that they are; for if they were not, it would go ill with our race, seeing "there is no man that liveth and sinneth not." *Here*, the wicked are loved and blessed; for here, we become perfect as our "Father which is in heaven is perfect," by loving and blessing our enemies; — a consideration of vast theological importance, lying far down in the ocean of Deity, undisturbed by the winds of contending textual criticisms that whip its surface. Here, the wicked are of so much importance, that God in Christ is looking after them continually.

In the resurrection, too, the wicked are of some account. "For the Scriptures positively affirm, that there shall be a resurrection both of the just and the unjust." And if the wicked are of some account *in* the resurrection, strange if they should be of no account afterwards. Why then are they raised up? "If they have no immortality, why are their slumbers disturbed?" This question, Mr. H. answers in part by saying, "it is as if the unjust, hearing the voice of God in the last call to life, should be putting on a glorious incorruption, and perish in the act." But surely, the act of putting on a glorious incorruption would seem the very last to *perish* in; especially, after having lain, according to Mr. H's theory, as nought, in the grave, for ages. And he who tells me that the wicked are *raised up*, as our author elsewhere says, to "languish back to nought," must excuse me from believing. For still, with God's elder Scripture in my heart and his younger in my hand, I will fast cling to my Father's skirts, and assure myself, not only that all his children shall have a resurrection, but that all shall be of some account afterwards. I can believe that *theologies*, which are the product of a soul, forced by education into unnatural connexion with monstrous dogma, may "languish back to nought," but not the *souls*, over which they wildly speculate.

We only add the reflection, that, if the wicked are

of no account in the future world, our prospects, and especially our prospects of re-union with departed friends, are very dark. For it is then, not only exceedingly doubtful whether they shall not be executed in the morn of the resurrection, but also, whether we shall not then be met by the angel of annihilation, and also stricken down to nought, while with them, in the very act of "putting on a glorious incorruption." For, who are the *holy* on earth?

But we need not pursue our chapter of illustrations farther. We have seen, in the cases cited in several preceding letters, that difficulty with the old penal theology, is felt by educated thinkers,—that it is a babel of confusion, from which they are scattered abroad, some into future existence, some into pre-existence, some into non-existence, and some, "the Lord knows where." Nor can we fail to see that this confusion increases as light deepens upon the world. And why must it not continue to increase? Certainly it cannot *subside*, till the Scriptures are so well understood, that man can walk in them, without trampling on the primary laws of his nature, and violating all the finer Christian sentiments of his heart. Then, and not till then, will the jargon be ended. Until that time, we may expect to see many a shipwrecked Theologian, like shipwrecked famished mariners, resorting to desperate expedients. And that time, I doubt not, will be, when the universal and everlasting Fatherhood of God shall be the greater light of all religion, and the practical Brotherhood of man, its lesser light, illumined by it and revolving round it.

And, now brother, if these letters shall find you in any plerplexity with *your* creed, you will not regard it as at all remarkable; but, I hope, think your way out of it, better than have some of your illustrious predecessors.

Yours truly.

LETTER XI.

SAFETY.

"I am safe any way"—Havoc of Creed—A Monster—Motive and Heaven—Heaven Lost—*What?* danger—The Old Prophets—*Where* Judgment—Lord's Prayer—Jehovah to be studied, not in vain—Universalism has Antagonisms—God loved for his lovableness—Religion, how valued—Worshipper like the Worshipped, illustrations—No rest from studying Jehovah—Must not be deceived in *his* Character, and why—Glory of "following the Lamb" —Sermon on the Mount—Earnest Question—Triumph of Universalism.

DEAR BROTHER,—

WE have seen how the doctrine of endless misery distresses and confounds men of the first mental qualities, and finest Christian mould. Perhaps, after all, *you* are not *quite* satisfied with it; so that, while I present you with what I deem a better faith, you may be saying, "I have no need to examine its claims, seeing that, if it *is* true, I am *safe any way.*" So, in substance, is it often said, though I think rarely by persons as intelligent as yourself. For the demoralizing influence of creed has, indeed, made sad havoc, when a man's notion of his religious obligations, has sunk down to the low level of mere personal safety; that very degraded level, trodden by "four-footed beasts, and creeping things."

True, safety is an element of human weal, which it were unnatural entirely to overlook. But, that a man should make safety his "*being's end and aim*," so that, being consciously safe, he should make that fact an argument for seeking no higher truth or nobler duty, were monstrous. It were as though in him were strangely joined, the reason of a man, with the instincts of the brute. In such a person, appears not a lineament of the Son of God. And, not until he comes to him, and learns from his lips and life, the higher lesson of self-sacrificing love, can he find the way to heaven, though he seek it "carefully and with tears." Heaven is, indeed, a place of safety, glorious safety. But its holy gates are forever barred against all who seek it as a place of safety *merely*. By the standard of Heaven, motive determines character, while character is the passport to it. Not to him, therefore, does its porter open, who is moved to seek admission only by selfishness, or the blind impulse by which a man flees from a mad tiger, or leaps from the jaws of an earthquake. The principle here involved is of vital importance,—the very pivot of eternal life. And yet, how blinded are the many to its practical value! How dim the light shed upon it by many a pulpit! Still is there abundant need of the prayer which we once heard from an excellent orthodox clergyman, in a union prayer meeting, "Lord, save sinners from seeking thee selfishly!"

Man is not to be indifferent to danger. But what danger? Or is there no danger save of *endless* woe? Not so thought the old prophets, whose earnest warnings, evidently, have no reference to such a woe. Even Jeremiah, whose "head *was* waters," in all his descriptions of the sorrows, in view of which he lamented, makes not the slightest allusion to such woe; nor even to woe beyond the grave. And yet, how many talk as though there is no noticeable danger of any other. How many pulpits are impressing upon their young auditors, that there is no other from which it is very *important* that they should escape; just as though God is limited, either to punishing none at all, or forever!—as though man must be whipped forever, or not whipped at all!!—and as though all this whipping must take place, only when the school is over, and it is too late for it to do any good!!! Whether this be so, or not, it certainly *looks* like the unnatural product of hallucination! It were more natural to suppose man's danger to be where his duty is,—his sorrow to be where his transgression is,—that the two things should dwell in mutual vicinity, and that God should "judge in the earth," as he says he does,—and that Christ should rather "come *into* the world for judgment," as he says he did, than that man should be carried *out* of the world for judgment; and this, especially, seeing that the whole matter, according to the popular idea, is *practically settled* before he is carried out!

Again, we say, man is not to be indifferent to danger. But *what* danger? Look at the "Lord's Prayer,"—that wonderful compend of devotion, adapted, like the "Golden Rule," to all time, place, and circumstance. That prayer contains no solitary intimation of escape and safety, as popularly taught; no deprecation of the danger which has been so popularly proclaimed,—no suggestion of the dreadful theme which has been so foisted into the chief place in pulpit discourse! Nothing of the kind whatever. But, rather, in its sublime simplicity, the simplicity of daily life,—it regards man as chiefly interested in his present relations and duties,—his present sorrows and joys. It contemplates a present sanctification of the Lord God in the heart, a present resisting of temptation, a present deliverance from evil, as wel as a present "daily bread." But not a word does it say about endless misery, or safety from it. And, right here, we submit the question whether, if Jesus had come into this world to save men from *such* misery, he must not have recognized deliverance from it, in the deprecatory portion of this universal prayer! Surely, if such had been his object, it must have so swallowed up all others, that any and all merely temporal evils, though such as had not been since the world began, nor yet should be, could not have commanded of him a moment's attention, a thought, or a tear! The fact, however, is far otherwise. Jesus regards temporal sorrows as of consequence, and bestows his labors in their removal; while the eternal sorrows of the creed, we think he does not recognize at all. But whether he does or not, it is equally true, that *mere safety*, as a motive to action, common to man and beast, is without a moral quality, and, therefore, without a moral value.

But further, what is man's work, as an earthly dweller beneath the star-sown azure, but "by searching to find out God." And though, with all the helps at hand, he cannot "find out the Almighty to perfection," yet, in the exploration of the fields of Deity, will daily search ever be rewarded with daily discovery. Jehovah has not said, "Seek ye my face in vain;" but, rather, "he that seeketh findeth;" "yea, if thou criest after knowledge, and liftest up thy voice for understanding; if thou seekest her as silver, and searchest for her as for hid treasure; then shalt thou understand the fear of the Lord, and find the knowledge of God." Certainly, too much of God cannot be known. So we agree; and, therefore, I ask, why you would limit your search for him, by the goal of safety, or why make your conscious safety a reason for declining to investigate the subject with which I present you,—a subject more deeply involving the character of God than any other ever broached among men,—a subject, the discussion of which *is* the discussion of that awful character.

So true is it, that Universalism, in contrast with all the opposing *isms* of the day, has something vastly important, for which to contend; nor can they fail the better to enjoy the Father's smile in the future world, who have faithfully defended his character in this. O, the moral grandeur of soaring benevolently and reverently to where the highest sense of safety is compassed by completely losing sight of it!

And, further still, "Love is the fulfilling of the law." The law is perfectly fulfilled, not by outward service, but by loving God "with all the heart." But even *God* is not to be loved *blindly*. He must be loved, if at all, for the lovableness of his character. There can be no other cause of *true* love. Whatever springs from other cause is but base alloy. If, then, our weal depends upon our love to God, and our love to him depends, as it certainly does, upon our apprehension of the lovableness of his character, shall we not, as we would perfectly fulfil the law, and be perfectly blessed by loving him perfectly, strive to find out his "lovableness" to perfection? And yet, do you propose to give up the search into it, merely because you feel safe against endless woe! That, surely, were a fearful coming down from the heights of Zion into the pagan plains of Ono,—a most disgraceful relapse into the darkness of the middle ages. I credit your Christian intelligence with no sentiment so gross and degrading.

And, yet further, is it not important what men *are?* And is not any religion valuable, just accordingly as it makes men what they *ought to be?* Nothing can be plainer. And is it not equally plain, that men gradually become like the God, or gods, they worship? Of this, the heathen nations are practical illustrations. In them, we clearly see the working of that law of sympathy between the worshipper and the worshipped, by which the former are gradually moulded into the character of the latter. But this law is peculiar to no class of religionists. It operates equally upon pagans and Christians, in New England and Hindostan;—equally upon *Stephen*, praying for his murderers, and *Calvin*, burning Servetus. The dark inquisitor of old Spain, coolly directing the tortures of his lamb-like victims,—was not he bolstered and nerved by his notion that Jesus Christ, the Son of the God whom he served was, forever, to direct the tortures of heretics, damned to everlasting pain! Who doubts it, or that the arm of the papal soldier was nerved by his penal creed, when, finding Zwingle, wounded by the wayside, he drove his bayonet to his heart, exclaiming, "*Die, heretic!*" Certainly, on the other hand, the better knowledge of God has ever brought the world the further on towards perfection. And the same must hold true, always. For the principle here involved lies at the basis of all true progress. It is the true stimulus to all true missionary religious operations. What are Christians sent to the heathen for, if not chiefly to improve their knowledge of God?

And now, brother, in the light of the above remarks, where is the point in the knowledge of God, which, being reached, I may say, "Now I need seek no further?" There is no such point. But do not a person's words imply that there *is*, and even that he has reached it, when he declines searching into a doctrine, so vital as that with which we present him, merely because, *if* true, he is *safe, any way*. Does he not, virtually, then say, "I know enough of God already, because I am good enough already? I do not wish to know any more that I may be made any better!" But far different is it with the person of right understanding. He says, "I would, by searching, find out more of God, that I may love him, and serve him better, and more cheerfully. I would not be deceived in *his* character, because I would not spoil *my own.* What though I, as an experimental Christian, am safe. Still, do I not earnestly desire to know whether there is any thing in the divine character, upon which I may repose hope for my fellow beings,—*fellow* beings,—bone of my bone and flesh of my flesh,—beings to whom I am bound by a thousand tender ties of fellowship and love, and to whom my whole Christian soul clings, in life and death! Surely, I must be very unlike any good divinity, so long as I can rejoice over my own security, in the presence of their *endless* ruin. So far from having the law of *God* in my heart, I am then rather acting upon the maxim, "*The devil take the hindermost!*" Such is the language of the man of true Christian understanding. To him, the discussion of the Father's lovableness is never like "spending money for that which is not bread." He talks, not of safety, but of duty. His concern is with his to-days, rather than his yesterdays and to-morrows. And lost, indeed, to him, is that day, which witnesses, for him, no deeper baptism into the knowledge and love of God. So is he fed with the abundance of God's goodness, and, exalted high above the miserable desert of religious selfishness, in which browse the lean and sickly ones, who only sadly and doubtfully hope that they shall "one day see the inside of heaven." But he is in a heaven already, and ever progressing into a richer one.

Safety from Jehovah's *everlasting wrath*, an excuse for not searching into his *character!* Let those who make it, go to the Sermon on the Mount, and learn what are the first "principles of the doctrine of Christ." For, surely, however skilled they may be in scholastic theology, they are ignorant of the Christian alphabet; and, however hopeful of heaven, they lack the primary element of its character and enjoyments.

And now, brother, though I am far from setting you down with the pitiful class just mentioned, yet it is possible that you, sometimes, incidentally think thoughts, and hastily drop words, which suggest some affinity with it. And I may again ask, in concluding this letter, whether, however safe you feel, and however well satisfied you may be, there are not times when you greatly need rest from the endless tossings of dreary, theological uncertainties! —rest from the "irrepressible conflict," ever going on between the heart God gave you, and the faith you have received! Be assured, Universalism is not always to be judged by the rags which orthodoxy is pleased to throw about it, in the presence of hoodwinked congregations. Its light is not always to be hidden by clouds of prejudice. Like the sun of the morning, it is destined to burn them all away, as it travels up the heavens. Man's whole nature, as well as God's holy word, is the sure guaranty of its ultimate triumph. This may seem strong language to you. But who knows but even *you* shall yet endorse it, as, viewing the divine character from some stand-point outside your creed, a new world shall open before you, bright with the effulgence of heaven? So we pray; and this the more hopefully, seeing that great changes are taking place in the theological world, and, unless all signs fail, are to continue to take place upon a broadening scale.

Yours truly.

LETTER XII.

UNIVERSALISM PRACTICALLY DEFINED.

Reader, not addressed as careless, utilitarian, or conservative—Skeleton creed—Nazareths and Jerusalems—Tradition questioned—Prejudice—Universalism practically defined at length—Involves difficulties—Harmonious with the heart—Sweet influence of.

Dear Brother,—

Permit me again to remind you that I do not address you as a person *careless* of his theology, nor do I address you as a theological *utilitarian*, who thinks of his creed merely in view of a present seeming availability; forgetting that the rod of terror, which forces the sinner down into the *position* of penitence, may, also, prevent his ever rising up into true Christian manhood; — filling his soul with crouching fear, to the exclusion of intelligent love. Nor, yet further, do I address you as a blind *conservative*, who, deeming that the dominant creed can have no errors to abandon, and no truths to adopt, is ready to stand over an antiquated sectarian altar, blowing among its dead, cold ashes, long after its fires have gone out; or, beside the old battery, long after its electric power has departed. You, I trust, have seen too much of theological change, to deem that no further change is needful. You perceive that the theological wheel of revolution is, even now, steadily revolving, and that, if its movement for the last half century shall be prolonged through the next half, the doctrine of endless punishment will have become but a fossil of the creed. Already more than ossified, it is often used as a fleshless skeleton, shaken in the face of that timidity which is more afraid of a dead human bone than of a living human arm, by persons who, judged by their appearance, care no more about it themselves, than the practical anatomist cares for the eyeless, grinning skulls of his dissecting-room, which frightens timid ones from its door! No, not as one, not as all of these, do I address you; but, as a person who thinks that, for *all* purposes, truth is better than error, and that the church may have many errors to abandon, and truths to adopt, before her light shall become "as the light of seven days," and her God her glory!

The orthodoxy of to-day was the heresy of yesterday. Why may not the heresy of to-day become the orthodoxy of to-morrow? The Jew, in his prejudice, scorned Nazareth, and yet that despised village was honored with the training of the son of Mary! *Jerusalem* could only crucify him! To-day, too, may have its Nazareths, in which are being trained, men of God, destined, wonderfully to bless mankind. And to-day, too, may have its Jerusalems, in which these men shall be crucified. Free inquiry is going abroad, and old traditionary foundations crumbling before it. Every doctrine is being more and more thrown upon the necessity of standing upon real merit, or not at all. Even the traditions of the papal church, are beginning to be called in question by its worshippers. Evidently the day comes hastening on, when, of all present religious Christian systems, that only, will remain, which, like God's word, cannot "pass away." The church may, indeed, be given into the hands of error, and lie in its thrall, "Yet for a time, times, and dividing of time;" but the hour advances when her eyes shall be lifted up to see "Jesus and him only!" Then will her deliverance have come!

"There is nothing of which a man may be so long ignorant, as of the extent and strength of his prejudices." I think I have seen this quotation credited to Bishop Butler. But no matter where it came from, it is profoundly true, and under the safeguard of a vivid apprehension of it, I wish you to read carefully the exposition of Universalism which I am about to write. You will thereby learn what it is, and whether your idea of it had, previously, been correct. I have put some of the leading propositions in negative form, that they may more directly meet certain mistaken views and assertions, which have been widely spread abroad. Throwing off technicalities, paying no regard to scholasticism and metaphysical subleties, I have endeavored that the exposition should meet the conditions and wants of the ordinary enquirer, in the plain, simple language of every day life.

What, then, is Universalism?

First, Universalism is not a Godless system. It is founded on the truth that "there is one God and only one;" and He, infinitely powerful, wise, good, just and holy. Its credal statement of the doctrine of God does not differ from that of other Christian denominations; though it may, indeed, lay more stress upon it, as setting forth the principle of universal government, and as providing the key for opening what would otherwise be the dead locks of Scripture difficulty. In other respects, for aught we see, it stands precisely with them, on the fundamental doctrine of all Christian religion — the doctrine of God.

Second, Universalism is not a Christless system. The God whom it glorifies is "the Father of our Lord Jesus Christ," which Christ, it cheerfully accepts, as "the only name given under heaven among men, whereby we must be saved." It believes that, "When we were yet without strength, in due time,

Christ died for the ungodly;"—that he became "a propitiation for our sins, and not for ours only, but for the sins of the whole world;"—that he is the way, the truth, and the life;"—that he is "the light of the world;"—that he lived "our example," died "our justification," and that, in "his resurrection," he becomes "the first fruits of them that slept." It knows nothing of particular atonement, while in other respects, it agrees with other popular theological systems, in regarding Christ as a practical and all-sufficient Saviour, "able to save to the uttermost all who come unto God by him."

As to the metaphysics of the Trinity, whose nice and blind questions, have convulsed œcumenical councils, shaken thrones, and laid the dust of empires with fratricidal blood, Universalism, *as such*, prudently lets them alone, satisfied to confide all to Christ, and to teach his all-sufficiency. Thus do Universalists exalt Him "above all principality and power," as the hope of the sinner, "the Saviour of the world." None, more than they, have occasion to sing—

> "In the cross of Christ I glory,
> Towering o'er the wrecks of time!
> All the wealth of ancient story,
> Gathers round its head sublime!"

or, to sing, with apocalyptic ecstasy, "Worthy is the Lamb that was slain, to receive power, and riches, and wisdom, and strength, and glory, and honor, and blessing." And none, more than they do hear, with the exile of Patmos, "Every creature which is in heaven and in the earth, and such as are in the sea, and all that are in them, saying, blessing, and honor, and glory and power, be unto Him that sitteth upon the throne, and to the Lamb forever and ever!" Thus is their faith not Christless, but full of Christ. Therein it is

"Him first, him last, him midst, and without end."

Thirdly, Universalism is not an *unspiritual* system. It worships God "as a Spirit," and believes that, "as a Spirit," he is everywhere abroad; and that man can do nothing without his aid, as a Spirit.

As to what are, and are not, special influences of the Divine Spirit, Universalists, like Limitarians, may differ in opinion among themselves. They generally think that much is credited to its *special* influence, which does not belong to it. For instance, here is a man of strong mind and will, full of nervous energy, versed in human nature, eloquent, and capable, therefore, of long sustaining the most pathetic pulpit appeal—capable of painting the most stirring pictures of endless woe, and eloquently and tearfully holding it up full before the imagination of his hearers. Now, when such a person preaches, we expect the people who attend, *confidingly*, upon

10*

his ministry, to be moved—moved to fly for refuge from the fears he excites, just as *naturally*, as a man is moved to escape from a house which he believes to be on fire. And, when we see this, we are not to regard it as the special result of divine influence, but simply, as the result of mind acting on mind,—alarm cries, acting on fears.

But, in all this, Universalism does not differ from intelligent Limitarians, while it agrees with them, that God's spirit is everywhere abroad, influencing the hearts of the children of men, "both to will and to do," of his good pleasure. If, in any thing, they differ from other Christian denominations, it is in giving to this Divine Spirit, a higher purpose and a wider field. For they suppose its motions by no means confined to temples made with hands, but that it is with all men, everywhere,—in shop, street, and counting-room, on mountain-top, ship-deck, and desert sands, — and everywhere whispering, in a still, small voice, "*This is the way; walk ye in it.*"

Fourthly, Universalism is not an unholy system. No class of Christians are more tenacious than Universalists of the vital truth, that, without "holiness, no man shall see the Lord." They believe that nowhere in the realm of Deity, can a sinner be truly happy—that nowhere can mere ritual service, catechetical knowledge of God, or intellectual culture, introduce an unholy person into the enjoyments of heaven. This, they teach and exhort; and not, as they "be slanderously reported," that men are to be indiscriminately swept into heaven *in their sins.* Universalists believe that sin *is* misery; and this, not the less, though committed on the golden pavements of the New Jerusalem, and under the very shadows of the throne of Love. So says Universalism, and so it wills that all Christian teachers affirm constantly.*

No, not *Universalism*, but *Limitarianism*, is more open to the charge of believing in an *unholy heaven.* For the latter generally teaches,—what all observation confirms,—that Christians are sinful till they die. It also teaches that death works no change from sin to holiness, and that there can be no such change after death. And, if all this be so, then either heaven must be an unholy place, or no pilgrim from earth can ever enter it. For souls unholy when they leave *this* world, and unchanged

* And yet how often have you heard ignorant or dishonest men attempt to get the laugh of their hoodwinked congregation upon us, by turning the heaven of Universalism to ridicule;—as, for instance, by telling how some little child said, of his nervous old *grandpa*, "If he goes to heaven, I don't want to;" or how some one asked, whether the murderer of "the babes in the wood," if he goes to heaven, won't kill them over again. The misrepresentations involved in this whole class of anecdotes are the result of either ignorance or villainy. But against him who makes them, we bring no railing accusation, but only say to him, as Michael to the devil, "when disputing about the body of Moses," "The Lord rebuke thee!"

on their way to the *next*, must be unholy on their arrival at heaven's gate; and, not sanctified *after* their arrival, must ever be "without," with "dogs and sorcerers." Or, if they go in, as our opponents affirm, then is heaven an unholy place.

But all this is foreign to the faith of Universalists. They believe, most sanguinely, that without holiness no man shall see the Lord—that only in degree as men are holy can they enjoy him. And, hence, Universalism yields to no other doctrine or system of doctrine, in its abhorrence of sin. It holds sin to be, *in itself*, sinful,—the foul and monstrous "mother of woe" and "death;"—that it touches but to blight and curse,—that it opens a burning hell in man's bosom, and would in the bosom of Gabriel, could it gain admission there,—that, could it enter the perfect paradise, it would be a frightful meteor, which must make holy ones pause upon their harp-strings, and flee, with terror and dismay, across the plains of light, to hide themselves in the throne of God. Universalists hold that sin is *so* dreadful, not because the Father is *vindictive*, but because of its own dreadful nature. It *hath* torment, and men must, in this or any other world, feel its tormenting sting, so long as they indulge in it. So they believe as a denomination. And, so believing, repentance is the burden of their ministry.

Fifthly, as is implied in the preceding remarks, Universalists believe that, for all the wicked, a change of heart is necessary. What they understand this change to be, is also therein implied. It is simply a change from sinfulness to holiness,—from sinfulness of *heart* to "holiness of *heart*." As to the means of this change, I know not that they differ from so-called evangelical denominations. As to the manner of it, perhaps they differ from some. Solomon says: "Train up a child in the way he should go, and when he is old he will not depart from it." Now if a person is already "in the way he should go," he only needs be cheered on. But if in the way he should *not* go, *he* needs be exhorted, persuaded, alarmed; for his sorrows will increase, as he farther pursues it. And when, aroused by the gospel, and brought to a stand, he "thinks on his way," turns round, and resolves on a holy life, then is he happy. And, in executing this resolve, is he regenerated, "conformed to the likeness of Christ;" and this, not by his own might or power, "but through the Eternal Spirit." Then has he peace with God, and his "fellowship is with the Father, and with his Son Jesus Christ;" then, like the eunuch, he goes "on his way rejoicing."

Thus we think Universalists *practically* differ less from the dominant sects in their views of a change of heart, than they do in their mode of expressing it. Throwing off theological technicalities, they use terms which the people can understand; as some physicians rule out the Latin upon their bottles, and let them speak English to Englishmen. Many a simple, in medicine, is often clothed with magical properties, in the eye of the patient, by being shaken from a phial, mysteriously labelled! To this, however, we have no disposition to file in any objection. But we do file in an objection to mystifying *discipleship to Christ*, by covering *it* up with unmeaning technicalities. These technicalities, Universalism aims to throw off, and to talk of discipleship in the language of practical life. As Jesus addressed Jews in language plain to Jews, so would Universalists address men of this nineteenth century, in language familiar to this century. And it is in doing this, that the latter sometimes *seem to differ* from their contemporary Christians, and where, really, they *do not.*

Here is a noble tree, sweeping the clouds with its majestic top. Two men stand looking at it. One of them says, "That is a "noble *white oak.*' O, no, says the other, that is not a white oak; that is a *macro carpa.* Both are right, for macro carpa is but the technical name for white oak. Two girls run for a flower. One says, O, is it not a pretty *buttercup?*" "Why, how you talk," says the other; "that is not a buttercup; that is a ranunculus.

But both are right, ranunculus being but the technical name for buttercup. So the Universalist says, "the Christian is one that loves and serves God." "O no," says his evangelical neighbor, "the Christian is one who has been born again." And here, also, both are right; for to be brought to love and serve God, is to "be born again," as that phrase is now understood by the church generally. And thus we find a practical harmony where many look for discord. And further, this being so, let no man hereafter say that Universalism does not hold to a change of heart.

Sixthly. Universalism believes the *means of grace* which God has ordained, *to be of infinite importance.* Among these, it reckons the creation, the Scriptures, Jesus, the Spirit, preaching, parental counsel, prayer, and every possible good influence "given under heaven among men." And of these means of grace, it believes that men must avail themselves.

But, do you say, men will be saved whether they use the means of grace or not? Then we reply, Never! Neither in this world, nor in any other can men be saved without the use of such means of grace as God affords them. Universalists only hold, in reference to *all*, what you do in reference to a *part*—that they will sooner or later, be led to the use of the means. If you are a Calvinist, then they only hold that God has *ordained* for *all*, what you say he has *ordained* for only a *part* of the human family. If you are an Arminian, then they hold that he *foreknew* for *all*, what you say he *foreknew* for only a *part*. And so they are, at least, *as consistent* as you are. Now, surely, you cannot suppose that Universalists should think less of the means of grace because they are to meet with a higher and fuller success. Here is a ship, off shore, stranded and going to pieces upon the rocks. The shrieks of the crew are in our ears. Here, too, is a boatman with two skiffs moored upon the strand. With the one, he can bring off only a part of the crew. With the other he can bring off the whole. Now, "which of the twain," do you think the most highly of, as a means of grace, to that sinking crew? "Why," you answer, "of the one that can bring them all off, of course!" Then, for heaven's sake, don't think it strange that Universalists esteem the means of grace which can save the entire human race, more highly than a means which can save only a part, leaving the multitude to perish miserably, from the stranded ship of humanity,—forever to blend their wail with the roar of wrathful billows, as they dash them about, and throw their fiery spray, high o'er the rocks of everlasting death!

Seventhly. Universalism believes that "though hand join in hand *the wicked shall not go unpunished*." This punishment, however long and severe, it believes to be, not vindictive, but paternal; and that, as such, it is designed to influence men towards ultimate repentance and good. It does not hold that punishment purifies, or pays any debt, or is, in itself, in any way a ground of pardon; but that its office is to awaken reflection, and thus to assist the sufferer into the way to heaven. As to the duration of punishment, Universalism only affirms that, as its object is repentance, it must continue till repentance is reached, whether in this or the future world. In a word, it believes that God punishes men, not as a being who delights in the endless pain of the souls he made, but as a good and benevolent Being, whom all creatures can love.

Eighthly. Universalism holds that the will of God is that all men shall be saved, and that he will ultimately save all. Save all from what? From hell? Yes; if by that you mean the hell which sin opens in every sinner's bosom. But the Bible says nothing about Jesus' coming into this world to save men from *hell!* It does say that he came to save men from their sins. Over the very gateway of his advent to earth, as on the very bright cloud that bore him down, was it written, "His name shall be called Immanuel, for he shall save his people from their sins." And the beloved disciple says, "Ye know that he was manifested to take away our sins." *This* was his mission to earth, — to "make an end of iniquity, transgression and sin." Will he succeed? Universalism believes that he will. It sees complete success guaranteed directly, by the Divine *promises*, and indirectly, by the Divine character. It believes that complete success was involved in God's plan in the beginning, and that all the means of grace which he employs have reference to its full accomplishment; that, as mercy is a divine attribute, the door of mercy is forever open, and that the Father will never be satisfied till the children by him created, and by him thrust under temptation, shall have all returned to holiness and heaven. So believe Universalists, and how reasonable and harmonious does their faith appear. And this, especially, when compared with the faith which makes the Father create myriads of immortal beings, and put them through the wilds of his providence, either foreknowing or foreordaining their endless damnation. Surely, in the light of this latter faith, we may well say, without irreverence, God is *darkness*, and in him is no *light* at all; whereas, in the faith of Universalism, we may exultingly exclaim, "God is *light*, and in him is no *darkness* at all."

Such, brother, is Universalism. I hope you will ponder it well. Doubtless you will say it involves difficulties. And doubtless it does. To man's feeble mind, what does not? And especially, what *system of theology* does not? But, compared with its antagonistic systems, I am persuaded you will, on careful examination, find its difficulties few and small. It neither sports with human affection, nor assaults the citadel of man's consciousnes. It neither drives Barnes into darkness, Beecher into cloud-land, nor Hudson into annihilation. But, joining all men in one brotherhood, and presenting them with the Fatherhood, it seems the natural way of Love and Rest. Softening, with its mellow light, the otherwise mysterious gloom of earth, it fills the human soul with a mild and blissful radiance, and lends a silver lining to all the dark clouds of Providence, with which man's mental day is overcast.

Yours truly.

LETTER XIII.

DESTINY — WHEN ABSURDITIES ALARMING.

Human destiny interests God, man, the glorified; and must forever, though human origin be forgotten—Author's interest—Last letter —Why absurdities will be noticed—Truth cannot fail.

DEAR BROTHER,—

The theme of these letters, — human destiny, — must, for depth of interest to human beings, be forever without a parallel. It chiefly interested Jehovah when he planned human creation. And that he is still interested in it, appears, as a golden thread, running through the entire fabric of revelation. Scarcely a page of the New Testament but discloses some vista to higher skies, through which angel fingers beckon us upward. And if it is a *necessary* truth, that the end of human existence should chiefly interest the author of that existence, it seems only a *natural* truth, that, in that Divine interest, man should sympathise. The question, "I came, but whence?" is important, *very!* The question, "I go, but where?" is important *infinitely!!* And, though we might *imagine* the former question to be forgotten, in the lapse of unnumbered ages, the latter can never lose its interest. For, though immortal beings may lose sight of their origin, never of their destiny! Origin is lived away from, — destiny is lived into. The latter must fill the contemplations of Eternity, and ever swell out in the song that wakes its echoes.

The announcement of the old patriarch is solemn, when he says, "*Man dieth and wasteth away;* yea, *man giveth up the ghost.*" But infinitely more solemn is his startling question, when he adds, "*and where is he?*" This is the question of questions, to every man who, filled with the light of Christianity, recognizes in every handful of human dust with which earth is bestrown, every human bone which the furrow reveals, the relict of a real brother. Infinitely more startling to him is this question than that with which Byron skeptically closes his apostrophe to a human skull:

> "Can all saint, sage, or sophist ever writ,
> People this lonely tower, this tenement refit?"

So grand is the theme of these letters. God forbid that you should turn away from them, because of its improper treatment. Bungling speech is often accepted by auditors, because of the evident pathos of the speaker's heart. And could I, my heart should so seal and spiritualize these words now dropping from my pen, that they should be read, if not for their literal import, for the spirit they breathe. Be assured, brother, they are the well-meant endeavor of a soul awed into humility, in the presence of his subject, and sighing along every line, because it is not receiving ampler treatment. But, brother, if I can but arouse candid investigation of the subject in hand, I shall be content. For sure I am, that candor and impartiality can hardly fail to conduct a waking soul, of your intelligence, quite away from the doctrine of endless misery, for the many, to the doctrine of endless life for all!

The doctrine of endless life, as holden by Universalists, I set forth in my last letter, and whatever else you may think of that doctrine, I presume you will admit, as I have before intimated, that it is harmonious with the generous and noble impulses of the human heart, that it has an air of naturalness, if I may so say, which commends it at once, as most believable to the unprejudiced mind, and that, whatever absurdities it seem to you involve, it involves none of the *ugly* ones, which so heavily burden the popular faith, sowing deep suspicion in the very hearts of its confessors. And now, with some of these letters, I propose to present you; less, however, by way of disproof of the doctrine which involves them, but as a means of stimulating further inquiry, in view of allaying the suspicions they excite. And yet, I must say that, though I do not put them on direct evidence here, they do seem to me, much of the nature of that circumstantial evidence, which, in civil courts, is often regarded as no less weighty than positive testimony, and sometimes more so.

To man, with his limited knowledge, the truest religious doctrines necessarily involves mysteries, and may, for the time being, involve absurdities. I say, for the time being; because, if the doctrines be true, the absurdities it involves, exist only in man's ignorance, and must therefore, fade away, as the light of knowledge increases. But when a religious doctrine involves many and obvious and radical absurdities, and when its absurdities increase, both in number and ugliness, with the increase of light, I think it may well be held under doubt. If the Bible is understood to teach such a doctrine, it is not skepticism, but zeal for the Scriptures, to ask, whether the teachings of that holy book have not been misunderstood.

We will now proceed to the inquiry, whether such, or such-like absurdities, are involved in the popular doctrine of endless punishment. In prosecution of this inquiry, I may have occasion to express myself strongly. But unless I am led widely astray, you shall have no occasion to suspect me of unfairness, as I trust I shall have none to suspect you of a want of Christian candor. With this inquiry, I may be a little lengthy, for it has deeply impressed my own mind, and is of sweeping importance. However, I hope not to be tedious. What I have to say, I shall merely throw upon the current of your thoughts, and leave it to work its passage to your convictions or otherwise. If aught I say, when well pondered, cannot bear its weight, let it fall. I shall be the last to prop it. It is then not of truth; for truth, having no earthly centre toward which it gravitates, can never fall, though it may be misunderstood. But I think I will defer entering upon the inquiry indicated, until the opening of my next letter.

Yours truly,

LETTER XIV.

FIRST ABSURDITY—MAN CREATED FOR ENDLESS MISERY.

Central Truth of Universalism—Absurdities of the Doctrine of Endless Misery—*First, That God should create in view of it*—Creator Independent, and " Love "—Probation short or long—God not obliged to create, or keep alive—God and Satan, how alike—Adam Clarke, Confession of—No Afterwards—Absurdity inseparable from the Creed—Suppose the *old* Doctrine involved such, what then?

DEAR BROTHER,—

Among Universalists, as among all other denominations of any intelligence, you will find persons holding more or less than is laid down in the authorized creed. (The Procrustean bedstead has never been made to work completely, even in the hands of the papacy itself; and we trust it is going out of use altogether.) But, as we saw in our ninth letter, Universalism proper contemplates one single truth, well worthy to swallow up all others, viz., *the Bible doctrine of the final salvation of all men from sin;* and this in opposition to their being forever annihilated, or forever damned. It regards other truths, compared with this, only as moments compared with eternity, or only as stars which meekly veil themselves, and retire when the resplendant sun appears. And now, rational and scriptural as all this seems to *me*, to you it may involve more or less of absurdity. Certainly, rational and scriptural as your penal doctrine seems to you, to me it involves the most *alarming* absurdities. Some of these latter I will now consider; and

First. Your faith implies that "God, the Father," casts vast multitudes of intelligent, immortal beings, in his own image, and places them in this world of trial, either foreordaining *that* he will, or foreknowing that he *shall*, damn them forever. And this seems to me an absurdity.

The Creator dwells in his own self-sufficiency. Of course, he is independent of everything outside of himself, and, therefore, can have no occasion, in creating, or in dealing with his creatures, to seek selfish ends;—a thing, which is alike forbidden, by the revelation of his essential nature. "For God is Love." Now that such a God should interest himself in begetting immortal beings, "*of his own will*, and in his own image, to feel his wrath forever—to be forever dying, but never dead,—to have their capacity for suffering forever filling up, but never full, does seem to me absurd in the extreme.

For, mark, no matter how long the creature's probation may be,—ten minutes, or ten years, or ten thousand years, or all the years of Beecher's imaginary pre-existence,—eternity equally follows; and the eternity of the creature's anguish was equally present to the Creator, when he set him up in being. You may say, as an Arminian,—not as a Calvinist,—that God did not *foreordain* the creature's ruin; but you will not deny that he endowed the creature with a susceptible nature, which, coming in contact with the world, into which he thrust him, he foresaw would work his certain ruin. And what you will not deny is, in the premises, all I ask you to admit. For, either way, the creature's endless misery was present to the divine mind, at the moment of his creation.

I do not intend dwelling long on this point, as it has been indirectly intimated in preceding letters, and must necessarily have an implication with the entire discussion. But permit me to ask if the doctrine in review, considered in its relation to the creating hand of God, does not appear to you absurd?—so absurd, that, as you *steadily contemplate* it, your whole soul does not reel and stagger as with the very giddiness of skepticism itself?

And here let it be borne in mind:

First. That it was optional with God whether to create the subject of foreknown, everlasting misery, or not.

Second. That, having created such a being, it is optional with him whether to sustain him in his anguish forever, or to permit him to sink out of it into nought.

And so much being borne in mind, how can we but stand appalled at the dreadful inconsistency between our ideas of the divine *character*, and our ideas of the divine *action?* For, allowing Satan a personal existence, and all the malice and cruelty ascribed to him, and to all this superadding infinite creative energy, what could *he* do worse than to create millions of intelligent, immortal beings, with such powers and circumstances that their existence should culminate in ceaseless misery? And if God do this, how is he better than Satan? *How* better? Seeing that his creating hand so abundantly supplies Satan with subjects for his torments. And then how are the words *godly* and *satanic* become synonymous!

Now to say that a God of infinite Love and Justice should sink under his endless curse, the beings whom he has thus created, endowed, and circumstanced!—well, brother, I do not ask that it shall appear to you as cruelly absurd as it does to me; but I do ask that you think of it *well*, and ponder still more carefully the paths of your feet along the wilds of speculative theology.

Dr. Adam Clarke, speaking of God, in his comment on 1 Peter iii. 15, says, "Do not suppose that he can do evil, or that he can *destroy*, when he *might* save." The doctor here assumes the *inability* of God to save,—an inability which *Barnes* repudiates.* But the Being who is too good to destroy (in the doctor's sense) one of his creatures, *only* when he *cannot* save him, is certainly too good to create a being, foreknowing that he must forever *damn* him.

But the doctor further says, speaking still of God, "Ever remember . . . . . that he can neither be, say, purpose, or do, any thing that is not infinitely just, holy, wise, true, and gracious." But wherein it is either infinitely just, or holy, or wise, or true, or gracious, in Jehovah to create multitudes of beings, with the seal of their everlasting misery distinctly visible upon their brows, has never yet appeared; but only the contrary. So that even Dr. Clarke himself, after having given the graphic and truthful description of God, from which we have quoted, immediately added, "What I have written above is not against any particular creed of religious people; it is against any or all to which it may apply; it may even be against *some portions of my own*," &c. Did not the great commentator here feel some of the "difficulties" which, Barnes says, "meet the mind when we think on this great sub-

* See Letter.

ject; and meet us when we endeavor to urge our fellow sinners to be reconciled to God, and to put confidence in him, . . . *real*, not imaginary difficulties? "Did he not feel, that the character with which he had invested his God, most truly *did* "lie against" his creed, or, as he says, "against some portions" of it? And did he not feel, in his heart of hearts, that it lay equally against all creeds, which make the Creator punish forever the creatures of his own will and power?

Indeed, as a man of sense, feeling, and reflection, how could he have felt otherwise?

We have already spoken of temporal evils, permitted to immortal beings, commencing upon a low plane of existence, and destined to endless progress, as admitting of explanation. They have a use, and an afterwards. But this absurdity of immortal evil, I think, can have none, save a terribly Hopkinsian or vindictive one.* Yet it is so involved in your creed, that its separation from it were as impossible as the amputation of the cloven foot of the devil. To shrink from it, therefore, is to shrink from your creed. To deny it is to deny your creed. To abandon it is to abandon your creed. If you have said that Universalism involves absurdities, pray ask

* Dr. Hopkins supposed, as we elsewhere quote, that the presence of the lost before the eyes of the Sacred, would abundantly augment the joy of the latter, raising it to "ineffable height." Stuart, that it will aggravate the sorrows of the lost.

yourself how it would show, if it involved *such an one as this;* and whether it would not then be thrown, by the dominant sects, into the waste-box of self-evident error!

Yours truly.

LETTER XV.

SECOND ABSURDITY—THE DEVIL.

Second Absurdity—the Popular Devil—God made him, foreknew him, and can control or destroy him—He is one of the great Family brotherhood—works in God's Strength—His Works cannot be overruled—"Friday's" Question,—why the Devil is not shut up *now*, *not* to be again let loose—What he has done for our Ancestors—Quotation from Milton,—made Himself a Devil, no Relief—Out-generals Jesus—Must be taken with the Creed that involves him!

DEAR BROTHER,—

In my last letter, by way of illustrating the character with which your creed invests the Father, I referred to the being called "Devil," "Satan," &c. And so I may as well here note

Secondly, That your creed implies that God, the Father, sustains a mighty being called Devil, filled with all malice against every thing good, in going about to effect the endless misery of his human creatures. And this all seems to me an absurdity.

In discussing it, no question need be raised about the personal existence, origin or character of this evil being, further than to say:

1. That, whatever Devil there is, God the Father made.

2. That, however he may have been originally created, and whatever evil character he may have since taken on, the Creator has not been disappointed in him.

3. That, whatever strength he now has to do mischief, the Creator gives him.

4. That the Creator can control him, or destroy him, at pleasure;—which is, indeed, implied in the third of these propositions.

The Devil, then, is the offspring of God, no less than we. And it is in God that he, no less than you and I, "lives, and moves, and has his being." He, too, is one of the Father's great family of intelligent moral beings, and, as such, is bound to all the other members, by the ties of a lofty relationship. But you say, he has sinned, and fallen into absolute, hopeless ruin, and that now, filled with hatred to all, and mightier than all, he goes about for the destruction of all—destruction absolute, endless. But, in all this, you are obliged to admit that he is fulfilling the divine idea in his creation; for the Creator has not been disappointed. And, too, the great Father is every moment strengthening the Devil for his constant work of spiritual carnage; so that, even he, lifting his hand, dripping with the blood of souls, plunged from the ship of humanity into the ocean of damnation, may truthfully exclaim, "By the grace of God I am what I am." He made me, he preserves me, and I do this work in *his strength.* And yet I defy him to bring any good out of this evil that I do; for the evil *itself* is *endless.* My hour is eternal! There is no afterwards in which He, almighty though he is, can either overrule or undo this fatal work of my hand."

Now that God should create such a being, foreseeing what he would be and do,—what havoc he would make of his other children,—and that, having created him, he should preserve and sustain him in his work of *inseparable* devastation through his realm, seems to us exceedingly absurd. And in view of it, we think the simple question of Crusoe's man Friday, "Why not God kill Debbil," was well put. Nor can intelligent Christians ever see anything but the most cruel absurdity in the notion that God the Father should create such a being, and give him the freedom of the universe for the everlasting destruction of his children. They, too, may well wonder why God does not, at least, shut him up, for the protection of the race on which he preys. We can easily conceive that, when such a being as this Devil enters Paradise, "damnation should follow." But we cannot conceive how it can be possible that, when the infant human race is nestling there in peace, a God of goodness should let him in!

We are indeed told, that the Devil shall yet be bound "for a thousand years," after which he shall be "loosed" again "for a little season." During that happy time, of course, his havoc of human souls shall cease, and perdition's supply of anguish be cut off. But the loving Christian heart, in view of the souls constantly dragged down to the pit all around him, earnestly asks, "Why *delays* that happy hour? Why comes not the angel with the chain *now?* Why is not Satan bound *to-day*,—this *minute?* Nay, why was he ever let loose? And when he shall, at least, be bound, why shall he ever be let loose again? And who can answer these questions, save by putting on true Hopkinsian boldness, and saying that God yet has made work for the Devil to do!—that perdition is not yet so full as he desires to have it!—that greater havoc of human souls is necessary before God shall be fully pleased!

These remarks may seem to you severe; perhaps satirical. But, be assured, they are made on the most sober and thoughtful earnestness. Why should they not be? For the Devil and his works, as understood by your faith, are matters of the highest, deepest, broadest, longest, most overwhelming interest. I feel it so, as I consider what he has already done, according to your creed, for many of my ancestors and yours, and what he is still doing. When he, himself, first sunk into the pit, Milton makes him exclaim:

> "Farewell, happy fields,
> Where joy forever dwells. Hail, horrors, hail!
> Infernal world! And thou, profoundest hell,
> Receive thy new possessor!"

And when I consider what multitudes he has dragged,—according to your faith,—dragged down with him, my gushing heart can but sympathize in the question of the simplest child of nature, "Why not God kill Debbil?"

But still you will, perhaps, seek relief from the terrible absurdity of your orthodox position, by re-affirming that God the Father did not create "that evil one" a *devil*, but that he has made a devil of himself. Be it so. And what relief is gained? Evidently none at all; for, *first*, no Philistine chance has happened to the Deity.* The devil is only the being that God foreknew or foreordained in his creation. And, *second*, if the question why God *created* him *were* satisfactorily disposed of, the question why he lets him run, have free course, and glorify himself in hell, by dragging others down into it by millions, still remains unanswered, or answered only with a glaring absurdity.

But I must say only two or three things more relative to this satanic matter. And

First, we know that God so loved all the individuals of the human race, that he gave his Son "a ransom for all, to be testified in due time," according to the Scriptures. And,

Second, you, through your creed, virtually affirm that God created the mighty being, called "the Devil," let him loose, and now sustains him in work-

*See Appendix.

ing the endless ruin of the responsible masses whom he gave his Son to save ;—so out-generaling the Son of God that, while the latter, by the mightiest exertions of his love, succeeds in winning only "here and there a traveller," into the "narrow way" to everlasting life, the former succeeds in perpetually thronging, with his captives, the broad way to the black caverns of endless woe ! And

Third, when asked how you will dispose of the dreadful absurdity here involved, you will say—I know not what. But for ourselves, we see *no* way of disposing of it, and feel bound to look, with not a little suspicion, upon whatever system of theology involves it. Such system, however time-honored, and however sanctioned by majorities, and by great and worthy names, should, to say the least, be accepted only after the most thorough examination, and under evidence the clearest and most direct from God. But every absurdity must stand or fall, be taken or left, with the creed that involves it. "For they twain are one." What God has naturally joined together, let no man attempt to put asunder. The Devil must be taken for better or worse, with anything whatsoever in which he dwells, or the thing itself be rejected.

Yours truly.

LETTER XVI.

THIRD ABSURDITY,—INFANTS SAVED, ADULTS LOST.

Bible, the standard, how read without profit.—*Third Absurdity, Infants saved, Adults lost*—Infant Damnation passed by—Few Adults regenerated—We may *know* who are lost, as well as who are saved—Absurdity *dreadful*—The Slave Mother—Infanticide—Truthful Illustration, but dreadful—The Infanticide and her Pastor—Illustration Tame—Mother's Dilemma—Don't turn away Brother—Dreadful Prayer—Heathen Infanticide—Mother's Prayer the Greatest Curse ! !—Earnest Question—Why not arranged to save all in Infancy—To live, perils everything—Objection, an Absurdity—Parents stronger than God—Parents responsible for the Child's *present* Condition—No Apology for Strong Language.

DEAR BROTHER,—

While we agree that the Scriptures are the ultimate standard of theological appeal, I think we shall also agree, that he who comes to them under the influence of strong prejudice stands but a poor chance for the truth. For the spirit with which he enters them will pioneer for him a sectarian way, dividing the texts before him, attracting these and repelling those, till what remains, to his mind, of the sacred word is certain to confirm him in his peculiar views,—till, covered all over with the texts which his idiosyncrasies have attracted, and forgetting all the rest, he becomes doubly sure that his views are right. I am, therefore, anxious that our discussion should reach the Scriptures rightly rather than hastily; and, consequently, must delay you yet a while, with the discussion of the absurdities involved in the faith which your prejudices all favor. For it is only when one's mind is in a condition to say, "I *may* be wrong," that he can hope to profit from any doctrinal discussion, however scriptural. But we proceed to say

Thirdly, that the popular creed implies that it is only at the most appalling hazard, that a human being survives its infancy on earth;—that, for it to die in infancy is to make its eternal salvation sure; whereas, for it to live to the age of accountability on earth, is to be exposed to endless woe, and, probably, to make that woe sure. And this, also, seems to me an absurdity.

We say, nothing, here, of the once prevalent doctrine of infant damnation, a doctrine which, a few years ago, it was heresy to disbelieve, and which has yet been dead hardly long enough to warrant safe burial! That shall pass for the present, with only the passing remark, that, we think its death forestalls the death of the entire class of dogma to which it belongs; and that, to us, the question of the prevalence of better doctrine, is only one of time. It is enough for our purpose here, to say that, whatever may be the *logical* limits of any modern creeds, the salvation of infants is now practically regarded as secure, — afflicted parents are now everywhere taught to dry their tears on the funeral of their infant offspring, under the comforting assurance, that the flower that bloomed so sweetly upon their bosom for a day, withered, not that it should die, but only in process of transplantation to more genial skies.

Infants then are saved — all saved. So says the church with one common voice. To affirm the contrary, were to shock the ear of Christian civilization, — even as, not many years hence, we think it will be shook by any affirmation that this life, so passionate, ignorant, and short, is to prove the anteroom to endless death, to multitudes of children larger grown.

Infants then are saved. And if the half and more, who breathe the vital air, die in infancy, then so many are saved, — saved, certainly and necessarily; and that, too, without the least possible spiritual peril or exposure. And thus, a great host is being gathered from earth into heaven, without any earthly probation at all. Such is the faith of the church to-day.

And now let us turn and look at the other half of our race, — that portion of it, which by dint of better constitutions, more care, and many prayers, survive their infancy — live on earth till they reach the hour of responsibility, — till they know the difference between moral right and wrong, and begin to act in reference to it.

Now, saying nothing about total depravity, or original, sin, it is believed, and very justly, that all these latter, become sinners. And becoming sinners, it is believed they are under condemnation to endless woe. And, further, it is believed that from this condemnation there is no escape save by a radical change of heart. * And, finally, it is believed that no such change can take place, beyond the grave. Of course then, all sinners who do not experience that change on earth are lost forever. But, obviously, that change is experienced by only a *very* small part of adult persons who go from earth to the tomb. And, therefore, only a very small part of them are saved; while all the rest sink to perdition! And thus, brother, according to your creed, it comes to pass, that, while infants are all saved, in Heaven, adults, — those who come to the years of accountability on earth — are nearly all lost.

Perhaps you may query, whether the fact that relatively, so few experience radical regeneration, is so obvious. But it seems to me your mind shall not

* See Appendix.

have gone over the present aspect of our race, and run back through the ignorant, barbarous, pagan past, before you will be satisfied, that, in the light of history and observation, nothing can be *more* obvious. For, if we know anything about the human race, up to the present time, we know that only an infinitesimal portion of them, have, in this life, been, in the orthodox sense of the term, regenerated, while all the rest have died in sin. From the orthodox stand point, we see just as clearly that the masses of human beings are lost, who have passed away, because of the character *they* bore on earth, as that *any* are saved, because of the character *they* bore on earth. From that point, the *only* evidence for joy or sorrow in contemplation of the dead, is character. And that evidence is just as valid for the one as the other. And in the actual state of the case, it proves very many of earth's past dwellers, to be now in hell, where it proves one to be in heaven. And, brother, so obvious is this in the light of your penal theory, that I think you will readily see and frankly admit it. However, the point we seek here is equally gained, whether you admit or deny, that by your theory, *so many* are lost.

Now we submit, whether it does not seem very absurd, that the Great Father should deal so differently with those who enter eternity very young, from what he does, with those who enter it only, not *quite* so young! — that he should take the former directly to himself in heaven, while he leaves the latter, a little time longer on earth, so exposed to the play of passions which he himself ordained, amid circumstances of temptation, which he himself provided, that, for the thousands of years of time past, their absolute endless ruin should be the *law*, and their final salvation only the exception; — so that, while very little children *all* ascend to Heaven, most of their parents sink to hell! The absurdity involved here, seems to me no less than dreadful. Yet is it part and parcel of the popular faith — inseparable from it. So that if that faith is true; this absurdity is true; and if this absurdity is true (I speak in a paradox) what an appalling truth for a family circle, and (pardon me, but I mean it all,) what a temptation to infanticide. Take breath and read on, but find no fault with our illustration unless it is severer than truth.

A few years since, a fugitive slave mother, overtaken by pursuers, took the lives of her children, rather than see them remanded into slavery. We judge not her bloody act here. Some pronounced it heroic; others diabolical. It was certainly very dreadful. But the maternal perpetrator of the wild deed, comforts herself with the thought that her children are forever free in heaven!

Here is a mother who believes the popular doctrine of endless punishment. Her only child is yet an infant. She looks upon it, loves it, considers its exposure to everlasting death, *if it grow up on earth*, kisses and destroys it. This done, she comes forward to the communion table. Arraigned by the church for her unnatural offence, she excuses herself by saying to her pastor in the chair, "You have taught me that if my child die in infancy, its eternal salvation is secure; whereas, if it live to years of responsibility, it probably must sink in hell forever. I could not bear to see it thus exposed to endless woe! No, I could not, for it was the child of my love! And because I loved it, I have saved it. Yes, my sweet little one is now in heaven! Safe, bless God! Safe! Satan cannot reach the little cherub *there!* Whereas, were it still on earth, according to what you have taught me, it would soon be so exposed, that I could chiefly expect only its endless ruin! O, sir, my child is safe now. I have, with these maternal hands, laid the dear one to sleep upon the bosom of God, where 'that evil one toucheth him not.'" And thus addressed, what can the pastor do, but either hold his peace, or deny his faith, or take refuge in mystery. If he says to the mother, "Verily, you have grossly sinned," she easily replies. "Be it so, seeing I have forever saved my child from sinning! It well becomes mothers to sacrifice themselves for their childrens' sake. This I have done!" And if the pastor say, further: — "God's great sovereignty must not be arraigned;" she easily adds, "Certainly not; I have not arraigned it, but done only what it demanded, at my hand, in view of my dear child's welfare! I have committed my child to God, in the only possible way to make sure of its salvation!" And if the pastor further add, with gravity, "You have by this act shut yourself out of heaven," she readily replies, "Be it so, seeing I have shut my dear child out of hell! And yet, how is it that I should be sent to that dreadful place for using the only certain, or even *probable* means of saving my child from it?"

Thus this infanticial mother might proceed. And what, I again ask, in all seriousness, could her pastor and church do, but take her strange case into charitable consideration? What could they do less than this, when they considered that she had acted only in view of the plain logical consequences of the creed they had put into her hands.

Perhaps you will shrink from this illustration, as *too dreadful!* And it were too dreadful for any purpose under heaven, other than that for which it is introduced. And yet, in view of that purpose, it falls infinitely short of the fact — it is tameness itself! For, infinitely more dreadful is the thing illustrated! Only just think of it, — an infant, immortal, crossing the line of accountability at the imminent hazard of everlasting death! Think of it, did I say? It cannot be thought of more than in part. For the damnation of the popular creed to which the little innocent is thus exposed, infinitely surpasses all knowledge, all thought. Its perdition is a wide-spreading wilderness, dark with woe, which no imagination can traverse; a boundless ocean of sorrow, over which no thought can wing itself! And how must the Christian mother, whose eyes are open to the subject, feel, as from day to day she hears the tramp of burning surf, nearer and nearer at hand, as her child nears the fatal line of accountability.* How can she then but wish her child secure? And what can seem to her too unnatural or rash, if it but promise it a safe asylum? How can she but wish it in heaven? And should she, in the phrenzy natural to her dilemma (for to such a dilemma frenzy *is but* natural), do as did the slave mother, mentioned above, would she not be, at least, *as* excusable? Nay, more? For what are the few years of hard bondage to which that slave mother could not bear to see her child doomed, compared with the endless bondage of black despair?

Now don't turn away, brother, unless you are sure that I overdraw the horror of endless death, or the feelings proper to those who anticipate it for

* See Appendix.

themselves or children! And if you do not, I am sure that you will not turn away at all. Nor will you then think me at all beside myself, or even rash, when I say that, viewing the matter from the stand point of your creed, were I the father of as many sons as Jacob, I must sincerely desire that they should all be laid in infants' graves! Nay, if I really believed with you, and my prayer for children had been answered, what could I do, as a good parent, but wrestle with God like Jacob, till I should see them early removed from these suburbs of damnation to a place of safety in the skies; so terrible would be my dilemma! And further, believing, as you do, what could I do but rejoice in all the infanticide of the heathen. For what are the jaws of the river monsters, or the beaks of soaring vultures, to the beak and jaw of everlasting ruin, — ruin, the most imminent exposure to which, is the dreadful condition upon which alone the heathen infant can survive its infancy, but which cannot *possibly* reach it if it does not. Happy, then, the babe, made a seraph by being cast away at birth! Happy the mother of many children, constantly written childless.

Now, brother, I ask, in all seriousness, if there was or can be, another absurdity, or group of absurdities, more glaring, dark, and dreadful, than is involved in this strange arrangement of an infinite providence—a providence of infinite good-will!—for separating infants and adults, parents and children, forever? Who, by coaxing and driving his imagination at the wild watch hours of midnight, can conceive such another? Why, brother, think of it. It surpasses every thing! In view of it, the most unmitigated evil, the most blasting curse, that can befall a human being, is, that God should hear the mother's prayer that it should outlive its infancy on earth, — for that is to outlive its safety from evil and curse, unparalleled,—imminently to expose it to evil and curse such as the very universe, under no other circumstances, provides, — to expose it to endless misery!

And, further, seeing that Jehovah can so save all the "little ones," why should we not wonder, as he desires the salvation of all men, that he did not contrive to propagate our species without any of them coming to years of accountability? Certainly he could have easily so arranged things, and then parents and children, *all*, would have lived together in heaven forever! A glorious consummation, indeed, it would have been! But no, instead of that, such is God's providence that, to live a little span of life on earth, is made to peril everything, and up to the present year of the world, to ruin almost everything. So your creed — so orthodoxy! And shall we not, as men of common sense, common candor, and common humanity, seriously suspect the truth of any exposition of the divine word which involves an absurdity so cruel, crushing, crazing; so dishonoring to our father God?

But here, you will perhaps be saying that parents have only to "train up their children in the way in which they should go," to make them secure of heaven. Now, not to stop to speak of the fact that, according to the popular faith, it is not training, but special regeneration, that the child needs, I remark that this, at best, but partially relieves, or rather affords no relief to one absurdity by inaugurating another. And the new absurdity is this: — that the feeble, sinning, earthly parent, (for there is no man that liveth and sinneth not), the parent who can scarcely stand himself in the hour of temptation, and who, in the midst of all the evil influences to which his child is exposed on earth, has the care of it, only for a few fleeting days at longest, can do for its *endless* weal, what God, and Christ, and all good angels, and the spirits of the just made perfect, cannot, or will not do for it, in all *eternity!* The earthly parent can train up his child directly into heaven. Whereas the child must sink to hell in spite of all the heavenly parent with all his aids can do, provided the earthly parent fail him. And thus, under this view, is the child greatly destined to endless life or death, according to the character of the earthly parent of which he chances to be born, and not according to the character, or will, or purpose, of the infinite heavenly parent, who gives being to parent and child both. To save the child, the earthly parent is powerful, even omnipotent; but for this purpose, the heavenly parent is powerless, without the earthly parent's aid!

How true it is that on absurdities absurdities grow;—each new one more glaring than that from which it sprung! But from the absurdity that God, the Father, who is more loving than all human parents, and perfect in prescience, power, wisdom, and goodness, and whose "years are one eternal day," in his best efforts to save, is utterly outdone by poor, weak, sinful, earthly parents, who can hardly, and, taking the world broadly, do, only rarely, keep out of hell themselves;—from *this* absurdity, what more glaring one can possibly arise.

And here to anticipate, in a word, an objection which seems to me as fallacious as it is plausible, and yet, one on which stress is often placed by careless thinkers, I remark that, evidently, God has made the *present* condition of the child very much to depend on the will and action of the parent, whereas beyond the sphere of the present, the great overruling providence takes the child and sees that no ultimate detriment befall it, and that the benevolent purpose of its creation be not frustrated. To *deny* such providence, were to make children the merest creatures of chance and human caprice, — to make them the mere exponents of parental folly, lovingly tossed about, and cruelly knocked about, at random, — some into heaven, and some into hell. Whereas to *admit* such providence, under the rule of a good God, seems to me equivalent to admitting all that is necessary to set the fore-mentioned absurdities in the strongest light. I leave them to your consideration. And in closing this letter, some portions of which I know are couched in horrid phrase, but which, as it becomes the subject matter, I deem needful of no apology, I find myself still praying that we may be led out of all error into all truth. I only add that the absurdity must be accepted, however dreadful or the creed in which it inheres, must be abandoned, however venerated.

Yours truly.

LETTER XVII.

FOURTH ABSURDITY.—CHILD OF "FIVE POINTS."

Freedom of Speech, man's birthright—Without it, the mind withers, —Restrained only by violence—Truth, terra firma—Going aloft—Absurdities multiform—*Fourth absurdity*—boy lost from "*Five Points.*"—Victim, born and bred in squalor—Soon dies—His probation a sham—Deserves recompense rather than endless punishment—Less to blame than his parents?—If hope for him, hope for all—Orthodoxy consistent with itself—Earnest question—The Beecher family—Relief needed, suppose the boy grows up, case not altered—Foolish shipmaster—The creed and its victim—The latter might as well have dropped into hell at birth!—Why not use strong language—The case mentioned not peculiar, in principle.

Dear Brother,—

In whatever else we differ, we agree that freedom of thought is man's birthright; and that only in so far as he practically asserts it, is he the "Lord's freeman;" that without its exercise, in spite of whatever pomp of circumstance, he is at the best, but a splendid slave.

Freedom of thought is the vital moisture at the roots of the mind, on which, its growth depends, and without which, of course, it withers, like the rush without water, or the tree in the desert. This freedom is recognized by our Lord when he says, "Yea, and wherefore of yourselves judge ye not what is right?" Why are ye bound by your old Jewish education, tradition, creed? "As a man thinketh so is he." This, too, is a *conscious* freedom. Hence the human mind naturally spurns all restraints upon it. It submits to them, only through its own ignorance, or somebody's violence. Such, brother, are my thoughts, as I seat myself for another letter.

I know not how my last, impressed you. And yet, we have so many mental things in common, that I can easily imagine. I think your criticism upon it must have provoked criticism upon your creed. As, turning to your creed,— you have said, "*if this is so*,"—turning to my letter,—you have added, —"*then this is so*," I can but imagine that you have thrown back upon the former a suspicious look. Nor need you be frightened, so long as you follow the Saviour's rule of judging the tree by its fruits. I am sure that you can receive nothing that I shall offer you, without sufficient evidence. I pray you may reject nothing, in spite of it. Fear not to advance boldly. Feel that truth only is *terra firma*, and that you are safe, only as your feet are upon it; while error is but a bowing wall or a tottering fence, or a deceitful mire. The man, established upon the truth, feels not a jar from the earthquakes which swallow up whole cities of tradition. The sailor, high up in the shrouds at midnight, with the strong yarn above him fast clenched in his veteran palm, cares little for the commotion of the elements, though the staunch ship dip her sails in brine; but, intent on duty, swings fearlessly over the darkling billows, and laughs in the very teeth of the gale. So, the man who goes aloft on bold religious enquiry, grasping with a vigorous faith the truth which heaven lets down above him, cares little for the billows of thought which swamp old creeds beneath him, but fearlessly swings in the welken, till, through the roar of the elements, he is drawn up into Heaven! The mount of religious enquiry is not always easy of ascent, but always heavenly.

But let us now return to our chapter of absurdities. I shall continue to present them as they have presented themselves to my own mind. Nor will you greatly err, if you regard them as notes taken by the way by which I reached my present theological status; or, as the disconnected soliloquies "of a mind shrinking with consternation from the necessary consequences of the faith it has been taught to venerate — soliloquies, showing up the same difficulty, in different forms, or as it strikes the troubled mind at different times; as, for instances, when it is met in the cesspool of a great city, in the murderer's cell, at the grave of a duellist, in the vicinity of idols, in rural districts of christendom, in dying chambers, in the funeral of the dead, &c., &c. For it meets the intelligent Christian thinker everywhere, whether he knows it or not, an omnipresent sorrow."

Fourth. The popular creed implies that the child, born and bred in the debauchery of some "*Five Points*," dying there at a youthful or later age, is consigned by "Our Father which is in Heaven" to endless woe! And this also seems to me, an absurdity.

Now it is but matter of course, that a child, thus born in corruption, and nursed at the breasts of licentiousness in a bed of shame, fed upon intemperance and every way debauched from uncradled infancy, should grow up, vile. The voice of prayer is never heard in its wretched home, nor does it learn the name of Jesus, save from lips of blasphemy. But in that home, if home it must be called, is ever found that concentrated atmosphere of death, in which, wedded intemperance and harlotry forever move. Without the bible, without the church, with only the worst examples to influence the formation of character, and, withal, and perhaps more than all, deeply tainted by hereditary transmission, of course, the vices, mid which that child moves, must "grow with its growth, and strengthen, with its strength." Groping its way beneath a pall of ignorance, which nothing but a miracle can lift, and under a constant pressure of passion, which scarcely less than a miracle can stay, its moral character is hurried through the several stages of bad and worse, with frightful rapidity, till, at length, a staggering mass of tumefied corruption, the poor creature, smitten with loathsome disease, dies early, is thrown into the dead cart, whose rumbling wheels seem to say, as it moves on towards the metropolitan Golgotha, where its load is to be forgotten,

> "Rattle his bones over the stones,
> 'Tis only a beggar whom nobody owns."

You very well know, brother, that cases of this kind are frequent, and that the fashionable faith is, that their young victims, drop, at death, into endless woe.

Now, I know not how this matter may strike you, but to me it seems extremely absurd, that the Great Father, should suspend the immortal weal and woe of a child of his own creation, upon such a probation as that boy had.

Why talk of probation! The poor creature had *no* chance! The die was loaded! The jury was packed! His freedom was but freedom to choose vice — freedom to fall. He falls of *course!* We expect nothing else, and are not disappointed! And your creed implies that he sinks to despair. Yet, it seems to me, nay upon my conscience, and in the name of the God of us all, I put the question, whether it does not seem to you, that that child, now in eternity, rather deserves a heaven in which to be compensated for what he suffered here, than an endless hell in which to be punished for what he did here? Why, that that child, whose misfortune, shame, misery it was to be borne into one hell *here*, should *therefore* be cast into another infinitely more terrible *hereafter*, — is it not too incredible for belief? And as you contemplate it, in spite of your best efforts at faith, are you not possessed with doubts which "go not out," even with "prayer and fasting?" Yet must it be believed, or the popular notion of punishment rejected, or both be held under suspicion. To doubt that that child is lost, is to lean toward heresy. To believe that he will ever be saved, is really, to be a heretic!

Do you say that the lad was less to blame than his parents. Perhaps so, for he was the child of sin. And yet, perhaps not, for his parents might themselves have had an equally miserable advent to earth. But, suppose the parents *are* the more to blame. The fact that the child goes into eternity with a miserably debauched *character*, is not thereby blotted out. With him the development of vice was so rapid, that at fifteen he was as unfit for heaven, as most sinners are at forty-five. He is thoroughly a sinner!

The question, how he became a sinner, is of no consequence to the creed, which, virtually, says, "as death leaves us so judgment will find us," and that "there can be no change of character afterwards." And thus, the lad, unfit for heaven, and in an eternity in which no fitness for it can be secured, is hurled down to hell,—buried forever beneath the night of Jehovah's frown. Now, perhaps, all this may look to you reasonable—believable! If so, we can only say, God help you. But as for us, we must be excused for regarding it with emotions of the profoundest horror and dismay.

We know, indeed, that many a holder of the popular creed, pressed by common sense, and common humanity, will seek to relax its meshes sufficiently for the escape of our young sinner,—will set the door of Heaven sufficiently ajar for him, somehow or other, at sometime or other, to crowd in! And, too, we know that to do this, were to strike the key stone from the arch on which rests the gray fabric of Orthodoxy itself. For if, for this lad's sake, you admit a probation, into the future world, by which he can be there fitted for heaven, then, can such a probation be found there for all men. If you set the door of Heaven so ajar, in eternity, that one sinner may enter in, then, for aught that appears to the contrary, all may enter in. In other words, if redemption be once admitted into the future world, for aught you or I can see, it will run among all the hosts of the wicked, and thus fulfil the Scripture which saith, that "it pleased the Father that in him [Christ] should all fulness dwell; and having made peace through the blood of his cross, by him to reconcile all things to himself; by him, I say, whether they be things in earth or things in heaven;" — or that Scripture which saith of Christ "He gave himself, a ransom for all *to be testified in due time.*"

For, just so explicitly as the Scriptures deny probation to *any* soul beyond the grave, they deny it to *every* soul. Orthodoxy is therefore consistent in denying it, or anything equivalent to it, either to *all* or to *none*. But it denies it to *all*. Its language is, every person who dies in sin is unsaved forever. So died our young and pitiful boy, and he, therefore, is lost forever! And this *must be believed, as the only alternative of denying the dominant creed!*

And now, whatever becomes of your creed, I earnestly ask you, whether or not, you can conceive of a greater seeming barbarism and absurdity, than is here involved? — involved in the notion that, under the government of a good and just God, endless woe should be the sequel of such mere sham probation as that child had? And what do you reply?

What *can* you, what can *any body* reply? Be silent if you will, think as you please, but do not, as is too much the fashion, with sectarian believers, when light falls around them, tighten the blind of creed and rush farther into mystery.

I am but presenting you with difficulties which, as I have before said, many have felt, and not a few acknowleged, — difficulties which have driven men in all directions for relief. We have seen how they drove Edward Beecher back into the dismal wilderness of the long past, and how, as the "wish is father to the thought," he found relief in the bold assumption of a long, pre-existent and forgotten probation. One of his brothers, I am told, finds relief from these *same* difficulties, not in the assumption of a *pre-existent* probation, but in the anticipation of a *future* one beyond the tomb. And while Henry Ward, seems to trouble himself little about the matter any way, and Catharine is trying to reconcile orthodoxy with common sense, the less dependent Harriet feels that a single doubt on the part of the mourner concerning the ultimate well-being of the dead, is sufficient to make the surviver miserable, and finds relief by virtually embracing the doctrine of Universalism, or what is the same thing universal restorationism. And the difficulties which this Beecher family meet, in the contemplation of the popular creed of the day, are by no means peculiar to them, but common to all independent thinkers. And this same noble family, thus broken theologically, all into pieces, is perhaps the best possible symbol of the dilapidated condition of the theological christendom of to-day.

Brother, I will try not to be tedious, nor over bold. But do you not feel the need of relief from somewhere, past, future, or present, as you look, through your creed, *down* upon that miserable boy of which we have been speaking? If you are not *afraid* to look *down* upon him, and not afraid to think of what you see, I know you must feel such need, and am praying that you may find it;—not, amid the dim uncertainties of a shadowy past or future, but in the plain discovery of the true word and Fatherhood of God.

We have supposed our young victim of hereditary and home vice to die at fifteen. But the case is but little weakened, as an illustration of absurdity, though he live to age, seeing that, under the circumstances, character is greatly *fixed* at fifteen; at any rate, so fixed that the church looks upon him as very nearly helpless; and this, especially if he continue as, with his established affinities, he almost invariably will, under the influences that spoiled him. And even if, as rarely occurs, he emerge from them, his reformation is regarded almost of the nature of miracle.

Now facts are facts, and, in religious matters, as elsewhere, it is dangerous to ignore them. Foolish is the shipmaster, who ignores evident rocks, because they are not laid down in the chart. His good ship will not, *therefore*, ignore them, nor be the less broken. So, in theology also, facts must not be disregarded. The creed may seem strong, but there may be facts stronger than the creed. And when these appear, they must not be put aside lightly. Rightly understood, they are God's elder Scripture, but by no means conflicting with his younger.

Here, then, is our creed, one which our fathers bequeathed us, or which has been provided to our hand—one which we believe and delight to cherish. *There* stands our ill-starred child of wretchedness, conceived, born, and bred in iniquity ;—*there* he stands, in filth and rags for which he is not responsible, blasted by passions bequeathed him, and which obtained fearful rankness, long before reason or conscience was developed for their control ; there he stands, confronted by the creed which points ever downward to his endless woe. For, however long he may stand in the flesh, so have the passions and appetites stolen the march upon his reason and conscience, under the influence of the corruption in which he was swaddled, that, as we have intimated before, not while the sin-struck body hangs about his soul, are repentance and reformation at all probable. He was as if marked for perdition before he was born! He was born as into the shroud of everlasting death. His lot would have been, practically, little different, had he been dropped into perdition at birth. His probation afforded but a chance to fall. And, therefore, to regard it as ordained of God to be his *only* opportunity to form a holy character, and thereby escape endless pain, is to put forward one of the most monstrous and barbarous absurdities that ever shocked the sensibilities of a good man, or excited his ridicule, contempt, or indignation!

You will say I speak warmly; and I certainly do, if I speak as I feel. I envy not the heart that can coolly follow our young sinner—any sinner—down into the pit of your creed. And, as I think of the multitudes that seem to do so, what were I, if, with the view I firmly held, my heart did not warm with zeal for the glory of the God of heaven, and with humanity towards the children of earth. Lukewarmness over such a subject were as criminal as it were unnatural.

But one thing I wish you to consider well. It is this: that to hope for that child of "Five Points," is to doubt the popular creed, whereas to believe that that child will be in some way saved, through God's righteousness, is to believe that the popular creed is, in some way, false, through man's ignorance. You may choose your horn of the dilemma.

And one thing further I wish to say here. It is this: That, as all human life is short, and full of temptation, and as eternity can be nought less than eternity, the notion that *any person whatever*, dying in sin, enters an eternity of sorrow, compromises the character of God, no less absurdly and barbarously, than does the extreme case which we have noted. This proposition may strike you at first as bold: but I think your reflection will have endorsed it, before the receipt of my next letter.

Yours truly.

LETTER XVIII.

FIFTH ABSURDITY,—MEN FIX EACH OTHER'S DOOM.

Conversation with a Lawyer, his Testimony ruled out—" Judge not, lest ye be judged."—*Fifth Absurdity*—Men send one another to Endless Woe—Illustrations, the Two Students, the Drunken Rowdy, Battle, and how War can be advocated !—The Duellist, the Highwayman, the Murderer, and his Victim—" Whoso can receive it, let him receive it."

DEAR BROTHER,—

Last evening, while awaiting the opening of services in a public hall, I incidentally fell into conversation with a certain lawyer. And, allusion having been made to certain court proceedings, to which we both had that day listened, I remarked, that I perceive that attorneys, like theologians, were quite liable to "shove by justice," in the pursuit of victory. "Yes," he replied playfully, "and of all controversialists, I think theological ones are most likely to do so." Making no denial of this charge, I replied, that only yesterday, I told my people that no other book had ever been so kicked and cuffed to make it testify falsely, as the very Bible itself;—that not even Blackstone, in the hands of interested attorneys, had so suffered from the wresting of passages from their true intent, and making them mean what their author never dreamed of! "I am glad to hear you say that," replied our amiable colloquist, adding, with a hearty laugh, "for I have never known any denomination, so given to that, as the one to which you belong." To this I replied coolly,—a group was gathered round,—"Either you are saying this playfully, or you are ignorant 'whereof you affirm.' The fact is right the other way. Nor is there one of you who dares defend the logical consequences of your creed." A few incidental remarks followed, when my friend remarked, "*Somewhere*, the Bible says, 'What more could I have done for my vineyard, that I have not done for it?'" "So it does," said I, and your now quoting *that* Scripture shows that you have never examined the Bible in view of this subject. For if you had, you would have known better than to have quoted it for your present purpose, inasmuch as it has no possible reference to man's future condition. It must be that you never have heard much Universalist preaching." "Certainly, I never have," he replied. And yet you dare make such broad assertions. Just as though I should sit in judgment upon your fairness, as a pleader, without having heard you make scarcely a single plea. The judge rules you off from the stand as a witness incompetent to testify in this case. The meeting was now called to order. And he *was* incompetent to testify. He understood law, from actual study. He understood Universalism only from rumor—only, as distorted by passing through the hostile medium of an orthodox pulpit.

You will perceive, brother, how humiliating it must be to us to be thus judged by excellent men, who know little about us; especially, while their mistaken judgment goes among the people as a pure coin, and also, at the same time, forbids that they put themselves in a way to learn that it is base. We commend to such persons, the Scripture which saith, "Judge not, lest ye be judged," though the measure they "mete" we have no desire to measure back again. But you, brother, I trust, are not the man to condemn an unpopular cause, before a hearing, or, from motives of policy or pride, or any thing else, withhold an honest verdict afterwards.

I have alluded to the logical consequences of your creed, as shrunk from by its confessors. I will further proceed to notice some of these, and will say,

Fifth, That your creed plainly implies, that men, both good and bad, may, and often do, determine the endless destiny of their fellow beings, by determining the length of their probation,—virtually putting them into heaven, by cutting off all liability to lose it, or into hell by cutting off all opportunity to escape it. And this, also, seems to me an absurdity.

We have already presented one illustration of the above proposition, in the supposed case of the mother who made the "calling and election" of her infant sure, by taking its life. Another is found in a sad accident, which occurred at one of our New England seminaries a few years since. Two young gentlemen were in their room, amusing themselves with a musket, quite unconscious of its being loaded, when the one innocently shot the other, thereby determining his soul at once to heaven or to hell forever.

And still another illustration is found in the death of the drunken rowdy, who fell, at the head of the rumsellers' mob, at Portland, a few years ago. The balls which, at the order of the resolute city marshal, laid him low, cutting off all opportunity for repentance, carried his soul directly to endless torment.

Illustrations to our purpose are also presented in war. Two armies meet. Fearful are the imprecations! Dreadful is the carnage! Balls and bayonets are the swift instruments of everlasting death! The soldier perishes forever, who might reform and be saved if permitted to return to his home of piety. At the hand of his fellow man, he falls lower than the grave. Nor may any tell how many of our revolutionary colonists are now, in endless despair, sent there by the hired Hessians of George the Third. Nor how many of those whose bones have been brought from the plains of Waterloo, as a fertilizer of British soil, are now in the endless despair to which they were consigned by the arbitrament of British swords. And this, especially, when it is considered, that, of all conditions, that of a soldier, in active service, seems least adapted to promote fitness for heaven. Of course, it is a mystery to us how orthodox Christians can advocate war, or their chaplains kneel mid guns, and swords, loaded and barbed with everlasting death! For these, in their view, are the terrible arbiters of souls' destiny, cutting off their probation, and thereby saying, as with the authority of the Infinite, *You shall have no more chance to escape.* These are they that rise up in the place of God, and "shut to the door" against their victims forever. Alas! for the orthodox advocate of war! Let me do him the justice to say, that I think he believes in his creed less than in humanity and common sense.

But, further, our point finds illustration under the operation of the *code duello*,—that miserable product of dark ages,—that foolishest, meanest mode of settling difficulties.—that wretched footman of chattel slavery, accompanying its desolating car, as it dashes into the fair fields of Christian civilization. The duel settles more than questions of chivalric honor. Instance a case. A and B meet at a public house, drink, altercate, challenge, and accept, choose their seconds, retire and fight. The question of honor is settled by the death of B. And not *only* that, but the question of B's endless damnation also. The fatal ball settles both. For, while A blows the smoke from his pistol, and retires a victor, leaving the *body* of the slain to his surgeon and friends, its spirit, prematurely driven out, and thereby excluded all chance of salvation, is met by evil angels in the threshold of eternity, and dragged down into the pit forever. Thus, according to your penal view, is a question greater than honor settled by the duel.

And what does the highwayman do? He meets the moneyed worldling in the way, robs him of his treasure and his life, and throws his body into the thicket, or leaves it in the ditch. But is that all? O no! He also robs his soul of all chances to repent, and tosses it into the thick darkness of despair, —buries it alive in hell forever! *So your creed.*

But the absurdity we are exposing finds a fuller illustration, in cases in which the murderer repents in prison, and finally dies, regretting that he sent the murderer into perdition. Such cases used to be, by no means, very unfrequent. We recently read of one, but have not the details now at hand. Let us suppose such a case, and see its bearing upon the subject in hand.

A young lady, respectable, but not converted, is

met and ravished, under a dark night, by a villain, who destroys her life to escape detection. Sent thus hurriedly to her God in sin, she is, by the conditions of your creed, of course, lost. No cycle of eternity but shall witness her unrelieved despair. Her soul is assassinated. Out of a dark night of time, she is hurled into a darker night of eternity. The brutal hand that cut her probation short off, thereby plunged her infinitely below the sphere of possible life, shut her up in woe, bolted the door upon her, threw away the key, and left her to pine in anguish forever. So your creed!

And now, leaving her there in her woe, let us turn to look after her murderer. As "murder will out," he is detected, arrested, executed. But, while in prison, blessed with a probation which he forbade to his victim, he comes to himself, heeds his spiritual advisers, repents, exhorts the multitudes from the scaffold, and swings from it into Paradise. And there, because he had much forgiven, he loves much, and never ceases to give thanks for the prison confinement through which the mercy of God reached him. Thus in heaven the murderer sings. But the young lady, his victim, where is she all this time? Lost! lost! *He* may have time for repentance, but not *she*. That was forbidden her, by the red hand that plunged the dagger to her heart. Mercy may come to *his* prison, but not to *hers*. That red hand of his, which might "the multitudinous seas incarnadine," may live to be washed, and forever twine wreaths for the immaculate brow of Him whose wrath *she* must forever bear.

Now, brother, your creed, taken in connexion with the history of crime, obviously involves multitudes of cases, similar to any and all which we have stated above. This, you will admit. And, admitting this, *can* you, as the heart of a man beats in your bosom, fail seriously to query whether that creed is not at fault? Can you be confident in that theology, which thus makes the frantic mother, the officer of justice, the warrior, the duellist, the highwayman, and the libertine, the arbiters of the eternal destiny of their victims; so that, in the case last stated, if it was the hard fate of the young lady to be abused, scared into phrensy, and murdered, it was her harder one to be, by her murderer's hand, consigned to the bottomless pit; while he, by the grace of God, which *he* denied to *her*, has space for repentance, and goes up to sing in heaven!

Now, is a doctrine involving such absurdities—I will not say barbarisms—heartily believable? To deny that the victims, in the darker cases cited, are lost, is to deny the sole principle of biblical interpretation, upon which your creed finds any scriptural support. In the last mentioned case, to admit hope for the young lady, is to admit hope for all; while to deny heaven to her murderer, is to deny heaven to all. For "all have sinned." And he gave the evidence of repentance, upon which we predicate hope for others.

But I forbear comment. Be your own commentator upon what I have said. The notion that the Living Father has made the endless weal and woe of men thus dependent upon the phrensy, ambition, lucre, lust, and brutality of their fellow beings,—well, "he that can receive it, let him receive it." But let him be very sure that he has an unmistakable "thus saith the Lord," on which to rest, a faith so at war with reason and all the humanities.

Truly yours.

LETTER XIX.

SIXTH ABSURDITY—ENDLESS REVENGE.

Revenge a dreadful Passion, not of God,—If it were, he would scorn to wreak it on puny man.—*Sixth Absurdity*—Endless Revenge!—Illustration from Hamlet—The murderer's soliloquy—Hamlet's soliloquy—Subject brought home—"Bridge of Sighs"—Pause, Brother.

DEAR BROTHER,—

I think we shall agree that, of all the fiendish passions that ever possessed, as devils, the human breast, no other is *so* fiendish as the passion of revenge. It is emphatically the passion of little minds, or of great minds belittled. It is anti-Christian every way, and in the most extreme sense. Therefore, notwithstanding the heathen speak of it "as the attribute of gods," and say

> "They stamped it,
> With their own great image, on our natures,"

it surely can be no attribute of the Christian's God, —of him who, as "our Father which is in heaven," is best seen in Jesus, and most fully in the prayer,

"Father, forgive them," which trembled from the cross up to heaven. No, God cannot be vindictive. His nature forbids it. Did it not, then he, like a vindictive mortal, were quite unlovable. And, indeed, did his nature admit of it,—the worst passion of the worst of beings, and culminating in the blackness of a demon's heart,—still, he must scorn to wreak it on beings his infinitely inferiors; and, especially would he scorn to wreak it on the puny earthy members of his great family, the human children of his creation, foreordination, foreknowledge, and love. Just think of it! The Great Cause of all,—Jehovah—vindictively tormenting one of his insect children between his fingers forever!

But, though revenge dwell not with God, yet it does, sometimes, dwell with men. And, when it does, the human heart-flower is no longer the rose, but "the serpent under it." Then do the soul's affections, which God would have shoot forth lovingly, become tormenting arrows, barbed with the most subtile, and virulent, and deadly poison, ever distilled from iniquity. As

> "The fairest action of our human life
> Is scorning to revenge an injury,"

so is the contrary action, the foulest. And this especially, when seen under the light of Christendom. Ugly is revenge, when reflected by the battle axe of the desert barbarian; but how much uglier when seen in the darkening brow of the Christian! And what could be said of it, did it disfigure and cloud the countenance of Jehovah! Then, indeed, were man's likeness to God to be looked for in his deepest depravity, for there it would then be found.

But, though there is naught on earth more fiendish and terrible than the spirit of a man "ranging for revenge, with Ate by his side," yet is it sometimes treated as respectable, and even made to stand boldly out in applauded characters, and especially those of the drama. Thus Shakspeare gives us his Hamlet, steeped in this passion to his very lips—caring for nothing else, if he may but "sweep to his revenge."

> "To this point I stand—
> That both the worlds I give to negligence,
> Let come what comes; *only I'll be revenged.*"

And others than Hamlet have said, with Shakspeare's "Gloster," as they have dashed upon their victims:

> "Down, down to hell, and say I sent thee thither;
> I that have neither pity, love, nor fear!"

And now, brother, let us return to remark

Sixth, that your creed enables any miserable wretch, whether acting from premeditation or impulse, and whether sane or crazy, drunk or sober, to take *endless* revenge,—not only to kill, but to kill forever. And this, which under the government of the Father, seems to me absurd, is so well illustrated in "Hamlet," that I will call your attention to it, though its principle is involved in the preceding letter.

Hamlet seeks to avenge himself upon his uncle Claudius, for the death of his murdered father. At length, opportunity presents itself. Finding his uncle alone, he approaches behind him slily, and with deadly intent. But, pausing, he overhears him penitentially soliloquizing about his bloody crime thus:

> "O my offence is rank, it smells to heaven!
> It hath the primal, eldest curse upon't,
> A brother's murder! Pray, can I not,
> Though inclination be as sharp as will;
> My stronger guilt defeats my strong intent,
> And, like a man to double business bound,
> I stand in pause where I should first begin,
> And both neglect. What if this curst hand
> Were thicker than itself with brother's blood,
> Is there not rain enough in the sweet heavens,
> To wash it white as snow? Whereto serves mercy,
> But to confront the visage of offence?
> And what's in prayer, but this two-fold force,
> To be forestalled, ere we come to fall,
> Or pardoned, being down? Then I'll look up;
> My fault is passed. But O, what form of prayer
> Can serve my turn? Forgive me my foul murder?
> That cannot be; since I am still possessed
> Of those effects for which I did the murder,
> My crown, my own ambition, and my queen.
> May one be pardoned, and retain the offence?

16

In the corrupted currents of this world,
Offence's gilded hand may shove by justice;
And oft 'tis seen, the wicked prize itself
Buys out the law; but tis not so above;
There is no shuffling; there the action lies
In its true nature, and we ourselves compelled,
Even to the teeth and forehead of our faults,
To give in evidence. What then? What rests? [*i. e.*remains.]
Try what repentance can. What can it not?
Yet what can it when one cannot pray?
O wretched state! O bosom black as death!
O serried soul, that, struggling to be free,
Art more engaged! Help, angels; make assay;
Bow, stubborn knees! And heart, with strings of steel,
Be soft as sinews of the new-born babe!"

Having thus spoken with himself, the half-penitent murderer kneels down in trembling silence, and seems to be offering up secret prayer. Hamlet, who had all the time been watching him, at first thinks this a good time to "take him off," at a blow; —and then again, he thinks *not*; because, if he kill him now, in the midst of his penitence, it would be to *defeat* his revenge, by sending the murdered soul to *heaven*. And so *he* now soliloquizes in turn, as he steps up slily behind the silently praying king:

"Now *might* I do it pat; now he is praying;
And now *I'll do't;* and so he goes to heaven?
And *so* am I *revenged*? That would be scanned:
A villain kills my father; and for that,
I, his sole son, do this same villain send
To *heaven!*
Why this is hire and salary, not revenge.
He took my father grossly, full of bread,

With all his crimes, broadblown as blush of May;
And how his audit stands, who knows save Heaven?
But in our circumstance and course of thought,
'Tis heavy with him; and am I thus revenged,
To take him in the *purging of his soul*,
When he is fit and seasoned for his passage?
No!
Up, sword; and know thou a more horrid hent;
When he is drunk, asleep, or in a rage;
Or in the incestuous pleasures of his bed;
Or gaming, swearing, or about some act
That has no relish of salvation in't:
Then trip him, that his heels may kick at heaven,
And that his soul may be as damned and black,
As hell, whereto he goes!"

Thus saying, the avenger leaves his victim till he shall have opportunity to strike him down in his sin, and thus not only kill him, but also send him into endless pain. Shakspeare's illustrations are always striking; but, in his entire writings, none is more so than is this incidental, but complete illustration of the absurdity under review. Hamlet will kill forever, and the creed of the church tells him how!

And now, brother, to come right home with our subject, do you not, as we have before intimated, find it hard to believe—nay, is it not really unbelievable, when under the practical test—that the infinite God has made the probation of one man, the result of one man's being, even his endless joy or anguish, to depend upon the deliberate malice, or the momentary caprice, or passion, or anger, of another? Yes, and even upon the *carelessness* of another, as when one man shoots, or otherwise destroys the life of another, unintentionally?—so that we must not only exclaim,

> "Great God, on what a slender thread,
> Hang everlasting things,"

but must also be amazed, that he has made the cutting of that "slender thread" to depend upon the rapier or bowie-knife of the assassin, or even upon the accidental thrust of a friend;—that he has left it to human accident and malice to determine when the sinner, hair-hung and breeze-shaken" over the pit, shall drop into it? Is not this hard to believe? *If* the Bible teaches it, (as I am sure it does not,) do we not feel that, in believing it, we are obliged to disbelieve every thing else within us and about us, and even to regard the textual Scriptures on which we rely for its support, as at war with all the humanities of the Bible, and with the very character of the God it reveals. I know not how it may be with all. I know not how it may be with you. But I see not how any attempt *really* to believe a doctrine involving such an absurdity, can, to a thinking, candid mind, looking upon it with open eyes, be any thing less than absolutely distressing. The bridge over which the Venetian despot caused his victims to be transported to a returnless doom, was well called the bridge of sighs. And so may the passage well be called, over which, according to *the* creed, human beings are transported to returnless woe. But what words shall express the emotion the thinking man must feel, all overwhelming as it is, who really believes that God has left it to passionate and ignorant human beings, to push one another over that bridge at pleasure!

Brother, pause, consider! Criticize the scope and details of these illustrations as you weill, ad still will be left, in their presentation, a body of absurdity necessarily involved in your faith, sufficient, as it seems to me, to shake the soul of the sternest of the John Knoxes of orthodoxy.

Yours truly.

LETTER XX.

SEVENTH ABSURDITY—THE PEOPLE AND THE PREACHER.

Blind side and "beam," different routs to conviction—*Seventh Absurdity,* illustrated by a rural scene— Scene described at length—The people lost forever, unless minister be sent, unlest he faithfully go, and unless he be of the right temperament—Indian anecdote—Knapps and Channings—Maffit—Not a word against revivals—How revivals are to be estimated—Gospel, the power of God, and should be sent everywhere—Its resources, the universe, its day, eternity—Something wrong in the creed.

DEAR BROTHER,—

If you should find these letters tedious, you may bear in mind that they are far less so, than the embarrassing and crippling experience in which they had their origin, and which at length aroused their author to the fact, that, while belaboring his fellow sinners for their obtuseness, he himself had his own blind side also—the fact that, if there was not a "beam" in his own eye, there was a "mote" there, as large as that which he had been trying to remove from his brothers.

But such may not have been your experience. Nor, if it has, can the author feel sure that the same considerations that moved him, can move you. There may be more of you to move, you may be more strongly entrenched in prejudice and tradition; and, too, your mind may be so differently constituted and educated, that conviction must enter it, if at all, by a very different route. However, as truth is never lost, he has no fears of his labors over these familiar letters being entirely wasted. They are freighted with the blessing of a brother who is confident that they will do good, in proportion as they receive candid attention.

The difficulties which are experienced with the doctrine of endless woe, are of shadings so numerously various, that they can be set forth only in part, while any attempt to do more than that, were likely to become wearisome. I shall venture however, to look at them further, still drawing upon my own experience. And now,

Seventh, I present you with another phase of the omnipresent absurdity, which you will easily detect in the discussion of the following true, pastoral scene.

A few miles from my late residence in ——, is a rural district, almost entirely destitute of what are called the ordinary means of grace. There indeed falls the shower of morning light, and there the clouds drop down fatness. There the streams murmur God's praises, and there the winds blow his hallelujahs. There *Nature's* means of grace are not wanting.

There, too, are the plain dwellings, from which a hard-working peasantry "go forth to their labor until the evening," when, coming in, they rejoice in the children of their love and care. Here and there is seen a store, a small school-house, and now and then factory-buildings, in some of which, the hum and clatter of industry is no longer heard. The highways are crooked, winding among farms, whose stingy soil, yields a scanty but healthful support to its toil-hardened workers. Cattle are seen grazing and browsing in the pastures, and men and boys at work in the fields, while the humble dwellings show that house-wives, and perhaps house-girls are not idle within. But with all your seeing, you see no sign of church or church-going!

Pass through this region as I have done, on the Sabbath, on my way to an appointment, and you will mark young men and boys abroad in the fields, and young ladies and girls regaling themselves under the family tree, and older persons abroad tantivying, while, doubtless, not a few sinewy men are fast asleep in the house, recruiting their exhausted energies for the hour, when the next rising sun shall again summon them to another week's toil. And, not least, at sundry corners and shops, you will be likely to see groups of persons whose general appearance indicates that drinking and gaming are more than thought of.

But as we have before said, you will see nobody going to church or Sunday-school , and this, for the simple reason that there is none save far off, to go to. Brought up without them, they know not the worth of them, and therefore feel not the need of them. And thus, without religious institutions among them, they are, as a matter of course, an irreligious people. Occasionally, to be sure, a loftier religious nature will pierce up through the superincumbent mass of ignorance and vice like a wild flower in the desert, and, amid the surrounding desolation, be marked as " an apple tree among the trees of the wood." Yet, as a general rule, the people are wholly given up to the idolatry of what is called irreligion. What they would have been under other stars we may not know—we can only imagine. What they are, we see. And what they are we doubtless should substantially have been, had we been born to their lot.

Over this community of churchless peasants and mechanics, the dominant church, glorying in its own salvation, and faring sumptuously every day upon the legacy of a better religious bequeathment, casts its eye, and says pitifully, " these souls are lost forever, unless the gospel be sent to them ; whereas, if it *is* sent, many of them will be saved forever.

And thus is the endless weal or woe of these countrymen, born to religious penury, made to depend upon the contingencies of somebody else's faithfulness. If some one be sent to them and faithfully go, they *may* be saved. If he play the Jonah, they are lost. If no *man* cares for them, then *God* does not. If men will let them sink, *He* will. If men, their brethren, scarcely able to stand themselves, will not open the door of their prison of ignorance, vice, and misery on earth, God their Father, infinite in goodness and power, will not, but leave them, *keep* them shut up therein to all eternity. "Whoso can receive this, let him receive it." But know all, that to reject it, is to reject the popular doctrine of salvation and damnation.

Let us not be misunderstood here. We easily and joyfully see that the preaching of the Gospel may be of incalculable benefit to such a people as we have indicated; and that therefore, it is the duty of the church to provide it for them. But that the Living Father should make their *endless* weal or woe depend on the preaching of a day or year; while at the same time that day's or year's preaching is made contingent upon the faithfulness or unfaithfulness of their fellow beings, weak, tempted and sinful like themselves, does seem to me an absurdity capable of staggering credulity itself. That the church's faithfulness to-day, delivers men to-morrow at a judgment whose decisions are final; or that the church's unfaithfulness to-day indirectly dooms them to-morrow, to a pit whose despair is hopeless —why, you tell me that, concerning this people, bred without religious opportunities, and I either disbelieve or am speechless. And I ask you, firmly as you may deem yourself grounded in your faith, if, when you attempt to believe all this, your whole soul, everything about you God-given and God-like, does not rise up and cry out in mutiny? And can you then avoid querying whether you have not mistaken a demon for an angel, or the thing you are *attempting* to believe?

But it is further to be noted that the absurdity here involved is cumulative. For, according to the popular idea, the salvation of this people is contingent, not only upon receiving preaching, but beyond this, upon the temperament of the preacher. If he be a man highly charged with sympathy, if he be impassioned and confident in his address, and withal make a fair show of sense, no prophet is needed to forestall the result. He will succeed in influencing many to feel as he wills them to feel. His own visions of God, and heaven, and hell, are sure to become their visions. In a word, if he be a revivalist, he will be about certain to have a revival. Whereas, on the other hand, if he be a calm, cool adviser and reasoner about salvation, speaking as a man of candor to men supposed capable of thinking for themselves, he may expect no such result. Under the phenomena of no popular revival, will he then be able to count up souls, suddenly recovered from endless woe, as the papers counted up the rescued survivors of the ill-fated Lexington or Austria—souls saved to-day, who, had they died yesterday, would have sunk in ruin to rise no more. All this you understand.

And now what are we to conclude? That God's saving power is so partial to certain *forms* of preaching? that the salvation of the people depends upon the mere *method* of *presenting* truth? That when two men, equally sincere, preach the same gospel, the one preaching according to his natural temperament, which is all fire, and the other according to his, which is cool and sedate — the saving power of the gospel is peculiarly partial to the former? that the people are more moved by the former, because more of the Holy Spirit inheres in his word? And, as we have intimated, are we to believe that God has made the eternal weal and woe of the people depend not so much, certainly not more, upon *preaching* than upon the *temperament* of the preacher? It may be that you can believe all this, — that you see no insurmountable absurdity in the notion that the great God thus hangs eternities upon trifles,—even upon trifling ministerial idiosyncracies!! It may be that, to you, it seems well that the anecdote which which we deem discreditable to the Indian, should receive practical endorsement in the popular estimate of pulpit power. Said the Indian, to his less eloquent brother, "You speak first, and when you have spoken, then me speak, and the power come down." But not the Indian only, deems that God is dependent on the presence of certain "*mediums*," for the communication of his "free gift" of everlasting life:—not the poor Indian only, is the victim of this sort of orthodox "*spiritualism*," practiced upon the high plane of the eternities. Nay, not he alone; for have we not all believed, is not the notion prevalent to-day, that certain peculiar ministerial gifts are about certain to make the power come down? To be sure this notion, so absurd, is now being abandoned by not a few. But that more than few, you will find, largely composed of persons, either fossilizing in the coolest Calvinism of the creeds, or swerving off from it upon the liberal highway which leads to Universalism — a highway now filled with travellers, whose orthodoxy has yet scarcely been suspected by others, or even by themselves.

In the ministry, there is, indeed, a variety of gifts. Some of these more stirring than others, move with greater power. But, whether the power comes more from above, may be quite questioned.

We think it is by no means certain that the saving power of the gospel is more partial to the Knapps than to the Channings. Knapp gets up revivals of *religion*, which, like "the crackling of thorns under a pot," go out in more permanent revivals of *infidelity*. Channing, less ambitious of show, more patient of results, and more confiding in truth and in God, plays upon the hearts of his generation with the sunny beams of love, loosening all their humanities, turning them upward to the Father, and, dying, leaves so much done, without drawback—done, never to be undone!

As to revivals, you well know, brother, that any man of the right kind of pulpit eloquence, and private address, can get them up in certain sections of the country, provided he knows how;—that is, provided he understands the mental action of the masses, and how to influence it. Maffit, the great revivalist, who figured so largely, and died so miserably, used to boast, in his palmiest days, as I was told at Hartford, that *he* knew *how* to do it. And certainly he did do it, most successfully. Whether or not he did it by any special aid of the Divine Spirit, is, I apprehend, a question on which you and I should not much differ.

Now in all this, let us not be understood as saying one word against true religious revivals; we believe they are greatly needed — revivals of practical godliness, which evince their divine origin, not by the flame with which they burn, but by the reformation of heart and life, in which they perpetuate themselves. Nay, we should go out of our way, here, to say anything, more than incidentally, against any *form* of religious revival. We only protest against the prevalent and absurd notion, that the escape of an ignorant and churchless people from endless woe, depends upon the contingency of a gospel minister of the revivalist stamp, or of any other stamp, going among them for a short season.

The gospel of our Lord and Saviour Jesus Christ is, indeed, "the power of God unto salvation." Let us not be understood as speaking lightly of it. It should be preached to all. It is capable of blessing all. We fully believe it eventually will. But eternity is the field of its bevevolent action, and not the narrow circumference of a single hour. As the power of God, its movements have a lofty purpose, which it is mighty to fulfil, for its resources are the universe. How then, shall it depend, ultimately, upon the weak, sinful, human preacher — put its trust in an arm of flesh, so that if that arm fail through infirmity or disobedience, its purpose is defeated, in the sinner's everlasting damnation?

I know not how the above considerations may strike you; but I hope that you will consider them well; not indeed as argument put forth in the defence of any religious theory, but as suggestive of the probability that there is something wrong in the popular creed, and that it becomes men, personally interested as we all deeply are, in the doctrine of retribution, if possible to find out the wrong, and rectify it.

Truly yours,

LETTER XXI.

EIGHTH ABSURDITY — HEATHEN LOST.

Exclamatory introduction—*Eighth Absurdity*, the heathen lost—Idolatry—Where are the swarms of idolaters of the past?—Paul would not have his brethren ignorant of those who had fallen asleep—Geology, and spiritual paleontology—President Wayland, quotation from—A shudder—Emblazonry upon the clouds of despair—Quotation from Rev. E. N. Kirk—Kirk and Wayland, true to the creed—More souls saved by *heathen infanticides* than by *Christian Missionaries!!*—To doubt that the heathen are lost, is to suspect Universalism true—No mild endless punishment—Kirk again—But two Orthodox receptacles for the dead, or but two conditions—Dr. Livingstone's query over the dead African—Does the Bible give no light on the condition of our departed heathen brethren?—Dreadfulness of the Orthodox view of them—Wilds of scholastic theology—*Ne plus ultra* of absurdity—Interdict upon common sense—Ghost of Banquo.

Dear Brother,—

This green earth, and you and I walking over it! These spangled heavens, and you and I walking under them! Grand conceptions. How they overwhelmed the Psalmist, when "at eventide," lifting up his eyes in the contemplation of the immensity of God's works, he exclaimed, "When I consider thy heavens, the work of thy fingers, the moon and stars which thou hast ordained, what is man that thou art mindful of him, and the son of man that thou visitest him?" But the Psalmist was, in this case, hardly peculiar. All thinking men are, sometimes, consciously wrapt in Jehovah, as king David was. And when I, in my humbler measure, have been so carried away in thought, I have felt a strong sympathy with the man who, on being told that an aged neighbor, recently deceased, was probably in perdition, coolly replied, "I think the Author of this vast universe can find some better business than to be damning forever that poor old man!"

But, you will say, this is a strange opening for a familiar letter; and yet, if you will consider it well, I think it will not prove an unprofitable one. But to bring our thoughts into line again, we proceed to remark,

Eighth, That a very large proportion of all who have lived upon and left the earth, up to the present time, have lived upon and left it, heathen. This is the fact. Your creed implies that they are lost. This is the seeming absurdity.

Idolatry very early appeared among men. It went with Ham to Africa, with Shem to China, and with Japhet to Europe,—or, at least, soon followed them. Its prevalence is attested by very early records, and from the dawning of historic ages down to the present time, it has been the law, and truer worship only the exception. Very important, therefore, is the question, what has become of the countless millions of our great brotherhood who have died in idolatry?

Paul would not have his brethren ignorant "concerning those who had fallen asleep," even though they had fallen asleep heathen. No more would we be ignorant of the condition of the multitudes of our heathen relation, who, after groping their dark and evil way on earth, have fallen on sleep. Well is it that the geologist deciphers the mazy records of material paleontology upon the charred tablets of our crusted globe. But far better is it, that the religious antiquarian should inquire after the spiritual, which accompanied the material — after the millions upon millions of immortal spirits which have, from age to age, been leaving their bodies behind them, in the dust of the grave.

This question of the heathen's eternity is a vast one, everywhere stirring men up, either to the abandonment of the popular penal creed, or to such modifications of it, as require the abandonment of the stereotyped plates from which have been stricken off a thousand editions of it.

This, as we have before said, is the creed.
1. Death does nothing to fit a soul for heaven.
2. No soul can be fitted for heaven after death.
3. Therefore all who die unfit for heaven are lost

forever. Under this view the heathen are disposed of in a syllogism, thus:

1. All who die unfit for heaven are lost.

2. The heathen die unfit for heaven, and therefore,

3. The heathen are lost.

With so simple a word, are the heathen of all ages disposed of under the popular creed, — the creed which, probably, finds no more truthful expositor, than the Rev. Dr. Wayland, long president of Brown University, one of the clearest reasoners and thinkers of the age, and whose published works are giving him a just celebrity upon two continents. In his "Moral Dignity of the Missionary Enterprize," a discourse whose sublime completeness, makes it well worthy to stand at the head of a volume of discourses on missions, the doctor says:

"We have considered these beings, [the heathen,] as candidates for an eternity of happiness or misery, and we cannot avoid the thought that they are exposed to endless misery. Hence, you will observe, the question with us, is not, whether a heathen, unlearned in the gospel, can be saved. We are willing to admit that he may. But if he be saved, he must possess holiness of heart; for without holiness no man shall see the Lord. It is in vain to talk about the innocence of these children of nature. It is in vain to tell of their graceful mythology. Their gods are such as lust makes welcome. Of their very religious service, it is a shame even to speak. To settle the question concerning their future destiny, it would only seem necessary to ask, what would be the character of that future state, in which those principles of heart, which the whole history of the heathen world developes, were suffered to operate in unrestrained malignity? No. Solemn as is the thought, we do believe, that, dying in their present state, they will be exposed to all that is awful in the wrath of Almighty God!"

Thus does this clear thinker and writer give the only fair and legitimate exposition of his creed, in reference to the heathen. All different ones set that creed at naught. To be consistent, we must either abandon the cardinal principle of that creed, or else believe that the vast multitudes of heathen who have, from age to age, swarmed up in the earth, and swept away into eternity, a broad deep rolling river of immortal beings, are now swarming in Hell; that they are there this moment, and there forever to remain, suffering "all that is awful in the wrath of Almighty God!" This was the thought which the doctor could not avoid without denying his faith. And, surely, it *is* "solemn," and can but make us shudder—shudder for the heathen, shudder for the honor of God, and shudder with the exclamation, what if we had been born heathen five thousand years ago!! But is not this thought so "solemn," that it degenerates into an absurdity? Is it not so expressive that it expresses nothing; so overdone that it does nothing; so shocking to common sense that the heart, on reflection, cares little for it. For, surely if the heathen do, for want of the Gospel, go thus quickly down to hell, over the sulphurous gateway by which they enter, to come up no more, might well be written in emblazoned characters, which should shine out like live coals upon the dark, "CHILDREN *of God, drinking the* WRATH *of God, for want of* OPPORTUNITY *to* ESCAPE *it!!!*" And, spanning the smoky abyss of their everlasting pain, might well be written "*millions of immortals* DESTROYED *by the* BEING THAT MADE THEM, *for lack of knowledge*, WHICH THEY COULD NOT OBTAIN!!! All this brother, all this, or the popular notion of endless punishment is a nullity!

The Rev. E. N. Kirk, speaking of the heathen in a published missionary sermon, says,

"If we examine their lives, considered in the light of a disciplinary, probationary, preparatory state, [and that is the only earthly state in which the popular creed considers them] we cannot believe that they go to heaven. They, as well as we, must be regenerated, and that in this world. But we find them as in Paul's day, infanticides, liars, adulterers, covenant breakers, bestial, sensual, devilish, murderers of mothers;" and so Kirk agrees with Wayland, that "these children of nature," in the sweet language of the latter—these "poor pagans," to use the language of the former—are lost forever. And surely as we have seen, they *are* thus lost, *or* the orthodox creed must one day *be* thus lost. If that creed be true, the link which binds it to these appalling consequences, was welded upon the anvil of eternity, and can be no more broken than that which binds the will of God to the execution of his purposes.

Kirk speaks of the heathen as "infanticides;" and they are so. Now for all who die in infancy, but three things remain,—annihilation, damnation, salvation. But Kirk, doubtless, believes in neither the first nor the second. The third, therefore, only remains. Infants are saved. And if saved, then, though the victims of infanticide, happy are they, compared with the victims of Kirk's earthly probation. Happy is the mother who sees her babe die, compared with the mother who sees her babe live. For it to die under the violent hand of the mother is everlasting salvation; whereas to lie upon her bosom, till reared from it into self-reliant responsible days, is everlasting damnation! And here culminates God's plan for separating parents and children forever to the wide extremes of glory and perdition. Here it is clearly seen that infanticides are, in the unblurred eye of the popular creed, the most successful *infant savers—that more souls are saved from endless woe by heathen infanticides, than by Christian missionaries!!* And I would suggest, whether an argument to the purpose of orthodoxy is not found in the fact, that a relatively larger number die in infancy in heathen than in Christian lands. May it not be that God, in his wise providence, takes more of the heathen away infants, because if he saves them at all, it must be at that tender age! A word to the wise is sufficient.

True, indeed, it is, that many, pressed with the absurdity, and barbarism we have been presenting as the consequence of their creed, are hoping that it is not so, hoping that the heathen shall in some way be saved. But plainly, just to the extent to which this hope is sound, is their creed rotten. So Wayland, and so Kirk, and so consistency. But however Wayland, and however Kirk, and whatever else to the contrary, there stands the creed with positive and unerring finger, pointing all who die unfit for heaven, directly downward to the shades of interminable woe. The creed that does not do this is "another" creed, on which the church deep lays its broad brand of heresy.

Furthermore, while there are many who seek

relief by hoping, against their creed, that the heathen shall, in some way, be saved, there are not a few who seek it, by dreaming that the sufferings of the hell into which the heathen fall, though endless, are not very severe—perhaps almost tolerated. But surely all they who hope for a mild endless punishment, under the popular creed, are only dreaming. For under that creed to quote from a missionary sermon by Dr. Kirk, "We can conceive of it, as nothing less than eternal banishment from light, and life, and hope, to regions prepared for the devil and his angels;" (not to add as Kirk does) "where the soul shall be enveloped and penetrated with a misery immense, infinite; where it shall find nothing more in all beings, but an universal hell—a hell within, a hell without, a hell in God himself!"

A mild endless punishment! And *can* there be such, to a creature like man? And if there can be, can that be such which involves the endless loss of God's favor, and the endless darkness of his power! Can the condition of a soul be anything short or more dreadful than language can express, or finite mind imagine, when the last ray of the light of God's countenance dies away upon it forever! Who can imagine, for the soul, a worse condition than that into which it falls, when, either by judicial decision, or by the operation of the common law of his universe, God puts it forever beyond the reach of all means of grace? Talk of a mild punishment of an endlessly damned soul! It is to talk at random. A soul left to wander forever from God, without the possibility of languishing into nought, must at length reach a point of wretchedness, at which, it would be a relief to be thrown into a literal lake of fire and brimstone! So dreadfnlly are all lost, who, under the popular view of retribution, are lost at all.

The doctrine is that the future world affords but two receptacles for all the dead, the one heaven and the other hell; and that these two are separated by an impassable gulf. Of course, all who are unfit for the former place, are banished from it into the latter. If you choose, you may regard these two conditions of the dead, as states, rather than places. It is all the same for our purpose. And now I leave it for any one to discover, either a gloomy corner in the orthodox heaven or a lightsome corner in the orthodox hell! Neither can be found, as we have already seen, and therefore must the above view of the future condition of the heathen be accepted, or the popular dogma of endless punishment be abandoned.

Dr. Livingstone, whose benevolent explorations in Central Africa are exciting so much interest, being present with a Bechuana tribe, at the time of the death of its chief, Sebituane, speaking of the circumstance, says :—" I never felt so much grieved by the loss of a black man before ; and it was impossible not to follow him, in thought, into the world of which he had just heard, before he was called away, and to realize somewhat of the feelings of those who pray for the dead." And he further adds, " the deep dark question, what is to become of such as he, must however be left where we find it, believing that assuredly, " the judge of all the earth will do right."

And is it indeed true, then, that even to the Christian missionary, (for such is Dr. L.) the Scriptures, which profess to bring life and immortality to light, give no clue to the future condition of the heathen—constituting as they have done up to a late date almost the entire human race? Are we still in utter ignorance of where the great, chief stream of intelligent human existence, which has been for thousands of years broadening and deepening and sweeping away, empties itself? or whether, as was once thought of the Niger, it loses itself in the sands of annihilation? We cannot think so. Orthodoxy, straight out, does not think so. To *it* the *question* of the future condition of the heathen is neither deep nor dark, though the abyss into which it makes the heathen sink, is both. It rather assures us, as we have seen, that the broad, deep, rolling tide of heathenism, compared with which, Christianity is but a little rill, has ever been, and still is, pouring itself an awful Niagara down the rocks of damnation into eternity's vast dead sea, ocean, of living woe. And, I repeat, this I must believe, as a votary of othodoxy, or part with its theory of retribution. I may wonder that God should have it so. I may be amazed that he has not been, and is not, in greater *haste* to send the gospel to the heathen! I may shudder at the compromise of his paternal love! I may deem it all unqualified absurdity, or something worse! But I must believe it, or oblique off into, what the church calls, heresy.

And now, brother, however you may be at first impressed with the presentations of this letter, I am persuaded that, on reflection, you will see that I have nothing overstated or overdrawn. So true is it that he, who *with his eyes open*, wanders where orthodoxy leads, oft finds himself in the gloomy depths of vast howling wildernesses, where, under the dark shadows with which his theory invests his God, he may well cry out in anguish, "all is dark, dark, dark; and I cannot disguise it."

So true is it—and while it is warm on my heart I will say it—that you may search the religious and mythological records of all ages, and not another doctrine can you find, written upon vellum or foolscap, by Pagan, Mahomedan, or Christian pen, involving directly, and by association, so many, so glaring, and so horrid absurdities as this same most Christian doctrine of endless punishment.

Do you say again, I speak strongly. Be it so. You will not say that I overstate anything. Nay, do I not understand everything; and this of necessity. Do you not feel that the doctrine I reject, whether true or false, by the terribleness of its absurdities, sets all human language at defiance! Are not some of them such, that, shrinking from their contemplation, your only rest and safeguard against what is called heresy, is in putting an interdict upon your common sense and consciousness. Do not some of the absurdities noted in these letters meet you at every turn, and often confront you so boldly, that you are obliged to attempt to deal summarily with them, while at the same time, you are astonished that they will not more readily "down at your bidding?" But these, unlike the ghost of Banquo, are "real, not imaginary difficulties."* We close this letter, praying that, under the sure guidance of the word and spirit of God, you may find your way out of them; and that way I think you will have discovered, when you sufficiently consider Jesus *as the exponent of the Father's love.*

Yours truly.

*Barnes.

LETTER XXII.

OBLIVIOUSNESS TO CONSEQUENCES.

Creed and consequences go together—Hard to separate the two in thought—Advice to a widow—*Ninth Absurdity* stated—Stuart's method of relief, remarks upon; 1, Link broken; 2, Natures of the righteous changed; 3, Why not of the wicked; 4, Ishmaelites in heaven; 5, Sense of God's goodness forbidden.—God will destroy sin rather than the Christian virtues—The good Professor rests—Second rate advisers—Perdition exposed, but not its victims!—Not think of the creed's consequences!—Hard to hold it, sometimes harder to abandon it—Veteran Soldier.

DEAR BROTHER,—

Perhaps you are saying, I am weary of absurdities. And if so, I think you may well be weary of the creed which involves them. That very creed you hold, say you are satisfied with it, and, I presume, intend to keep it. But if you keep it, you must keep these wearisome absurdities. For they are part and parcel of it — as inseparable from it, as darkness from chaos. I know, indeed, that, pressed with their hideousness, many a theologian, under the deepening light of Christian civilization, is striving hard to divorce them from it. But all in vain. They are fixed to it, like serfs to their soil. No shrewdness of management can ever secure a bill of their divorcement, in any court of common sense. Joined together like cause and effect, if the one be taken, the other cannot be left. If the one be left, the other cannot be taken. It is in vain that you invite the Devil to dine, with the polite request that he leave his cloven foot behind.

Perhaps the best thing that those can do, who feel that they *must* hold the popular creed, is to be as oblivious as possible to its consequences — a thing which many are attempting; but which, to *live* minds, were like attempting to forget the dead whose ghosts nightly haunt their pillows. Yet, I once heard a weeping widow publicly advised to do so, by the minister, at the funeral of her wicked husband,—advised not to think at all of his condition in the future world. But what advice! How comforting! Not think of her dear husband! And had she not his miniature in her bosom, and a lock of his hair in her drawer, and loving words he had once spoken, in the hour of their plighted faith, embalmed in her memory, — and dear children by her side, bearing his image, and asking, "*Where's father?*" And touched by their tender and ingenuous questions, does she not often turn away to weep? And yet, is she cruelly told, not to think of her husband! Or shall she think of *him*, but not of his *condition*. Impossible! The father and his believed condition must appear only together upon the tablet of her memory! They admit of no dissociation in her widowed mind. Yet such *was* the advice given. And cruel as it was, it was, perhaps, the best possible, under the dominant creed. With no kindlier and more comforting words, can *its* Christianity minister to many of the broken hearted victims of bereavement. And, to accept such words, is to do the greatest violence to our holiest affections, and the greatest injustice to those whose condition we attempt to forget. For myself, may nobody think of me, when I am dead who will not sympathetically follow me into the future world. And this brings me to a

Ninth absurdity, involved in your creed, and which I will formally note. It is this; that it requires its votaries to believe that all the generous sympathies with our fellow beings, which our holy religion teaches us to cherish in our hearts *here*, and which are here the glory of the Christian character, are, in *heaven*, to be so completely "extinguished," that we shall be able, without pain, to listen to, or contemplate, the wailings of unrelieved despair. By that creed, the loving husband is required to believe that, in heaven, among the "spirits of the just made perfect," he shall so cease to pity, or care for, his own excellent but unconverted wife, that, after having hung tearfully over her in death, regretting only that he could not divide with her the anguish of its struggle, and after having survived her to drop many a tear upon her miniature, he shall, all at once, become so indifferent to her fate, as to answer her endless wailings, with endless hallelujahs! And this seems to me an absurdity.

But whether an absurdity or not, it has involved great and good souls in difficulty. Instance, Professor Stuart. Speaking in reference to it, he says, "If parents, husbands, wives, brothers, sisters, must see those dear as their own life, perish at last, while they themselves are saved, heaven, in mercy, will either extinguish their social susceptibilities, or else give them such a sweet and overpowering sense of the justice and goodness of God as shall not permit the joys of the blessed to be marred, nor the songs of the redeemed to be interrupted, with sighs of sympathetic sorrow. How this will or can be done, we may never know in the present world; nay, we may have many a distressing hour, while enquiring how it can be done, unless our natures are wholly changed." So speaks the Professor, and what meaning is in his words! What must be the strength of that necessity, which, in such a mind, hypothecates such assumptions — *social susceptibilities extinguished! natures wholly changed!* And on these we may well remark,

1. That, if the nature of souls is to be so

"wholly changed" on entering the future world, we see no such connexion between this world and that, as can make our conduct in this, determine our character and consequent destiny in that. For then is our resurrection in the future world, just about equivalent to a new creation. The link of moral connexion between the two worlds, is then completely broken. But *this*, Orthodoxy very justly denies; and, in denying it, virtually denies the hypothesis of Stuart, that our natures are to be so wholly changed.

2. We remark that, if, consistently with the Divine plan, the natures of the *righteous* can be so changed in the future world, that they shall cease to pity the hopeless sufferings of their lost fellow beings, we see not why, upon the same principle, by an act of God no more arbitrary—the natures of the *wicked* may not be so changed, there, that they shall cease to love and desire sin. And this latter especially, seeing that it is evident that the motives of sin are largely "in this mortal flesh," which is put off in the grave. As above intimated, *we* advocate no such arbitrary change, any way. But its admission were fatal to the Orthodoxy which says, "As death leaves us, so judgment will find us."

3. But more than this should be said. For, to the intelligent Christian, the entire revealed charac-

ter of God, becomes ground of inference that whatever change of nature is arbitrarily wrought upon the soul as it leaves the body, that change must be in favor of virtue rather than of vice—must be rather to soften and sanctify sinners, than to harden and deprave saints—to "*extinguish*" earthly vices rather than Christian virtues!

4. And further, the idea that God shall "so extinguish "the social susceptibilities" of the glorified, strikes the mind with peculiar horror. To do that, were to fill heaven—if not with Ishmaelites, every spirit's hand being against every other spirit's hand—at least, with sorry anchorites, sitting, every one by his own solitary fire, and without a neighbor, all over the deserts of eternity. For, certainly, with "social susceptibilities" extinguished, there can be no society. The ability to pity, is but a form of the ability to love. With the extinguishment of the former, therefore, must go out also the latter. And so because the saints must not pity, they must be disabled for love; and hence the many voiced song of social praise must be hushed before the throne, forever! hence must darkness gather over the eternal hills of light, and paradise lie in its final shroud. But,

5. Unless the natures of the redeemed *are* wholly changed, the very perpetual act of God in keeping their friends alive in endless suffering, must forever

forbid to them that "sweet and overpowering sense of the justice and goodness of God," which, the Professor supposes, may reconcile them to it. The more "sweet and overpowering" is our sense of God's "goodness and justice," the more severe and distressing is our heart's struggle with the notion that he inflicts endless pain, directly or indirectly, upon our fellow creatures—"bone of our bone and flesh of our flesh."

But thus did the heart of Stuart struggle, and thus did his head speculate. Nor could he, on reflection, fail to see that, as "God is love," we should look for his extinguishment of the sinner's susceptibility to sin, rather than of the saint's susceptibility to pity—that whatever arbitrary change is to be wrought in disembodied souls, must be to destroy the vices which the Incarnate denounced, rather than the virtues which His life and teachings exalted. And certainly, among these virtues, is the charity which loves all, pities all, and seeks the good of all, enemies as well as friends. How then shall this virtue, or the susceptibility to it, be extinguished, even though it be, as our Professor supposes, to prevent heaven from being eclipsed in the dark shadow of hell. But enough.

Thus did the heart of Stuart struggle with his penal creed. The spectacle of his struggle is indeed sublime. It severely taxed his ingenuity. But it is now ended. The good man rests. Nor do we believe that his excellent "nature is so wholly changed," or his "social susceptibilities" extinguished, or that, by any other means, he is brought to rejoice in the endless woe of those whom he, as a Christian, necessarily loved on earth.

But Stuart, so far as we know, said nothing about relief sought by forgetting the dead. It is only second class thinkers who thus advise. And even these second rate advisers are even *pointing us to* the miseries of the lost, to deter us, as they say, from going to their "place of torment." So inconsistent are they. Why, I have seen the excellent minister, referred to above, as advising the mourning widow, eloquently lead his audience, to use nearly his words, "up to the verge of the pit, that they might look down over the battlement of hell upon the anguish of the damned." But he would not have the widow do this, lest she should descry her husband among them, "treading the burning marl."

The doctrine of endless woe is deemed so fundamental and efficient, that the creed from which it is excluded, is deemed more than useless. But that dark item were certainly, valueless, if unthought of. And yet those men who value it so highly, tell us not to think of it, or to think of it only abstractly; which is to do the impossible thing, of thinking of the sufferings of hell, without thinking of the sufferers. And what wisdom is here! What consistency.

Hold a creed, and not think of its consequences! Why, we need a creed, only in view of its consequences, just as we need causes, only in view of their effects. If the contemplation of the consequences of a creed is unprofitable, then drop it. It is not of God. If any part of it is thus unprofitable, drop that part. So much of it as *is* of God is profitable to contemplate, and so much, therefore should be cherished; its damnatory clauses not excepted. Its minister should see that its hell stand as fully exposed, as its heaven, and that the damned walk before the eyes of the living in the darknes of despair, as distinctly as the saved in the light of Paradise! Thus only shall they be well assisted,

"To escape from hell and fly to heaven."

Not think of the consequences of your creed! not even when it involves our fellow men in an almost universal and overwhelming everlasting ruin! and when it involves the government of God the Father, in almost every variety of seemingly, palpable, evident, self-evident, absurdity and injustice.

Not think of the consequences of your creed! As well be a "dead man out of mind." As well were the creed itself dead! We rejoice to see it dying!

Not think of the consequences of your creed! You, brother, will not say so. For you must clearly see, that, to be blind to its consequences, is equivalent to its abandonment. I think you will *try* to, either boldly face it, or openly abandon it. I do not impute to you the unmanliness, which declines to do either. I will be charitable. My own experience has taught me that, to do either, is sometimes, only like doing the hardest of things. It is only under the pressure of a terrible necessity, that mourners submit to go wild in the funeral of the wicked dead. They *will generally hope*, though their creed go to the winds. The heart God gave them will believe the dead in heaven, or in hopes of it, even as though, to believe them there, actually tore them from the meshes of their creed, and put them there. Too true is it that

"Hope springs eternal in the human breast."

So hard is it to face the consequences of the popular creed! Whereas, its actual abandonment, is, if possible, harder still. *That* is to be hoped for, only in the last extreme! The veteran soldier surrenders, only when his last gun is silenced, and the flag-staff of the enemy is upon the wall. And yet you know, brother, and I pray that you may feel, that immortal man is never more thoroughly a conqueror, never more exalted in his humble consciousness, never in stronger sympathy with the angels that excel in strength, and never more God-like, than when he meekly surrenders himself to his own convictions!

Yours truly.

CHAPTER XXIII.

A POINT BETWEEN TWO MOMENTS.

Theological reform gradual.—Dawn upon the close of the dark ages.—The Bramin's microscope.—Visit to a dying sinner.—Heart query.—Title to heaven secured in a moment.—Lorenzo Dow.—Repentance always profitable.—A moment, a century, eternity.—Eternity depends on a point of time between two moments.—Catholic Priests.—Young man's funeral.—Last hour of life an excited one; so is every hour.—Heart rebels.—Query comes.—What if any other system of faith involved *such* absurdities!

DEAR BROTHER,—

I shall stop writing of absurdities. But you will, (as I have before intimated), be relieved of their tediousness, only by the abandonment of your penal creed. You cannot turn them out of doors, because they are part of the house. Nor can they fail to glare more sharply up, as the light of your heart deepens. Such, I think, has been your experience thus far, and such must it continue to be.

It was only very gradually, that the light of civilization dawned upon the close of the dark ages. And just so gradually, did the church expurgate her creed of the more obviously absurd of its damnatory clauses. The doctrine of infant destruction, for instance — who can tell when it ceased to be believed? It only melted into a better faith, before the deepening light, as night melts into day. We only know that the church, from holding it firmly, at length, impressed with its absurdity, came to hold it loosely, and finally, turning to the Bible, found that it was not taught there, and so, repudiated it altogether. And so also, at this day, are other things equally absurd and obnoxious, appearing in the popular creed, brought out under the increasing light, as new stars are brought out under the increased power of the telescope. And shall not these also pass away. Already are they driving thinkers into all sorts of shifts for relief. Every day are they becoming more startling and appalling. And shall they not pass away? They certainly must. And this, in just so far as thinking minds turn, impartially, to the patient study of the Scriptures!

We have referred to the telescope. It does not make stars, where before all seemed starless. Neither does light upon the mind make absurdities, where before all seemed reasonable. It only *reveals* them. They were always matters of fact; as were the living creatures, in the water drank by the Bramin who smashed the microscope. We will imitate the Bramin, neither by resisting the light, nor affecting to ignore the absurdities it reveals.

For, in the language of Barnes, as before quoted, they "are real not imaginary difficulties." And the more the believer in endless woe studies God in Nature and in Grace, the more will they meet him at every turn. For instance,

You, as a minister, are called upon at midnight, to visit a member of your congregation, suddenly and dangerously ill, lying at the point of death. Like a faithful shepherd, you heed the summons. Hastening to his house, his sisters meet you at the door, with an air of the deepest sadness. Sad are they because they are to lose their brother, but sadder, because he is likely to lose his soul. For he has been irreligious, and perhaps profane. They feel that, according to your teachings, his eternity depends upon a momentary treatment of his case. Of course, they entreat you to do all for his salvation, possible; a thing for which you are quite ready. You enter the sick room. The dying man stretches out his hand to you, or barely gives signs of welcome. Evidently the tide of life is ebbing rapidly away. You seat yourself by his bedside, and —— but you can fill up the picture, brother.

And now, in that dark, dying hour, comes there not a deep heart-querying, whether God has really ordained that the popular alternatives of life and death to that man's soul, shall depend upon a midnight dying hour? an hour when he is abnormal with pain and anodyne, and fear? Comes not the query, lurking among the shadows, whether, if the sick man is prepared only for endless woe *this* hour, anything that you can do for him, can, under grace, so change his relations to the universe, that, dying the *next* hour, he shall be fit for the society of angels forever. Ah, brother, if you are the man I mean, then, well do I know how deep are your queryings here, over what you had taught, and what your creed involves, and what, I am confident, must pass away. For, of all hours for transacting important business, a dying hour, with its weakness and pain, and excitement or stupidity, is least fitting; save perhaps in some cases of the calmest Christian peace.

For the present, however, this idea of sudden conversion in the hour of death extensively prevails —prevails co-extensively with the popular creed. So that, thousands upon thousands are now deemed to be in heaven, who secured their title to it in a brief moment of that hurried repentance, into which they were frightened in the hour of death. But is it so? Does it not, in calm reflection seem to you *too* absurd? Not only are the subjects of this supposed change, in the worst condition for transacting spirit-work, but have you not seen that, when disappointed in dying, they, by their return to their former thoughtlessness, show that the change, on which heaven would have been predicated in their funeral, had they died, was, after all, only imaginary? And when you have seen this, have you not been staggered? Do you say, "I don't believe in this dying bed repentance?" Very well. But to say that, is to thin the ranks of the redeemed and to thicken the ranks of the lost. To say that, is to dash the fond hopes and anticipations of thousands of mourners, by casting their dead out of heaven into hell!

Lorenzo Dow said what he had a mind to; and among other odd things, that "sinners will burn the candle of life all out, and then hope to appease everlasting wrath, by throwing the snuff in God Almighty's face." But, brother, do you not find it hard to believe that with that *snuff*—that miserable residuum of a life of sin, the sinner can secure an eternal reprieve from perdition, and an eternal right to heaven?

We are not here saying one word against sincere repentance, at any time and place. God hears his children, always. But that he should say to the sinner, "give me this last bed-ridden moment of your life, and I will give you an eternity of blessing; withhold it, and I will give you an eternity of cursing!" that seems too much for intelligent belief. But is it not involved in your creed? practically involved—so involved that about all the holders of the one, hold the other also?

A Roman Catholic priest, speaking of the victims of the fall and flame of the ill-fated "*Pemberton,*" comforted their surviving friends, by hoping that they had time to make their peace with God, before they died. And is not this the comfort that Protestant clergymen often give, at the funerals of the irreligious dead? "He might have found God, between mast head and deck." Only recently we heard a minister, in the funeral of a young man, after cautioning the audience not to delay seeking God, by referring to the fact that the deceased was so delirious in his sickness that he could not be so much as "pointed to Christ," add, for the comfort of the family, that "just before he died, he had a lucid interval, and *might* have got a glimpse of Christ." And now brother does your hope for the dead hang upon such uncertainties, as fill up the medicated, and delirious experiences of a poor mortal's dying hour?

But *if* you say you do not believe in this death bed repentance; then I reply—but you *do* believe in the repentance of this *life*, as determining the creature's eternity. And what you do believe in this matter, involves an absurdity just as great and glaring as that involved in what you do *not* believe. For one single minute, or even the millionth part of a minute, bears the same relation to eternity, which is borne by the largest conceivable period of time.

In other words such a period of time bears no relation to eternity, which is not borne by the largest conceivable period. Hence it is equally as absurd to believe that God should ordain that man should determine his eternity of weal or woe by the action of a century, as by the action of a second. All limited periods of duration stand to eternity, only in the simple relation of the finite to the infinite. Hence, if you hold that the creature's eternity is determined in this *life*, you may as well hold that it is determined by the last moment of this life, seeing that you hold to what involves precisely the same principle.

But further; I think your credal theory is, that every person is at every moment in such condition, that, dying, he would go direct to either heaven or hell. And this being so, it follows that, to every person redeemed, there must have been a *moment* in which he was fit for destruction, followed, *immediately*, by a moment in which he was fit for glory. And hence, in these two consecutive moments—nay, at a *point* of time *between* them, or on an imaginary line separating the two—the soul must have been completely redeemed—taken from the "stones of the pit" to the threshold of heaven—from endless night, to endless day. And thus, by a logical necessity of your theory, eternities mightier far than the universe, turn on mere pivots, *points* of time.

And this being so, why should the notion of salvation in a *last* moment,—"between mast-head and deck"—be at all questioned. If eternity depends upon a single moment, why may it not be the last one, as well as any other?

But, as we seem to have changed sides you may say, "the last hour of life is generally an excited one." And so it is. But what of that? Is not every hour of life an excited one—if we except the hours of sleep? Are not most men more than half intoxicated with something or other, all the way along from the cradle to the grave. It may be with business, it may be with pleasure, it may be with politics, it may be with scholastic theology, it may be with wine. "Childhood is restless ever," and so is age. And that, under all the passionate excitement through which man makes his way *to* the earth, and under which he is born, and into which he is thrown, and midst which he is obliged to live, he should be expected, or rather necessitated, to settle the appalling questions of Orthodox eternities, were, to me, as great a wonder as, that this eternity-work, should devolve on a last moment of life; and this the more especially, seeing that the creature knows nothing, only as he learns it, and is obliged, therefore, to live one life, to learn *how* to live. The principle involved in the two cases, is, in the last analysis, entirely the same.

Shuffle the matter as we will, to this nicety do we at last come, making the man's eternity of positive joy or sorrow depend on some single moment of his ignorant and excited earthly life. And perhaps, you deem that you can meet the difficulty it involves, with ease. But, on reflection, and after all, do you not find the heart God gave you, charged with an inalienable idea of justice and goodness, rising up in rebellion against it? And this, especially, as you visit the dying sinner, and attempt to comfort mourners around the coffins of death-bed repentance? or, even as you look out upon the face of society, organized under the eye of heaven and in the midst of all the good which comes down from the Father of Lights?" And will not the query come, and *stay*, whether the creed which involves such nicety, may not, *must* not, be false? And does not such a query, oftimes greatly weaken the confidence with which you assert the doctrine of doom, and exhort and persuade your fellow sinners, whether in the church, in the chamber of the dying, or at the funeral of the dead? And if any new system of faith were presented you, involving such absurdities as we have seen that *yours* involves, would you not reject it, without so much as examination? O the power of a false religious education. It almost conquered even Luther himself.

Yours truly.

LETTER XXIV.

THE DIFFERENCE BETWEEN MEN'S HEARTS.

Expounding the Judgment parable; line drawn, reflection afterwards—Query in social meeting—The exhorter and the exhorted—The shattered man's remark—Difference between men; too small for the eternities—If we could see *hearts*, would the difference seem greater?—If so, would the increase of difference be in favor of the righteous?—The Revivalist and the Philosopher,—which soundest before God?—Gradation of character — The scale cut—A pause in sermon-writing—"Are you sure the Lord says so?"—Punishment before judgment—Cursed out of sleep into endless woe—Future suffering forbids what the suffering of this life seeks—Satan's thanksgiving---Items jotted---The spectral camp.

DEAR BROTHER,—

You are expounding the parable of the sheep and the goats,—making it separate the human family, right and left, to the wide extremes contemplated by your creed. And when you have made parents and their children part—"part to meet no more,"—you proceed to ask your audience, who of them are prepared for the "right hand" of the Judge, and who for the "left." And perhaps you earnestly cry, "should the Judge descend this moment in a cloud of flame, and draw the line of eternal judgment through this audience, on which side would you individually fall?"

Your sermon is ended. You shake hands with A, B, and C, the congregation disperse, and you are at home. And now as you sit there, quietly, do you not seriously query, whether there can be difference enough between, even the best and the worst of your congregation, to make the former fit for, or worthy of, endless life, in heaven, and the latter, of endless death, in hell. Some of them profess to be Christians, others do not. Some of them are really better than others. But viewing them from any stand-point, other than their profession, and especially viewing them from the stand-point of reason and common sense, do they not seem too much alike,—to have too many good and bad things in common,—to be the everlasting antipodes of the moral universe! When in your "conference meeting," sitting quietly by the altar, you hear one of your brethren exhorting his neighbors to repent, are you not often asking yourself whether, if that brother be saved his neighbors can hardly be lost? He may be a brother well worthy of your confidence. But even yet, after bating his habit of formal religious service, and, judging him by his daily life and spirit, *does* he differ so very materially from those whom he exhorts, as his profession, in the eye of your creed, indicates? Is he less devoted to gain, or more benevolent? Is he less *sharp* in trade? Is he more industrious, or has he less self-conceit? Is he more consistent with his profession? Is he less ambitious, or does he do more to harmonize society? Is he less careless of his tongue? Has he fewer sides, or do you better know where to find him? Is he a better citizen? In a word, his profession and ritual service aside, does he appear so very materially different from his non-professing neighbors?

Said a shattered man, "The Lord knoweth them that are his, and it is well that he does; for if he did not, I don't know who under heaven could." And, brother, do you not often feel the force of this remark, as you look out upon the face of your congregation, or upon the church generally? Do not its deacons and ministers, almost equally with its laymen, give unmistakeable evidence of selfishness, ambition, jealousy of place. I scarcely know a minister, seemingly more ambitious than one whom I heard put in the fact that *ambition* did not inhere in, or depend upon the human body, and therefore would not be thrown off with it, as evidence against the doctrine of universal holiness. So true is it that men may be "proud of their periods thundered against pride," that

——"all men have flaws,
Some men have few, and some are flaw all o'er,"

and when a man finds himself intent on marking the

sins of others, and deeming himself worthy in comparison with them, he would do well to remember the exclamation of Scotia's bard,

> "O wad some power the giftie gie us,
> To see oursels as ithers see us!"

Now, in all this, let me not be understood as calling experimental religion in question, but the contrary. Nor am I to be understood as doubting that, taking Protestant Christendom through, professed Christians are, as a general thing, the more godly part of community. But I am to be understood, as saying that the difference between their moral character and that of others around them, and intimately mingling with them, in their neighborhoods and households, seems quite too small to become at death, an impassable gulf, dividing them to heaven and hell forever. And, if I am not mistaken, the absurdity here involved, sometimes so glares upon you from your creed, that your soul is, for the time being, paralyzed for its defense; and this, especially as you mingle with your promiscuous parishioners, sit in their families, acknowledge their kindness, and see their contributions falling into a common treasury.

Perhaps you will say, "Man looks on the outward appearance," and that, could we look at the heart, we should see a greater difference between the so-called regenerate and the unregenerate, than now appears." And perhaps we should. But is it certain that the increase of difference would be in favor of the former? I think not, and that the contrary were the more probable. For, does not the professed Christian feel a special necessity for keeping his external character smoothed up to the level of his profession, to meet the public expectation? And is not his external character, therefore, a *little* less likely to be the true exponent of his heart? Whereas, the worldling, without any particular profession, is, I think, the more likely to pour his internal character, right out upon his surface life. So that, I think it should be regarded as, at least, very doubtful, whether, could we see the *hearts* of men, we should find the increased difference of character thereby revealed, to be in favor of professed Christians.

But further; I think it is not certain that, could we examine hearts, we *should* find the difference between men greater than appears in their lives. Though we might find their hearts *all* the worse, why might not the *difference between them*, be all the less? For, in the heart estimate, as God reckons it, knowledge and ignorance, happy and unhappy stars, modify the result.

George Whitefield vainly besought Benjamin Franklin to seek religion as the former understood it.

The great preacher deemed himself saved, and the great philosopher lost. But could you have looked into the hearts of the two individuals, even at the time when Whitefield was preaching to congregated thousands in the open air, and Franklin, removing farther and farther from the stand, was philosophically estimating the compass of the human voice, might you not have found the heart of the philosopher as *sound* in the sight of God, as that of the revivalist. So I am inclined to think. If the latter fulfilled his mission, did not the former fulfil his? What human being ever had a mightier mission than Franklin,—inspired men excepted? And could you look upon the hearts of your parishioners, I am inclined to think that you would find them to differ, even less than they seem to. Certainly, all that I have seen of testing hearts, by throwing them under circumstances calculated to bring out what did not before appear, goes to favor such a conclusion — to show that hearts differ less at the centre, than at the surface. And so I think you find no relief from your perplexity, by appealing from the visible to the invisible character of the people.

We have around us every grade of character, ranging from the highest good to the lowest bad. Now, to suppose a line to cut the scale at any point, separating all above it to heaven, and all below to hell, were to suppose a seeming absurdity. For the one next *above* the point where the scale is cut, must differ from the one next *below*, only by an inappreciable quantity. And when, in obedience to your creed, you suppose such a line to be drawn, separating the different members of your congregation,—of the families of your parishioners. and of your own family, to infinite extremes of joy and woe forever, I think you sometimes stagger backward,—that then, if you are engaged at writing a sermon, you sometimes pause, lean back in your chair, turn upon your elbow, drop your head upon your hand, look thoughtfully at the window till the ink dries in your pen, and then, slowly wetting it again, and turning to your growing manuscript, you ejaculate, as you resume your work, "Well, the Lord says so, and I suppose I must believe it;" and so your sermon is completed. But were I present, just then, I should ask, "are you quite sure that the Lord says so?" You have been taught and trained from a child that he does, and studied theology through text-books, based on the assumption that he does, and as I look at your library, and see how *exparte* is the evidently *used* portion of its theological works, I am bold to ask, whether after all, and frankly, you have ever impartially examined the subject pro and con. And if not, how dare you feel so confident what the Lord says about human destiny? This is a matter to be looked after, especially when it is considered that, "there is nothing respecting which a man may be so long unconscious, as of the strength and extent of his prejudices."

You are preaching about the last judgment as you understand it. But while you are teaching your hearers that it is to occur at the end of the world, and only after all questions of character shall have been fully settled, and after both saints and sinners shall have been long in heaven and hell respectively, (or in an unconsciousness from which the latter must be cursed back into life again,) are you not sometimes struck with the seeming absurdity that the Father should bring them up from their flames, and down from their bliss, to be again mingled together for a judgment day, and then separated, right and left, to where they were before, or as some suppose, respecting the lost, to a worse place —to sorrows deepened and heightened forever.

Or if you take the ground that both saint and sinner lie in unconscious sleep till the end of time, and that then both are aroused for judgment, by the trump of the archangel, are you not met by the cruel absurdity that the Father should curse the sinner back to consciousness, make him sensitive again, merely that he may pour upon him his wrath forever? Why not let him slumber on? Why awaken him to have "no rest day and night," in the dismal tossings of absolute despair! Who may say why any being less than an infinite despot, should do so cruel and barbarous a thing. But such is not "Our Father which is in heaven."

Or further, if you take what I deem the only consistent orthodox ground — the ground that as judgment is not till the *close* of probation, there is no punishment *during* probation, that is, during this life — then you are met with the absurd notion that the good Father withholds punishment, so long as it can possibly do any good, and then, when it is too late for it to do any good, pours it out upon his children forever. Or, if you admit that God punishes sinners in this life, then are you glared upon, not only by the absurdity that he punishes forever, when too late to do any good, but that the punishment which he inflicts in the future life, should be of a nature absolutely to *forbid* the reformation of character, which in this life it is designed to *promote*. So that Satan, at length, should have occasion to thank God for barring the way of his victims from hell back to heaven again.

But this letter is long enough. Its several items are jotted down as leading indices to a long series of absurdities which we have not time to compute,— absurdities which are meeting the open orthodox thinker at every turn, and in every form — absurdities which multiply and become more hideous with the increase of light, and in whose presence reason and common sense must bow themselves, as the vassals of the Vatican before the image of Saint Peter. "Gigantic shapes," "midnight phantoms," as unreal as the creed which grows them is untruthful, a "spectral camp," they

> "Beleaguer the human soul."

I leave you, brother, to buffet them, earnestly praying that with the Bible in your hand, wide open towards the light of heaven, you may yet sing,

> "Down the broad vale of tears afar,
> The spectral camp is fled;
> Faith shineth as a morning star,
> Our ghastly fears are dead."

Yours truly.

LETTER XXV.

THE ARGUMENT FROM TEMPORAL SUFFERING.

Reasoning from limited to endless suffering—The two things infinitely unlike—The former limits itself, the latter knows no limitation—Supposed Analogy—Paul—Argument applies to both the righteous and the wicked—Suffering in this world a *means*, endless suffering an *end*—The former has an afterwards, the latter not—The true analogy—Tables turned—Lafayette at Olmutz—Prisoners of the Inquisition, eternal prison—A caution—New scientific discoveries dissipate old fears—Illustrations, Thunder, Moon, Comet—Think.

DEAR BROTHER,—

While the absurdities which we have mentioned seem quite *real*, you will very likely try to prove them *imaginary*. For if they are absurdities in fact, then is your penal creed an absurdity in fact,—a chief absurdity, involving all the subordinate ones,—greater than *any*, because comprehending all. But such an admission you will not readily make. Against it, you will be likely to argue.

For instance, in reference to the absurdity that the living Father should create children for fore-known or fore-ordained endless suffering, you will fall back again and again, to say, "Absurd or not absurd, it is a fact, that God either fore-ordained or foreknew, suffering for the creature in this life; and if in this life, why not in the life to come? Why may not the latter be matter of faith, seeing that the former is matter of fact." And to this I reply, very well, what of it? It affords no relief to the difficulty in question. For that lies, not against the doctrine of pain or of punishment, in this or any other world; but only against the doctrine of *endless* punishment. We have seen that, on the question of punishment in the future world, Universalism, as such, is silent. It is against the doctrine of *endless* punishment that it utters its protest.

And here, perhaps, you will again say, "It is a fact that *temporary* suffering enters under the Government of God; and that the principle upon which temporary suffering enters, equally opens the way for the entrance of endless suffering." But if you say this, you certainly say what needs proof, and what no thinking mind will accept without it.

And now let us again "look and see," whether temporary and eternal suffering are so alike, that the principle of the former, necessarily involves the principle of the latter. We think they are not.

1. Because the two things are infinitely unlike in duration. The former is but a span, a point of time; the latter is like God's "eternal day." Here, then, is a difference between the two things, which no

language can set forth, the extent of which no heart can imagine ;—a difference which does not begin to be set forth by the difference between a point of time and an incalculable number of incalculable ages—a difference infinite. And, surely, an infinite difference may well be regarded as quite *essential—so* essential that the principle of the less does not necessarily involve the principle of the greater. For illustration : I was this moment called from my study to assist in comforting a daughter distressingly sick. Now it is by God's will, or permission, that that daughter is in extreme pain. But relief is evidently at hand. Her pain is temporal. And now am I to believe that upon the same principle upon which her temporal pain is reconcileable with our idea of God's fatherly goodness, her eternal pain, (supposing her present pain to be drawn out forever,) would be. Even now, while I am writing, she is relieved, and we are all enjoying the "*afterwards.*" And were no new principle involved, and were God just as paternal, even though he kept my daughter in her distress forever !

2. But I remark, further, that the pains or punishments of this life, involve a principle essentially different from that of endless punishment or pain, inasmuch as the former, unlike the latter, tend to limit and destroy themselves, either by exhausting their cause, or working a change in their subjects,

incompatible with their continuance. This is clearly seen in physical life, when the pain of a sick person, considered as an effect, reacts upon its cause, and the sufferer is relieved; and also, when the pain, becoming extreme, disorganizes the nervous net-work of the body, and relief comes by death.

If we had instances of persons lingering on for all the years of earth,—from creation till now,—in all the agony of a death-struggle, without any indication or hope of change for the better, such instances might, perhaps, afford imperfect, seeming, not real, analogies to the purpose of those who attempt to scale, with their logic, the wide gulf between the sufferings of earth, and eternal suffering. But such instances are entirely wanting, and must remain wanting, so long as physical pain appears so essentially incompatible with its perpetuity.

Paul was for a night in the stocks of a cruel dungeon. And am I told that precisely the same principle of the Divine government was thereby involved, that should be, if he had been kept there till now, and would be till all eternity! Paul is for a moment under the hands of the executioner. And do you say that the permission of this, involves the same principle of the Divine government that would be involved, by his being hacked forever by the cruel headsman, without hope or possibility of ever either dying or arising from the block. Do you say that the cases are completely analogous. I know you will not; and yet I think you must say it, or abandon your analogical argument for endless pain.

Do you say Paul was a righteous man, and of course he could not be punished forever. Then we reply, that that does not alter the argument at all, seeing that your proposition is, that whatever God can justly influence, or permit, or suffer, for a day, he can justly inflict, or permit, or suffer, to all eternity. If your proposition does not involve this, I think it involves just nothing at all. If a righteous man suffers *for a day*, there is a reason for his suffering *for a day*, which may not be equivalent to, or compatible with, his suffering *forever*. If a wicked man suffers for a day, there is reason for his suffering for a day. And why may not that reason, also, be incompatible with *his* suffering forever. Who shall say, who can conceive that in the latter, less than in the former case, the suffering shall not tend to an end.

Do you say, this may all be true of physical suffering, but not of spiritual. Then we ask you why? Do we not see the same general law operating in the latter as in the former? Does not mental anguish, too, work a change in the condition of its victim, which appears equally inconsistent with its eternity? When it reaches a certain extreme, does it not, at least seemingly, obtain relief, by divorcing the soul from the body, and putting it into entirely new relations in that world beyond the grave, to which our logic of analogy cannot follow it with confidence, and to which we can entrust it only as we confide in the goodness of the Living Father. But this thought will be better elaborated, as we say,

3. That suffering in this world appears to be a means, and not an end. It is a means, when by a slight pressure of it we are admonished to leap from the jaws of mutilation and death. Nature has clothed man with a skin so sensitive, so susceptible to pain, as a means of grace, to guard him against danger. Suffering is a means of grace, when it teaches to appreciate and enjoy freedom from it. And how much we are all indebted to it, as such a means, few are aware, and probably none, fully. It is a means of grace when, by its experience, we are disciplined in the higher Christian virtues. Even Jesus "learned obedience from the things which *he* suffered." And the Psalmist said, "before I was afflicted, I went astray, but now do I keep thy commandments." It is a means when, as in the inimitable parable,

> "It stopped the prodigal's career,
> And caused him to repent."

To be sure, in this world, we do not always, or often, see the end perfectly gained, to which suffering is a means. Not always does it make the prodigal repent, or stop his career. In spite of it, he sometimes goes quite into his grave, bound fast in the chains of wicked habits. But before he dies, if sane, he admonishes others against them, and often says, if he had not twisted his bands of evil habit, he never would. But as it is, he sees the right, and yet the wrong pursues. So he dies. And then, what more reasonable than that, with the fleshy organism in which his passions and appetites were nourished up to a rankness that almost defied his endeavors at reform, thrown off, and, at the same time, the better prepared to begin anew by all his remembrances of the past, he should find all the sorrows he experienced on earth, a means of deterring him from sin, and wedding him to holiness.

Perhaps it is enough to say here, that all the sufferings of earth, as man is an immortal being, have an eternal afterwards, in which their subject *may* undergo infinite changes of circumstance, affecting his moral condition in as many different ways as his Creator shall please, and by which deliverance may at last reach him, and all his past but magnify the glory of his future,—whereas eternal suffering can have no afterwards, but is itself the bitter never ending end of his being.

Reasoning this matter, as we have done, from the particular to the general, I think we can hardly fail to see, that all the penalties of the divine law are underlaid with a benevolent intent, and that not one of them is incompatible with the blessedness of the sufferer. To doubt this, were dreadful. For if any single one of the penalties of divine law is thus incompatible, then all may be; and so the whole law be but a concoction of Almighty malevolence. To find a penalty in the law of God which is against the good of the violator, is to find a stitch dropt in the web of providence, and its whole economy *ravels out.* It is *God good to all,* or to *no one.* God in *all,* or *no where*—his tender mercies are over *all* his works, or over *none!* Now limited suffering, as we have seen, is consistent with the divine benevolence towards the sufferer. But not so eternal suffering. That, without an afterwards, is to the creature, the great end—the absolute fore-ordained, or fore-known; at any rate *fore-fixed* finality of his being. And, certainly it seems, therefore, of an essence entirely different from that of temporal punishment. And so we think you are quite mistaken when you say that the principle upon which temporal suffering enters the government of God, equally opens the way by which eternal suffering may enter.

But though the analogy you institute relative to the subject under consideration is unsound, yet there is an analogy capable of being instituted having nature for its basis, which seems to us of great value, in this discussion. Nature's teaching relative to suffering, is that it is protective, corrective, remedial, limited. This we have seen. For at death admitting the soul's immortality, there is nothing to indicate that suffering will accompany the soul into its new mode of life, and new world of circumstances. And as suffering in the world *below*, is a means, and limited, we must infer, if we infer any, that it will be thus limited in the world *above*. And so the analogy in which you sought relief, but increases your embarrassment, and confusion. For, as we have seen, "doth not nature itself teach" that the tendency of all earthly suffering is in some way to limit itself—that it is *not* the ultimate product of an immortal creation, but intended by the benevolent Creator, to work some change, under which it shall give place to an "afterward" of good.

Lafayette, after lying long in the prison of Olmutz, bound in the chains of Austrian despotism, was at length set free, under the influence of the revolution of empire. But there can be no change in the empire of God, and no change in the condition of the victim of *endless* wrath, under which he shall be set free from his dungeon of "outer darkness." Its gate is forever closed upon him by the wrathful, relentless purpose of Jehovah. By that purpose eternal, no death is permitted to come, and "heave the massy bar," to set the sufferer free. It was kind in God to permit the wasted victims of the inquisition to die out of their loathsome, lightless, subterranean dungeons, into the glorious "afterwards" of heaven. But no such kindness comes to the victim of the prison of future woe. Even though the Living Father should, as Stuart supposes, "in mercy extinguish the social susceptibilities" of the righteous, he has no mercy to extinguish the susceptibilities of the lost sinner, or rather to extinguish the sinner himself. Endless punishment is indeed a long lane; for it never turns, only as it turns forever downward through shades of night, even darker and more dismal.

And here it may be well to say, that great carefulness should be used in reasoning, analogical, from things temporal to things eternal. "The constitution and course of Nature" is even yet but imperfectly understood. We know too little of her operations and their results, to reason very confidently from *her* details to the details of *theology*. But our increasing knowledge of her is all in favor of goodness. Science, busy among her dark mysteries, is ever making discoveries, all quieting to human fears; so that, whereas our ancestors saw a "God in anger" when the thunders were abroad, we then only see a God in kindness, purifying and adjusting the elements, for the good of his creatures. And the blazing comet, which, as a fell harbinger of Divine wrath, drove our ancestors into hiding places, but invites us forth to wonder and trustingly adore. From the moon's approach to the earth, science has also taught us to have no fear, by the discovery of a law which forbids that she ever impinge upon it. And thus, from what science has already taught us, (and we are yet but upon the shore of knowledge,) we may easily infer, that, what is dark she will yet illumine, and, that in the highest and best sense, God, in Nature, does all things well. And with the Bible in one hand, we know that he does all things well in Grace.

But I must close this letter. I have dwelt thus long upon the supposed analogy between the principles involved in limited and limitless pain, because I know it to be a favorite resort of persons of your faith, and because, when considered, as I trust you will consider it—it plainly throws its entire weight into the scale against you. I have only one single word in conclusion. It is this, "*think on these things.*"

Truly yours.

LETTER XXVI.

THE THREE STAND-POINTS.—BIGOTRY, CONSERVATISM AND PROGRESS.

Three Stand-points—First, Bigotry—The Bigot Characterized—His favorite syllogism—His creed, his rock—Bigots everywhere—Impervious to logic—Eyeless fishes — Not so the reader — Second Stand-point, *Conservatism*—Conservatism characterized — What is, is best, and *presumed* about right—Getting along pretty well — Fault with Luther, Knox and Jesus — Brahminical quiescence —Tempest—Feeling for the foundation — Skeptical — Living sinners and dead—Texts dropping out—Tendency to freedom—Alarm of the N. Y. Observer— Its correspondent — Universalism, on the heels of the revival of '57—*The catastrophe! !*—Third stand-point. *Progress*—Who occupies it? —Why so few?— *Positive* testimony needed—Exparte reading—Endless punishment flees as light comes —Drops of water save!—Questions to the reader.

Dear Brother,—

I think every believer in the doctrine in review, who contemplates its absurdities at all, must contemplate them from one of the three stand-points,—*Bigotry*, *Conservatism* and *Progress*. His impression, of course, must depend upon which of these he occupies. For, in morals and religion, not less than in physics, does the view depend upon the relative position of the viewer. Boston, seen from the

"*Monument*," is very different from Boston seen from the *State House*, or *Commercial street*.

First, then, let us suppose the viewer of the difficulties we have been mentioning, to occupy the standpoint of *bigotry*. How then, is he likely to be affected?

The bigot is a person "unreasonably wedded," or *blindly* attached" to some religious creed; one who, hugging his peculiar faith, as absolutely true, and, of course, rejecting all opposed to it, as absolutely false, sees no occasion to open his mind to reasoning; but, impervious to logic, and blind to facts, his mind is a barren rock to the seed of any better theology. If a Pharisee *to-day*, he will be *to-morrow*, whether Servetus burn, or Christ be crucified. For, if at any time, coming suddenly upon some glaring absurdity in his creed, he is startled for a moment, he is sure to find speedy relief in his favorite syllogism, always at hand, thus:

1. Whatever lies against my creed, is false;
2. This absurdity lies against my creed;
3. Therefore, this absurdity is false.

And thus, completely satisfied, he slumbers again, as Luther, while yet but partially emancipated from the thraldom of the Papacy, when defending the doctrine of transubstantiation against Zwingle, satisfied himself, *most provokingly to his opponent*, by simply holding up a parchment on which he had inscribed the words, "*This* IS *my body*," so the bigot easily disposes of all objections to his creed, by holding it up and exclaiming, "*This* IS *true*."

Fixed fast in his faith, like a living creature on a rock, he can neither move nor turn round. Imbedded in thoughtlessness, his fossilization is susceptible of no check. Whether the points of his faith are true or false, they can no more be wrested away by the power of logic, than a star from the belt of Orion, or from the brow of Taurus. His creed is "his rock, and his fortress, and his deliverer." Under its "shadow he reposes." Within its defense he feels safe! And it delivers him from the inconvenience and danger of thinking for himself.

Such is the person, who contemplates the religious aspect of the world, from the stand-point of bigotry. And such persons, whether few or many, are scattered among all denominations. So that for a person to suppose that *his* denomination is free from them, were to show himself the bigot of his generation. If any of this class should chance to glance into these letters, very well. But wrapped in a covering, tougher than that which defends the monsters of the Nile against the attacks of the musketeer and the spearsman, they will hardly be affected by them. Having lived in darkness till they have become blind, as fishes in subterranean pools are said to become eyeless, whatever error

22

they have, must die a natural death. Its dissolution can be hastened, neither by facts nor logic. They *will* believe all that they *agreed* to believe. To do this, they feel bound, as by the most solemn of oaths. At any rate, they act as though they did. For they either decline reading or hearing anything against their views; or else, read as though they read not, and hear as though they heard not. Yet it is not for *us* to blame them. They *may* be honest, after all. They have our best wishes and earnest prayers, while we regret that, viewed from their stand-point, our writing for their benefit, must be vain.

But to this pitiful class, I think you, brother, do not belong. You are not so dogmatically sure that you are right, that you cannot listen to, and appreciate an opposing argument. But, while you *will* not bear the *close* confinement of the class mentioned, it *may* be that you shrink, somewhat, from roaming *far* beyond "the liberty of the yard," freely over the rich and inviting fields of theological enquiry. But,

Second; supposing such a discussion as the foregoing, to be contemplated by a believer in endless punishment, from the stand point of *conservatism;* how is *he* likely to be affected by it?

And who is the conservative? The conservative, as we use the term, is a person who would keep things as they are, not because he knows them to be *right*, but because they are *as* they are. That a policy is settled, is to him a sufficient reason for sustaining it, without asking many questions about its exact righteousness. That a certain system of religious faith prevails, is to him, evidence that it should prevail. Of course, therefore, he is the foe to innovation. To be sure, he would not support a faith which he *knew* to be false! Nor is he very confident that the prevalent one is *true!* Whether it is or not, is a question lying back of his sphere of thought. He is willing to *presume* it true, and that some others *know* it to be true. If objections to it are put forward, however plausible they may appear, he is satisfied with presuming them unfounded. If it seems to involve great absurdities, he is quite willing to presume that they are *only* seeming, and so give himself no trouble about them. Such is what we have called, the conservative.

Now, whenever any of this large class, chance to hear or read things against their popular faith, they are, as we have said above, very likely to assume them to be false; or that, if true, they are truths which had better not be spoken. For they get along pretty well with things as they are. They are members of a respectable society, and *doing a good business.* Their pew is eligible and easy, and the pulpit does not trouble them. Their society, too, is united, and makes a good appearance on the Sabbath. To be sure, they don't like all that the preacher says, and his creed has a rather hard look; but then, they never have examined it, and are unprepared to disbelieve it. Perhaps they care little about it, because they have too little faith in it, to be moved by it. And, though they have as much faith in *that* as they have in *anything*, they would by no means, be regarded as skeptical. Indeed, if they *did* believe it *false*, it were little matter, seeing the minister preaches as though he believed it false also. Sometimes, indeed, in a lucid interval of religious thought, interposed between the waves of worldliness and conservatism, they have a confused notion of a better state of things—a state of things more worthy of the God-like, thinking mind. But then, stocks are up, and all is quiet. Whereas, innovation, in matters of faith, would certainly produce a downward tendency and discord, sadly injuring "the oil and the wine."

Schisms, they cannot bear. Schismatics are unendurable. Their spirit would seem to say, "Luther should have kept his place;" "John Knox should have held his peace;" "the Wesleys, should not have lighted their incendiary fires;" and even "Jesus of Nazareth should have left his 'sword' of disunion behind him in heaven, and not kindled a fire of excitement, under which, the peace of families should be broken up, and a man's foes become they of his own household." Nor would *they* have so disturbed the Jewish church, living quietly as it was, before the great agitator came among them!

So these conservatives would seem to reason. Of course, they are greatly unmoved by anything that can be written or said against their creed, save at intervals, when the sun of righteousness reaches them, through the thick mists of their carnal policy. Until they feel that the church has higher ends to gain than a present peace, and that the individual soul has God-like energies to develop, the awakening of which depends on the breaking up of stereotype theological fashion, it were as vain to ply them with facts and logic, as to sow wheat upon a rock! The Bramin finds perfection in perfect quiescence. His great god is absolutely perfect, because his sleep is absolutely undisturbed. And so these conservatives seem to find the perfection of the church in the perfect quiescence of the religious mind. To them, therefore, every faith is good enough which disturbs not her rest, while every faith is bad which *does* disturb it. They have not learned, what Jesus knew, and Luther felt, and philosophy teaches, and observation shows, that the well-being of the church, —the conservation of her healing virtues,—often requires the descent of the angel of agitation,—that

22*

she be lashed into excitement by winds of unpopular truth, warring with the winds of prevalent error,—and that, healthful, ofttimes, is the very whirlwind which sweeps up the hat of the Cardinal, and robs the Pope of his mitre. As the tempest strips the trees of the forest of their dead leaves and limbs, so does agitation strip the church of its dead faith.

Agitation,—why it is God's remedy for all evil, and therefore should not be feared, so long as it is but the result of truth. Yet is there nothing which these conservatives so much fear. And though, perhaps, not bold enough to object to any innovating theological proposition, provided they *know* it to be true, yet, as they never examine, more than exparte, and, therefore, never *know*, they ever satisfy themselves with pushing it aside, as a disturbing element which is *presumed* to be false. And, in all this, they may be very sincere, acting with an eye single to the oil and the wine of evangelical piety. But though sincere, and, therefore, hardly to be censured, how be pitied.

And here it should be said, that, among the large class in review, are many different shades of theological character. Some of them are scarcely distinguishable from the bigot, while others of them are living on the verge of liberal, independent thought. Not a few of them are becoming every day more dissatisfied with their mere policy, and secretly and anxiously enquiring after something better. At the instigation of their awakening thought, they are throwing out their feelers after the foundation of their faith. Yet are they like a person off in a river, who, with the waters up to his chin, hardly durst step for fear of sinking deeper. Truth is beginning to seem to them a primary rock, fit to become the headstone of the corner, though rejected by master builders; and error, but sinking sand, though accepted by the church, and relied upon as fundamental. As they think that, in *past* ages, the thoughtless masses of the church have been led into the widest and the wildest errors,—errors from which God has remarkably and miraculously interposed to deliver them,—they begin to enquire whether the *present* age is so free from false leadership, that the mass of thoughtless followers are perfectly safe. And thus enquiring, they become restless. That a thing seems politic, no longer fully satisfies them. They would know whether it is true. Hence are they sometimes more than half ready to go to *thinking* and *reading* independently for themselves, and abide the consequences. Yet are they still conservative, carefully concealing their troublesome misgivings, and still regarded as orthodox to the core.

As is implied above, many of these conservatives are quite skeptical. They may not be consciously so, they may deny that they are so. But after all,

I think they are. The absurdities of their faith, though assumed to be false, are, nevertheless, quite sufficient to make them suspicious whether it is true; and hence it is, that it seems to sit as lightly upon their hearts, as a thing without length, breadth, or thickness. And hence, too, if they preach as though all *living* sinners are going to perdition, they are not impressed as though all *dead* sinners are already there, and all dying sinners, just ready to go there. If, for the living, their dogmatic faith is stronger than their Christian hope, for the dead, their Christian hope is stronger than their dogmatic faith. And so they write comfort on the tombstone of their unregenerate brother, and stand in calm Christian trust above his grassy grave!

But, brother, all this you well understand, and therefore I need not dwell.

Now to this indolent, skeptical, traditionary class of church-goers, believing everything, believing nothing, I think you do not belong. You, I trust, tread not the same ground with them, unless it be upon its extreme verge, where it is ready to impinge upon the region of independent enquiry. You are a conservative of a better school; thinking more of the truth than of any error or doubtful thing, which ignorance or tradition has foisted into the place of Truth, and given its name and honor. You are awake, I trust, to the fact that great error may now, as in time past, have great church patronage; and that, therefore, the credit of the church now as in time past, may not be so good as to make it quite safe to receive her theology on trust. As her doctrine of *infant* damnation was once found counterfeit, and as she has often been proved guilty of other base issues, you see no reason for holding her doctrine of *adult* damnation, as *necessarily* true. And having never examined it *thoroughly*, you are holding it very loosely; and this, the more especially, as you begin to perceive that the cruel absurdities, which, as light increased, drove the former doctrine out of the church, lie *equally* against the latter!

Indeed, brother, as you proceed with enquiry, are you not surprised and even startled, at finding how many things, bearing on the doctrine in review, are different from what they had before seemed? Have you not been surprised to see how the proof texts of your faith have been dropping out of the Scriptures? So that you have sometimes asked, whether they will not all be gone by and by? And has not this the more startled you, as you have thought that such a faith as yours, a faith involving such absurdities, should be received only upon the *fullest and most positive proof?* It may not be so, with you, but I am persuaded that it is. Whether it is so or not, I do not set you down to the conservative class of which I have been speaking.

But, furthermore, if you *are* occupying the stand-point which I am supposing, you will have anticipated the remark, that a tendency towards freedom is very manifest, throughout this vast mass of enslaved conservative mind. Such is the tendency of the age, and it is with the hope of strengthening it that these letters are written. Nor can I doubt, (*me judice*) that every conservative Orthodox reader of them, dealing as I think they do, with facts and common sense, must feel quickened towards enquiry. The absurdities they present, must excite, in every mind, a healthful distrust of the creed that involves them. Such we think, must be the private experience of all our conservative readers; while we are hoping that some of them, shall, by this humble effort of one who feels that it may be his last, be brought quite out into the open fields of free and independent enquiry.

And indeed such a coming out is now rapidly taking place—so rapidly, as seriously to alarm the fears of conservative, theological periodicals. *The "New York Observer,"* in a late number, after referring to the fact that a man was recently ordained to the Orthodox ministry who "held [among other things] that the gospel is not absolutely necessary to the salvation of adult heathens, some of them being undoubtedly saved without it;" and that, "after death, and before the final judgment, there is a state for all souls, where some who had died impenitent, some who had rejected Christ in this life, would have a new offer of Christ and salvation, and the gift of the Holy Ghost, and be saved; so that, if called to the death bed of an impenitent sinner, and knowing that he had but a short, definite time to live, he would not shut him up to faith in Christ within that time, or final ruin," proceeds with comment, in the course of which, it says, "apostacies are generally gradual. Scarcely any great defection in church history, however, has been so rapid as that which is now rushing to its crisis, in New England. To turn back the tide of corruption, to strengthen the things that remain, to save the rising generation from being borne away into the mire and misery of Pelagianism and Universalism, is a work that should command the active and untiring energies of every sound man in the church. . . . . Daily we behold the gathering evidences that a new reformation of the nineteenth century must be preached."

In such and such like language, does the "*Observer*" express its alarm. And as it partially institutes a comparison between the nineteenth century and the century of Luther, it were improper not to say here, that we think the *Observer* is now occupying exactly the conservative position in the church, which was, in the sixteenth century, occu pied by the very papal hierarchy with which Luther had to contend. We do not mean to degrade the Observer to the level of Rome by the statement of this fact; but we do mean to intimate, that, like Rome, it is the practical enemy of theological progress. We do not say or mean that it is dishonestly so. We only state the thing as it is. We agree with the "*Observer*" that we do need a reformation, like that under Luther. But if it come at all, it must come by *innovation*—the very thing which the *Observer* deplores. It must come, if at all, along the way of free enquiry—the very way, which is leading to what the "*Observer*" deems alarming consequences. In a word, if it come at all, we think the *Observer* must be among the first to feel it, as an antagonistic force.

In the article from which the above extract is taken, a correspondent is quoted, as saying, "My strong conviction is, that, unless there shall soon be a mighty outpouring of the Holy Spirit, the day is not distant, which will witness a more extensive and appalling apostacy in New England, than we have ever before seen, and that apostacy will be into Universalism." And we doubt not, there will be *such* an apostacy. And no doubt, too, it is likely to be to many, as appalling as was the apostacy of the sixteenth century to the Orthodox masses, disturbed by the eloquent tongue and pen of Luther.

But what is quite remarkable, is, that the writer above quoted by the *Observer*, should regard a mighty outpouring of the Spirit as likely to cure an evil which he finds so very rank and rife *immediately upon the back of the mightiest outpouring of the Spirit, ever enjoyed on the Western Continent.* Really, one might well query whether that outpouring had not some responsible connexion with the so-called apostacy, which the writer bewails—a thing which is certainly quite probable, and to our mind, quite certain. For every religious agitation of the popular mind, but carries it another step towards, what the writer regards as a *catastrophe*, —it eventually makes better men, and makes men find a better God.

But we have quoted from the "*Observer*," chiefly to show that the tendency of the age is all towards Universalism, and that this tendency is becoming so strong that Orthodoxy is taking the alarm. The masses of *silent*, acquiescing unbelievers in the doctrine of endless woe, are certainly and rapidly tending towards positive and active disbelief of it. Multitudes there are, in our Orthodox churches and congregations, who, while supporting the dominant sects, are saying in their heart, as said an Episcopalian, a little time ago, "as to endless punishment, the day is gone by for believing that." And what is more, perhaps, its seeming *advocates* are often among its real *doubters*. So that, should the private conversation of the lettered clergy, come to the ears of the unlettered and unthinking laity, it would, not unfrequently, fill them with amazement.

Third. But I must pass to say a word in reference to the third class—those who contemplate the absurdities of Orthodoxy from the stand point of *progress*. And who are these, but they, who in spite of their creed, have reached the point of free and impartial enquiry. Unhappily the number of such is not yet very large; comparatively few, are yet so freed from the bondage of creed, the blindness of prejudice, the toils of fashion, and, what is not least, the bias of *Orthodox friendships*, as to be prepared for the impartial search necessary to the discovery of the exact truth.

But, happily, the number of such is increasing, and all they who are, as upon occasion, they meet with the absurdities and barbarisms of their creed, do feel, as said an orthodox brother a few weeks since, "*It has a hard look, hasn't it?*" And scarcely will they have set off in their free inquiry, before they will be saying to themselves, this creed can hardly be true, *if we are made in God's image*." And soon and deeply will they feel that it should be believed only upon the clearest and most positive Scripture proof—that, compromising as it seemingly does, the character of God, and rending, as it does, the affections of man, it is not to be rested upon any poetic Scripture of confessedly doubtful signification. And to the Bible they will at length turn, to see for themselves, whether these things are so. Nor will they study the Scriptures by the light of their old exparte commentaries, merely. They perceive, at last, that to do so, were only to equal the folly and wrong of an "unjust judge," who should solemnly charge the obsequent jury to hear but one side of the question which they had sworn to settle impartially.

In a word, we think anything like a fair view of the bearings of the doctrine in question, must lead all who are not the victims of bigotry the most intense, and indifference the most stolid, — all whose manhood is not completely sunk in the sectary,—all whose humanity is not hardened into misanthropy, whose milk of human kindness is not turned to gall, whose every generous and noble impulse is not dead —all who care for the honor of Almighty God, and of his Son Jesus Christ;—in a word, all whose religion has not proved to them the most unmitigated curse, to search the Bible diligently, and, as we have intimated, with all the helps, pro and con, which Providence has put into their hands, to see whether the church, since the middle ages, has not, very generally and materially mistaken the will of God relative to human destiny. Before the middle ages, we know that Universalism prevailed. Origen, the first scholar in the early church, was a bold advocate and defender of it, nor have we the least evidence that it was then regarded as heretical. It is only since the church emerged from the darkness of those ages, covered all over with the errors which her ignorance attracted, that the brand of heresy has been laid upon it. This, we think, is pretty well understood. And every person, who takes anything like a plain view of the doctrine of endless woe, must needs suspect, whether it does not belong to that large brood of mediæval dogma, which wastes as light increases, and whether *it*, also, is not to pass away in the wake of retreating barbarisms.

Somebody has said that he dares think that the day is not distant, when men will look upon war as they now do upon the African slave-trade. And we dare think that the day is not very distant, when the doctrine of endless misery for adults, will be looked upon as the church now looks upon the doctrine of endless misery for infants. The latter, recently believed, is now thoroughly repudiated. The former, now believed, shall ere long, be repudiated. And the latter change will be no more remarkable than the former. The condition of eternal salvation was once believed to be the *sprinkling of a few drops of water upon a baby's temples!* It is by many, now understood to be the hurried prayer of an excited hour. The former act used to snatch the soul from the jaws of unending woe. Now the latter is supposed to do the same. The former, the church has repudiated as *too* absurd for belief, as well as too unscriptural to be true. And just so, must she, ere long, regard the latter. Such is the conclusion towards which we think every unfossilized and frank enquirer about human destiny, must ever find himself tending, and which all shall eventually reach.

And now, brother, if I regard you as a representative of the class of impartial enquirers, mentioned above, may I not conclude that the language I have used in reference to their perplexities and misgivings over their creed, and their tendencies away from it, is none too strong? For, is it not a fact, in spite of your education, your old exparte reasoning, and all the proof you have assumed from the Bible, — in spite of all, in the face of which, doubt must arise, if it arise at all—that you *do doubt*—doubt *strongly*, and the more so, the more you think upon the subject? For, of the class of dogma in debate, as affected by the increase of religious light, we may well say, as say the Scriptures of the beast of the field, " The sun ariseth, they gather themselves together, and lay them down in their dens." Ps. civ. 22. And further, do not your doubts so deepen, as you trace your creed in its consequences, that you sometimes fancy you feel them hardening into disbelief? In a word, are you not sometimes saying to yourself, in reference to your penal creed, "I must either cease to think of it, or cease to believe it?" Or, if you have not yet reached *that* point, are you not conscious of being on the way to it? And, therefore, may I not prove the truth of what I have been saying, by an appeal to your own frank heart?

Finally, in closing this letter, permit me to recall your mind to the old question, whether the doctrine in review can possibly have had its origin in the harmonious character of "the God of all grace." Many are thinking not, many are saying not. And the number of them is rapidly increasing as Christian enlightenment advances. And my heart shall still be praying, that you, with the Bible in your hand, wide open towards heaven, may soon be among the number.

Yours truly.

NOTE.

Several letters intended for this series, and which would have broken the seeming abruptness of its conclusion, are here omitted to bring the book within suitable limits.

SECOND SERIES.

SECOND SERIES.

LETTER I.

THE BIBLE AND ITS MEANING.

Theme, solemn—Dean Swift's critic—Indirect disproof—Soliloquy of the reader—Heart-doubt, tenacity of—No dispute about *Bible-words*, but about their *meaning*—Assertion balanced by assertion—Romishness—The real Question—To the Scriptures.

DEAR BROTHER,—

The theme of these letters forbids that they be written with an eye to safeguards against hyper-criticism. You, in reading them, unlike Dean Swift's critic, will not be "altogether conversant and taken up with faults, blemishes, mistakes and oversights," or like his "young critic," intent only on "spying out the worst parts of the play." For eternities are not trifles on which to practice "intellectual gymnastics," but too awful and appalling for any thing but seriousness, candor and awe;—and this, whether to the dead, who are already dead," or to "the living, who are yet alive." In the former series, I familiarly noticed, among other matters, some of the difficulties of the doctrine of endless woe, which have impressed my own mind, and, as therein shown, other minds far greater,—difficulties, "real, not imaginary," deep seated and aggravated as light increases. And, though not introduced as direct disproof of that doctrine, I think they have but to be thrown into logical form, to amount to little less. To put them in that form would have been less in keeping with our design, which was, simply, to arouse attention to the general subject and leave the reader to state and sustain whatever proposition he pleases. For, as we have before said, no person is really convinced till he convinces himself.

Though the arrow be true, the bow may be badly sprung. I know not, therefore, how the former series of my letters have impressed you. But, as we are both human, must needs imagine. And if I am not mistaken, you have sometimes been in a mood to soliloquize something on this wise:—"Well, these difficulties are serious! I cannot say that they are overdrawn! No, for *I* see other depths beyond them! I confess I don't exactly know what to do with them! It is a *hard* doctrine that involves them! And yet I must believe it,—I *suppose*. But after all, *may* it not be *false*. Other doctrines have proved false,—why not this? Soul, *between you and me*, I am inclined to think it at least half false,—or else I am not made in God's image, and my reason and consciousness are a stupendous lie! But what am I saying? *False?* This doctrine of the *Father's* false! Nay, it only *seems* so! It cannot *be* so! *Seems* so? And what have I to do with *seems so!* Here is my *Bible!* Who am I, that I should array my idiotic reason against it. This is God's word, and I believe it. It is "forever settled in heaven, and woe unto him who attempts to unsettle it. It is a rock, and however the angry billows may dash and surge about it, I will not fear to stand upon it. For though the ocean be dried up, and the star-sown heavens be harvested, it '*shall never pass away.*' Anchored to it, my soul drifts no more. Away, pride! Now balanced on the true centre of gravity, I stand firmly! Let others bow the knee to plausible error, or fall in or out, with coming majorities or minorities,—I *never.* Am I not taught that vain philosophies are dangerous, and that evil comes to him "who leans to his own understanding?" Be it mine to lean upon *God's* understanding! What he says is true, and who shall dare be wise above it. Nor will *I* do so, though tempted "forty days and forty nights" in a wilderness of absurdities *darker* and *more* appalling than that with which my brother has presented me. Not so shall *I* be frightened from the truth! And yet, —well—."

Ah, yes, brother, I think I understand you. "*And yet—well—*" And yet your misgivings will not down at your bidding; or, if they seem to flee before *your* "scourge of small cords," it is only to come thronging back again, as from the cold summits of your creed, you descend to a common sense view of practical life. You believe and you disbelieve. So that while in the act of affirming your penal faith strongly, you are sometimes startled by a voice like that which sounds in the soul of a witness who feels a little doubtful about the subject of his testimony, just as he comes upon the stand! When you say, "God says it, and I believe it, it is but a moment, before the heart *God gave you* denies it, and you doubt it. And this doubt is sometimes aggravated by the thought that, what you doubt, as unreasonable, but try to believe as being Scriptural, many wise men absolutely disbelieve, as unreasonable and unscriptural both. Or if it is not so with you, then you are not the person I mean.

When you say of the Bible, "it is God's word, and I believe it," you say well. We have both set to our seal that "God is true." That is but an axiom in theological geometry, given of heaven for our common benefit. But, if you say, *the Bible teaches that God will punish sinners endlessly;*

then, what you say may be true, and may not; certainly it needs proof. Your assertion that it *does* thus teach, weighs just as much as my assertion that it does *not*. Your confidence that *you* are right, but just counterbalance my confidence that *I* am. You have miraculous evidence that the Bible is true. But have you miraculous evidence that you hold the *true meaning* of it? The question is not what the Bible *is*, but what it *teaches*,—nor what are its *words*, but what do they *mean*. You have your honest convictions of their meaning. So have I mine. But for either of us to assume our *convictions* of their meaning, as the basis of reasoning in the very *discussion of their meaning*, were the most bald *petitio princippii*,—the favorite resort of the narrowest of bigots. By such assumption, you might say, "Jesus says of the wicked, 'these shall go away into everlasting punishment,' and that settles the question." And so might I reply; the Bible says, "The Lord will not cast off forever," and *that* settles the question. But you see we have only settled it into grand confusion.

Neither you nor I would differ much from the Romanist about the *words* of Jesus in reference to men's forgiving sins. Yet about the *meaning* of those words, we should differ with him widely. We are not Romanists. And yet may we not be a little *Romish* in *our* assumptions for a *protestant* dogma?

We both mean to be fair; especially when reasoning out of the book which opens under the awful shadow of the throne of God. But after all, have we not from childhood been so accustomed to hold some certain meaning of it as *necessarily* true, that the idea of that meaning's being either confirmed or overthrown by reasoning out of the Scriptures, strikes us oddly. It may not be so with *you.* But no suggestion is profitless, which leads to a more guarded study of the words of life.

Finally, brother, we agree that *if* the Scriptures teach the doctrine of endless punishment, that is final. But do they? That is the question, over which you and I hang, counterpoised upon our affirmation and denial. What shall turn the scale? We both answer, "*the Scriptures.*" To them then let us turn, not to receive *confirmation*, but as newly installed learners, to sit meekly at the feet of the Master, and listen to whatever gracious words shall proceed out of his mouth.

Yours truly.

LETTER II.

PENTATEUCH, VERSUS ENDLESS PUNISHMENT.

Positive proof needed—The question—1. Moses as a *Historian*,—What he doesnot see or hear—Garden threatening, the death meant, not of the body—Wild notions—Error flies from the simple-hearted—Not eternal death—Nothing in the language to *suggest* it—Then were all lost at once—The death meant, that which took place at the time—2. Moses as a *Lawgiver*—His silence, significant—God's silence—Origin of the dogma—Why Moses did not incorporate it—3. Moses as a *Prophet*—Sees not endless punishment—What he did see—Five important reflections.

DEAR BROTHER,—

As we now enter the Scriptures, I think we shall agree that if the doctrine in question is taught there at all, we should expect to find it taught most *positively* and *explicitly;* and this, not only because of its vast importance; but because it is not in the nature of the enlightened human mind to receive a doctrine, involving such obvious absurdities as we have had under review, unless it is so taught. With this single remark we enter at once upon the enquiry, *Do the Scriptures teach the doctrine of endless punishment.* And,

1. Is it taught in that portion of them,—their first five books—written by Moses.

Moses was a prophetic historian of the past. His inspired eye and ear, pierced and listened back to chaos, while his inspired pen wrote what he saw and heard. But he wrote nothing of any place or victim of endless misery. He speaks of the wicked and of their fearful overthrows; — of nations of them swept away by flood, of cities, full of them, sinking down in flame. But not the slightest intimation does he give, that endless misery awaited them in the future world. So much is plain to his simplest reader.

No such intimation is given, even in the *garden threatening.* To be sure, men have made the death therein mentioned, mean "death temporal, death spiritual, and death eternal." But never was assumption more bald, or *so* bald!

The record is simple. "In the day thou eatest thereof, thou shalt surely die." The *death* is certain, and the *time* of it. But *what* death? The death of the body? That cannot be, seeing the body did not die at the *time specified.* Indeed, the death threatened, so far from *being* the death of the body, is represented as limited *by* the death of the body. For the unhappy results of the transgression, summed up in the sequel, are spoken of, only as continuing until the transgressor should return to the ground. And, too, that return *to* the ground, so far from being predicated upon the *transgression*, is spoken of as a natural consequence of having been taken *from* the ground. "For out of it wast thou taken." "For dust thou art, and to dust shalt thou return."

There have been many singular and wild opinions about the consequences of the first sin. It has been thought and taught, that, before that event, what are since beasts of prey, were without carnivorous teeth, carnivorus stomachs, and taste for blood; or, that if they possessed their present brutish forms and instincts, they were held in check by some strange sort of animal conscience, which they, unfortunately, lost when Adam fell. And so, also, has it been thought, that, prior to that event, the seeds of thorns and thistles were lying dormant in the ground, waiting the fertilizing influence of the transgression, as rain and sunshine, to develop their noxious growth!—notions which, not only set common sense at defiance, but which are absolutely exploded by scientific research. Tigers were always tigers, man was always man, and Eve might have pricked her finger in a rose tree, before sin entered paradise.

Milton has it, (poetry, to be sure,) that the earth received such a shock from the transgression, that the hitherto vertical rays of the sun, obliqued off from paradise, leaving it damp and chill. And so, also, will many have it, that the unnumbered millions of all subsequent ages, of all climes and conditions, were doomed to total depravity for the first sin of Eve ;—for I know not whether Adam's sin was necessary to complete the ruin ! !

But this whole brood of error flies from the person who, with childlike simplicity, reads the narrative of the fall. Certainly, such person sees therein no connexion between the sin of our first parents and their return to the dust.

Again we ask, *what death is threatened?* Do you say *eternal* death? To this we object more strongly still. For, while the term "die"* is of commonplace and widely variable import, and while there is nothing in the context to indicate, or even *suggest* for it, so *fearful* an import, it were just the term which Jehovah would be most unlikely to use to *express* such import, and then, (as we will show,) leave its true meaning to be evolved, only after vast millions affected by it, should have been swept into despair upon the deep, strong tide, of, at least, *four thousand years.*

And still further, if it mean eternal death, then *all* suffer it. For the language is positive, leaving no loop-hole of escape. Then *the day* our first parents

*Hebrew,—"Dying, thou shalt die."

sinned, their sun went down, and the dark night of their Creator's frown settled upon them, a pall and a shroud forever. But enough. He who can find endless punishmsnt in the garden-threatening can find it anywhere, and manufacture it where he cannot find it.

Do you ask, what death *was* threatened? Why, of course, the same that was executed at the time specified — that which the guilty pair suffered the very day they sinned — death of innocence and peace — death of the sweet consciousness of the divine smile which they had ever before been experiencing — death in sin and shame,— the truc Bible death, — the death of those of whom the apostle speaks, as "dead in trespasses and sins,"—the death which the apostle himself experienced when, (as he says of himself,) "sin revived and I died." Such was the death threatened, and executed in the garden, and which Jehovah has been threatening and executing in the world ever since. But not eternal death; nor is such anywhere intimated by Moses, as a *historian.* Let us now turn to him as a LAWGIVER.

In considering Moses as a Lawgiver, it should be borne in mind that the government which he administered was a pure Theocracy, in which the creed of the Church blent with the constitution of the State. Standing, therefore, as he did, at the head of the Church, next to God, and mouth for him to the people, importance attaches to whatever he says about the penalty in question. And what does he say about it as a Lawgiver? Nothing? Yes, *just* nothing.* And what does this silence argue, but that he was ignorant of it, save as a heathen dogma. Many are the penalties he proclaims, but they are all temporal. Did he know of another, infinitely greater than all, and which for saving the people is (as we are told) more efficient than all, and keep it a profound secret from the people! Many were the penalties which God, *through* Moses, revealed to the people. Did *He*—the Father—purpose one infinitely greater than all, and keep it a secret with himself; so that, not the people only, but Moses even, was liable to enter endless woe by the way of sin, *blindfold!* For even *Moses*, meek as he was, sinned, and must, therefore, then have been exposed to it!

Importance is here. And I ask you, brother, whether it were like God's servant, *Moses*, to practice such concealment from the congregation he loved? or whether it were like the *God* of Moses? And this, especially while manifesting so great an interest in their temporal welfare, admonishing them against every variety of temporal calamity, and delivering them out of their distress, so that they

*Read his legislation and see.

should sing, "O that men would praise the Lord for his goodness, and for his wonderful works to the children of men." Was it like the Lord, after all, to sweep them, unadmonished, into *eternal* distress—distress which knows *no* deliverance, —to reveal a *law* and conceal *such* a penalty?

The doctrine of endless punishment took its rise among the heathen. At first but a conception of their poets, it was at length canonized as a Draconian means of coercing the obedience of the people. Why did not Moses incorporate it into his church-and-state-creed? So available as it is! So available as the later church would have it! I answer, just because Moses, being only Jehovah's amanuensis, could write neither more nor less of law and penalty than Jehovah dictated. It was optional with him to follow no mythological or ecclesiastical Draco. Hence his silence as a *Lawgiver* upon the penalty in question. Let us consider him as a Prophet.

For Moses *was* a prophet. And as a prophet he foresaw startling events. To him was opened the fearful vista, down which succeeding prophets also gazed upon the tribulation such as had "not been since the world began, neither indeed should be." And thus, in part, he describes it to the congregation awaiting his decease in the plains of Moab:—

The Lord shall bring a nation against thee from far, from the end of the earth, as swift as the eagle flieth; a nation whose tongue thou shalt not understand;

A nation of fierce countenance, which shall not regard the person of the old nor show favor to the young:

And he shall eat of the fruit of thy cattle, and the fruit of thy land, until thou be destroyed: which shall not leave thee either corn, wine, or oil, or the increase of thy kine, or flocks of thy sheep, until they have destroyed thee.

And he shall besiege thee in all thy gates, until thy high and fenced walls come down, wherein thou trustedst, throughout all thy land: and he shall besiege thee in all thy gates throughout all thy land, which the Lord thy God hath given thee.

And thou shalt eat the fruit of thy own body, the flesh of thy sons and of thy daughters, which the Lord thy God hath given thee in the siege and in the straitness, wherewith thy enemies shall distress thee:

So that the man that is tender among you and very delicate, his eye shall be evil toward his brother, and toward the wife of his bosom, and toward the remnant of his children which he shall leave:

So that he will not give to any of them of the flesh of his children, whom he shall eat: because he hath nothing left him in the siege, and in the straitness, wherewith thy enemies shall distress thee in all thy gates.

The tender and delicate woman among you, which would not adventure to set the sole of her foot upon the ground for delicateness and tenderness, her eye shall be evil toward the husband of her bosom, and towards her son, and towards her daughter,

And toward her young one that cometh out from between her feet, and toward her children which she shall bear: for she shall eat them for want of all things secretly, in the siege and straitness wherewith thy enemy shall distress thee in thy gates.

If thou will not observe to do all the words of this law that are written in this book, that thou mayest fear this glorious and fearful name, THE LORD THY GOD;

Then the Lord will make thy plagues wonderful, and the plagues of thy seed, even great plagues, and of long continuance.

Moreover he will bring upon thee all the diseases of Egypt, which thou wast afraid of; and they shall cleave unto thee.

Also every sickness and every plague, which is not written in the book of this law, them will the Lord bring upon thee, until thou be destroyed.

And ye shall be left few in number, whereas ye were as the stars of heaven for multitude; because thou wouldst not obey the voice of the Lord thy God.

And it shall come to pass, that as the Lord rejoiced over you to do you good, and to multiply you; so the Lord will rejoice over you to destroy you, and to bring you to nought; and ye shall be plucked from off the land whither thou goest to possess it.

And the Lord shall scatter thee among all people, from the one end of the earth even unto the other; and there thou shalt serve other gods, which neither thou nor thy fathers have known, even wood and stone.

And among these nations shalt thou find no ease, neither shall the sole of thy foot have rest: but the Lord shall give thee there a trembling heart, and failing of eyes, and sorrow of mind:

And thy life shall hang in doubt before thee; and thou shalt fear day and night, and shalt have none assurance of thy life:

In the morning thou shalt say, Would God it were even! and at even thou shalt say, Would God it were morning! for the fear of thy heart wherewith thou shalt fear and for the sight of thy eyes which thou shalt see.

And the Lord shall bring thee into Egypt again with ships by the way whereof I spake unto thee, thou shalt see it no more again: and there ye shall be sold unto your enemies for bondmen and bondwomen, and no man shall buy you.—*Deut.* xxviii. 49-68.

Such was the latter end of the Jewish nation, which Moses foresaw, "laid up in store" with Jehovah, "sealed up among his hid treasures." He heard Jehovah say, "I said I would scatter them into corners, I would cause their remembrance to cease among men." But nothing did he hear Him say of driving them into perdition beyond the grave, and making their sorrows ceaseless there. If any one doubt this latter proposition, let him read the Pentateuch, and be satisfied.

And here, dismissing Moses from the stand, let us make reflections upon his silence upon the matter in question. And

1. It is the silence of the first five books of the Bible, historically covering more than *two fifths* of the age of the human race, and embracing the only revelation of recognized authority which Jehovah gave to man during that long period.

2. It is to be noted that, during these thousands of years, in which, of course, men were swarming away into eternity, Jehovah was frequently revealing his judgments. How fitting to have revealed *this!*

3. It should be also noted that, of all the dispensations, that by Moses is justly regarded as the most severe. It was by him that, from Jehovah's "right hand, went forth a *fiery* law." Yet among

all its penalties, is there no intimation of any one which, compared with *endless woe*, is so much as the prick of a pin, compared with the torturous death inflicted by the concentrated malignity of the Spanish Inquisition. And yet, further, why should not the severe dispensation have the severe punishment? Why look in a milder dispensation for a severer? *

4. This entire absence of all allusion to endless punishment is the more significant, in the fact that Moses, brought up in the court of Egypt, must have

*Archbishop Whateley, after a lengthy argument on the subject, says:—"Is not, then, the conclusion inevitable, that, if the doctrine of future retribution had been to be revealed, or any traditional knowledge of it confirmed, we should have found it explicitly stated, and still more frequently repeated than the temporal sanctions of the law? And when, instead of anything like this, we have set before us a few scattered texts, which, it is contended, allude to, or imply, this doctrine, can it be necessary to examine whether they are rightly interpreted? Surely it is a sufficient reply, to say that, if Moses had intended to inculcate such doctrine, he would have clearly stated and dwelt on it in almost every page. Nor is it easy to conceive how any man of even ordinary intelligence, and not blinded by devoted attachment to an hypothesis, can attentively peruse the books of the Law, abounding as they do with such copious descriptions of the temporal rewards and punishments which sanction that Law, and with such earnest admonitions grounded on that sanction, and yet can bring himself seriously to believe that the doctrine of a state of retribution after death, which it cannot be contended is even mentioned, however slightly, in more than a very few passages, formed a part of the Mosaic Revelation."—*Thayer's Origin and History of the Doctrine of Endless Punishment, p.* 37-8.

been familiar with it. For the Egyptians nominally believed in it, and formally consigned their wicked kings to it. That Moses should have left it behind, therefore, when he forsook the Egyptian court—what does it argue, but that he regarded it but as of a piece with the other superstitions of those who worshipped apes and monkeys, leeks and onions. Or, considering that Moses was but mouth for God, what does its absence from his writings signify, less than the seal of Jehovah's disapprobation stamped upon it!

5. All things considered, and as *God is good*, and was always good, as good to the ancients as to the moderns, must we not infer from the fact that the people of the patriarchal and Mosaic ages, were never admonished of endless punishment, *that they were not exposed to it.* This inference seems natural and necessary. If any choose to deny it, and say that the unadmonished masses of those early ages are now, somewhere in Jehovah's empire, actually suffering on, and to suffer forever, they have a right to their opinion. But for ourselves, we have no language to express the horror with which such an idea, set in the divine goodness, fills our soul! And we can but rejoice that the later Scriptures fully authorize its denial in favor of a better opinion of "the Judge of all the earth."

And here, brother, let us pause, and see just

where we are. We have passed over the plains of Paradise, through the land of the patriarch, *by* the mountain that burned with fire ; and leaving it far behind, now find ourselves in the " plains of Moab, before Jordan." So that, chronologically, nearly one-half of our Bible-discussion is completed. And the result thus far has been to show, either that God had no design to punish his children forever, or that, having such design, he carefully kept them ignorant of it. Which of the two things is most in keeping with His Justice and Goodness, as our " Father " in heaven, I leave you, brother, to judge, praying that you may judge nothing rashly, " but judge righteous judgment."

Yours truly.

LETTER III.

JOSHUA — PSALMS.

Passage over Jordan—History silent—Job silent—Psalms silent—Exposition of text " The wicked shall be cast into hell, &c," and incidentally of the text, " thou Capernaum, ... shall be brought down to hell."—Concluding observation.

Dear Brother,—

Our last letter brought us down all the way from Eden to where Moses died " before Jordan." And in all that long journey, under the guide of Moses, we discovered no trace of the doctrine we seek. Let us now "pass *over* Jordan." What remains of the Old Testament covers a period of a little more than a thousand years. Does this residue teach the doctrine in question?

As to the historical portions of it, it is enough to say that we know not that anybody supposes *them* to teach it. We therefore pass them at a step.

Job,—tried as was his patience, I think it is no where supposed to be intimated, either by himself or his friends, that he was liable to have it tried by the fiery ordeal of *endless* pain. Leaving him, therefore, with his comforters and his potsherds, we are greeted by the melody of the *Psalmists.* Nor with them also should we be detained more than a moment, had not the sentiments swept from their lyres been singularly abused.

Passing along the Psalms, one naturally catches their inspiration, and finds himself exclaiming, "O Lord, our Lord, how excellent is thy name in all the earth." Thus he sings, till, approaching the 17th verse of the 9th Psalm, he is startled by the announcement that therein is the lurking place of endless punishment. Pausing he reads,

"*The wicked shall be turned into hell with all the nations that forget God.*"

And now, brother, let us examine this text. Does it teach endless punishment? We think not for the following, among other reasons.

1. Because such a meaning seems forbidden by the context. The Psalmist is evidently upon the subject of temporal judgments,—judgments by which "the Lord is *known.*" For while in verse seventh, he says "He hath prepared his throne for judgment," in verse sixteenth he says, "The Lord is *known* by the judgment which he executeth;" the obvious meaning of which, is, that his judgments are matters of *observation,*—abroad in the earth; that, "verily he is a God that judgeth in

the earth." To such judgments, the Psalmist is accustomed to refer, as they occurred all along the line of sacred history. But surely, judgments in the *future* world—the casting into endless woe *there*,—were not judgments by which he could be said to be *known* to men on *earth;* certainly not, without such a revelation as in the Psalmist's time, at least, had never been made. The awed camp of Israel knew God by the judgment he executed upon the rebellious companies of Korah, Dathan and Abiram. The judgment which swallowed them up, they could see from their tent-doors. But surely, they could not see them enter upon eternal pain, that they should know God by *that.* The same general remark might be made in reference to other judgments of which the Psalmist speaks, and is, doubtless, equally applicable to whatever judgment is meant in the text under consideration. And this conclusion is confirmed by the fact that, *if* this text teach endless woe, it is, as we have seen, an entirely new outburst of light from above, or rather of darkness from beneath. But, further, we think this text does not teach endless punishment.

2. Because, whatever the judgment meant, it is inflicted upon nations.

Nations are turned into hell. Can that hell then be in the future world? We all believe in national sins and national judgments. God setteth up one nation and pulleth down another. As "Judge of all the earth," and as a God who "judgeth in the earth," and as he whose son came *into* this world "for Judgment," he tries, condemns and executes nations. So has he dealt with nations of old. But does any one suppose that Babylon or Greece, Macedon or Rome, were turned into a region of endless woe in the future world,—that they are suffering there now, and shall forever? The idea were simply preposterous. But I further object to making our text teach endless punishment.

3. Because there is nothing in its Hebrew to even *suggest* such punishment.

The word covered up by the word hell is *sheol*, which, as we will show, means simply the invisible world—the grave—and, by an easy and natural figure, a condition of solitude and desolation comparable to that of the grave. It is in the Scriptures frequently *translated* grave. To show that it does not mean a place of endless punishment, perhaps the argument *reductio ad absurdum*, will be briefest as well as most conclusive. Admit then that it *does* mean the popular hell, and what follows. Why, then you have made Jacob think his son Joseph in hell, and that he himself is to follow him there. For he says, translating the word *sheol* as in our text, "I will go down to *hell* to my son mourning." Gen. xxxvii. 35. Then, too, does the same patriarch make his going to that awful place, to depend upon any negligence of his sons on taking care of Benjamin. "If mischief befall him by the way which ye go, then shall ye bring down my gray hairs with sorrow to *hell.*" Gen. xlii. 38. Then, too, is David made to charge Solomon to cast Joab into hell, and to see that Shimei is brought down to it with blood. 1 Kings ii. 6, 9. Then, also, is Job made to pray that God would send him to hell,—"O that thou wouldst hide me in *hell.* Job xiv. 13, and, further, to say that he must go there any way." If I wait, "*hell* is mine house," xxvii. 16. Then, too, is the Psalmist made to pray that the wicked may go into *hell*, and go quickly, (Psalm xxxi. 17, lv. 15,) and to say that "our bones are scattered at the mouth of *hell*, cxli. 7.

These references (which might be multiplied) are sufficient to show the absolute absurdity of making *sheol* mean a place of endless misery. For what a bedlam! Joseph in hell and Jacob going there, and cautioning his sons not to send him there. Job praying to go there and the dying Psalmist charging his son Solomon to send Joab and Shimei there, and praying that all his enemies may go there *quickly!* All this, and more, while from not one of the Bible worthies do we hear of so much as a prayer or a wish that any may escape going there.

Such is the bedlam into which we are thrown by

making *sheol* mean a place of endless punishment. Whereas let it mean as it naturally does, the region of the dead—the grave,—and by an easy figure, desolation like that of the grave, and all this chaos at once comes to order.

And now, having seen for ourselves what the word *sheol* does *not* mean, we are prepared to hear the learned orthodox, Dr. Campbell, say, that

"Sheol signifies the state of the dead without regard to their happiness or misery."

And also to hear the equally orthodox Whitby say, that

"Sheol, throughout the Old Testament, signifies not the place of punishment, or of the souls of bad men only, but the grave only, or the place of the dead."

And of these authorities, it is enough to say, there are none higher.

Having thus settled it that the word *hell* (sheol) in our text does not mean a place of endless punishment, nothing further is necessary to our purpose. We will, however, spend a moment upon the enquiry, what our text *does* mean, as it will afford opportunity to refer to the Great Commentator—Jesus. According to Matt. xi. 23, he thus addresses Capernaum, "And thou Capernaum, which art exalted up to heaven, shalt be brought down to hell." And here note,

1. That the Greek word *hades* here used by the Master, and translated "*hell*," is admitted *on all hands*, to be just equivalent to the Hebrew word, *sheol*, used by the Psalmist in the text in question, and therein translated "*hell.*" And

2. It will be admitted that whatever be the hell meant, the words of the Saviour, "*brought down to*," are equivalent to the words of the Psalmist, "*turned into.*" And hence,

3. It is seen that to learn what the Saviour meant by Capernaum's being "*brought down to hell*," is to learn, substantially, what the Psalmist meant by wicked nations being "*turned into hell.*" So much seems plain.

What then did the Saviour mean. I think he meant that as men go down into the silence of the grave—hades—and are forgotten, so Capernaum should go down into desolation and be buried in oblivion. But I will neither assert nor argue what seems to me so clear, but simply refer you to orthodox commentators. I quote only Clarke and Barnes. On the clause "*shall be brought down to hell*," the former, in his commentary, says "Here it [hell] means a state of the utmost woe and ruin and desolation, to which these impenitent cities should be reduced. This prediction of our Lord was literally fulfilled; for in the wars between the Romans and the Jews, these cities were totally destroyed, so that no traces are now found of Bethsaida, Chorazin, or Capernaum." Barnes, upon the same clause, says,

"This does not mean that all the people shall go to hell; but the city which had flourished so prosperously, should lose its prosperity and occupy the lowest place among cities. The word hell, is used here, not to denote a place of punishment in the future world, but a state of desolation and destruction as a city. . . . . . This has been strictly fulfilled. In the wars between the Jews and Romans, Chorazin, Capernaum, &c., were so completely desolated that it is difficult to determine their present situation. (*See Com. vol.* 1, *p.* 138.) Then, for cities to be "brought down to hell," is to be brought down to a state of desolation—buried from the world. Therefore, as we have seen, for "nations to be turned into hell," can mean nothing else; so clearly does the Saviour explain the Psalmist"—the New Testament throw back light upon the Old.

Thus have we shown what the Psalmist certainly did *not* mean in the text in question, and also what he obviously *did* mean. Nor have we given so much attention to this text, because it deserves it, but only because careless readers almost habitually stumble upon it. And now, after having halted so long about it as the traveller in the Holy Land halts to decypher an inscription upon some ancient ruin, we add a new string to our harp, and pass on through the Psalms, singing as we go, "O sing unto the Lord a new song for his mercy endureth forever." And as we leave them behind, let us pause for an observation.

We have now passed over the first three thousand years of the world's sacred history—that is chronologically, more than half of it,—and yet have failed to discover the least trace of the doctrine of endless punishment as threatened, feared, or thought of. We have, indeed, heard threatenings and seen the smoke of burning cities. But we have heard nothing of the threatening and seen nothing of the smoke of endless torment. We have seen Jehovah's judgments all abroad in camp, court, and temple,—turning cities and nations into *sheol*, but we have heard nothing of *the* judgment to which evangelical ? Christians appeal. Relatively to *that*, we have found all silent as *sheol*. And *how* significant is this silence of thirty centuries of Divine Revelation, I pray you, brother, ponder well!

Yours truly.

LETTER IV.

PROVERBS — MALACHI.

Silence of *Solomon*—Threatenings of *Isaiah*—His use of the word *gnolem* (forever)—The worm that dieth not—Isaiah *not evangelical*—*Jeremiah*, sadly abused, why he wept, also *not evangelical*—*Ezekiel*—His threatenings, temporal—Silent upon the doctrine in question, "Why will ye die,"—*Daniel* also silent—His figure of the Resurrection examined—Concluding remarks upon our review of the Old Testament.

DEAR BROTHER,—

We now come to the writings of Solomon,—Proverbs, Ecclesiastes, and the Canticles. With these, we need be detained but for a moment. For, though, "because the preacher was very wise, he still taught the people knowledge," he is silent upon the doctrine under discussion. In Ecclesiastes, he glances towards the future world, only enough to say, "the dust shall return to the earth as it was, and the *spirit to God who gave it;*" and in his Proverbs, only enough to say, the "sinner is driven away [from earth] in his wickedness." We pass over both with a step, and listen to oriental strains along the spicy groves of the Canticles. But here, too, we find no business; and, therefore, as we prefer business to pleasure, we hasten through them, to where our ears are greeted by the lofty and energetic strains of the evangelical prophet.

"Isaiah is very bold." And thus he cries, "Hear, O heavens, and give ear, O earth." And listening, what do they hear? They hear the principle authoritatively announced, that it shall be well with the righteous and ill with the wicked. They hear of judgments upon Israel, Assyria, Babylon, Moab, Egypt. They hear of the desolating march of armies, of the overthrow of cities, of regions swept with the besom of destruction. But nothing do they hear of endless woe.

"Then said I, Lord, how long? And he answered, until the cities be wasted without inhabitant, and the houses without man, and the land be utterly desolate, and the Lord have removed men far away and there be a great forsaking in the midst of the land."* Thus the prophet agrees with the Psalmist, that Jehovah "judgeth in the earth." For thus he further cries, "Behold the Lord maketh the earth empty, and maketh it waste, and turneth it upside down, and scattereth abroad the inhabitants thereof." Thus does he speak of the overturnings and overturnings, in the long line of providential preparation for the advent of *Messiah*; and of *Him* in his glory, and of the gatherings of the nations to

* vi. 11, 12; xxiv. 1.

him, and of how, under his reign, with joy, men "shall draw water from the wells of salvation," he has very clear visions. But of any place of future woe, as receiving the souls of the multitudes of the wicked, whose death, by famine, pestilence and war, he foretells, all vision is denied him. No judgment does he announce which looks beyond the death of its victims;—unless it be that pronounced upon the King of Babylon: "Thou shalt not be joined with them [other Kings] in burial,"*—a judgment, quite harmless to the dead.

Do you say, Isaiah makes the people cry out, (xxxiii. 14) "who among us shall dwell with the devouring fire? Who of us shall dwell with everlasting burnings?" And so he does, but is speaking of the overthrow of the Assyrian army which he compares to the burnings of lime. Henry paraphrases the ejaculation thus, "Who of us shall dwell with this devouring fire, before which so vast an army are as thorns, with these everlasting burnings which have made the Assyrians as the burnings of lime." And how the prophets use the word *gnolem* (translated everlasting and forever) is seen in what he says of the smoke which should go up from burning Idumea,—"the smoke thereof shall go up forever."† Is it smoking still!

Do you say Isaiah speaks of the "*worm that dieth*

*xii. 9. †xxxiv. 9-10. Terms denoting duration in a future letter.

not?" Certainly he does, in the last verse of his prophecy, and also explains himself to have reference to what shall take place during the *moons of earth.* His language there is the basis of a simile employed by Jesus, which will be considered in its place.

Thus do we find Isaiah, like all his inspired predecessors, silent upon endless punishment. Why then is he honored with the title, "*evangelical,*" as those at *this* day, who repudiate that dogma, are *not?* But no matter; for, standing, as they do, with the old Bible worthies, though pushed out of the synagogue, they are not punished into bad company.

But here we come to Jeremiah, the *weeping* prophet, whose tears are so frequently referred to as being shed over the immortal ruin of souls. And yet, singularly enough, and, for the credit of the ministry, *sad* enough, he makes not a single allusion to the subject — not a single allusion, which, so far as I know, has ever been argumentatively pressed into the *service* of endless punishment.

Jeremiah tells us *why* he weeps. It is "for the slain of the daughter of my people"— that the city "sits solitary"— that "she weepeth sore in the night, and her tears are on her face" — that "among all her lovers she hath none to comfort her" — that "Judah is gone into captivity," "dwelleth among the heathen," and "findeth no rest" — that the ways of Zion [Jerusalem] do mourn, and none come to her solemn feasts,— that "all her gates are desolate,"— that "her adversaries are chief, her enemies prosper" — that "Jerusalem hath grievously sinned, and therefore is removed." "For these things," saith the prophet, "I weep; mine eyes runneth down with water, because the comforter that should comfort my soul is far from me." "My children are desolate, because the enemy hath prevailed." "Mine eyes do fail because of tears; my bowels are troubled, my liver is poured upon the earth, for the destruction of the daughters of my people, because the children and the sucklings swooned in the streets of the city." "They say unto their mothers, where is corn and wine. Behold, O Lord, and consider to whom thou hast done this." "Shall the women eat their fruit and children of a span long? Shall the priest and the prophet be slain in the sanctuary of the Lord?" "The tongue of the sucking child cleaveth to the roof of his mouth, for thirst. The young children ask bread, and no man breaketh it to them." "For the punishment of the iniquity of my people is greater than the punishment of the sin of Sodom." *

The above texts sufficiently indicate why the prophet wept, while he gives no intimation of endless punishment. Shall not *he* also be stricken from

*Jeremiah saw no endles woe for Sodom; but only woe, less than Jerusalem was *then suffering.*

the roll of the *evangelical?* For to say that he believed in endless misery, and yet, did not speak of it, in his zeal and pathos, were to say that though his head was a "fountain of waters," his heart was a quarry of stone.

And now we pass to Ezekiel, "whose hot hurried breath we feel approaching us like the breath of a furnace." We see him portray Jerusalem upon a tile and then lay siege against it; we hear him say of Jerusalem, "I will give it into the hands of strangers for a prey, and to the wicked of the earth for a spoil. The fathers shall eat the sons in the midst of them, and the sons shall eat their fathers; and I will execute judgment on thee, and the whole remnant of thee will I scatter to the four winds." "Ye have multiplied your slain in this city, and ye have defiled the streets thereof with the slain; therefore, thus saith the Lord God, Your slain whom ye have laid in the midst of it, they are the flesh, and this city is the caldron."* "And they shall know that I am the Lord, when I have scattered them among the nations, and dispersed them in the countries."† This, and much more do we hear Ezekiel say, after the manner of Jeremiah, and upon the key note of judgment struck by Moses in the "plain of Moab." But not a word do we hear him say of endless misery. He speaks indeed of dis-

* Not, *eternity* is the caldron, or furnace!
†Ezek. iv. 1, 2. vii. 21. v. 10. xi. 6, 7. xii. 15.

persion, but not into woe in the future world. To rise to *that* grand conception is the province of profane poets — poets, not divine, but Miltonian. Moreover, the object of punishment, as stated by Ezekiel, *demands* that it be limited in duration. "And they shall bear the punishment of their iniquity; the punishment of the prophet shall be even as the punishment of him that seeketh unto him; that the house of Israel may go no more astray from me, neither pollute any more with all their transgressions. But that they may be my people, and I may be their God, saith the Lord."*

Thus Ezekiel, like his brother seers, is also silent upon the doctrine of endless woe. One text which he uses, however, has been pressed into its service. It is this, "Why will ye die, O house of Israel," (xxxiii. 11.) Relative to this, however, it is enough to refer the reader to the remarks I made upon the garden threatening. And yet, as *conclusively* settling its meaning — *very* conclusively — I will quote from Hosea. The prophet is speaking of Ephraim and Judah,—that is, of the tribes that rebelled, and those that stood loyal to the house of David when he says, "When Ephraim spake tremblingly, he exalted himself in Israel, but when he offended in Baal, he *died*."† Now we know, historically, what Ephraim's death was — the being sunk in wretchedness and carried away into captivi-

* xiv. 10. † xiii. 1.

ty. Such was *his sheol.* Does any one dream that Hosea has reference here to the future world? Such a *dream* were ridiculous. Then, why dream so about his brother Ezekiel. The whole prophecy of the latter shows what *he* meant. We leave it behind without finding the least intimation of endless woe, and pass to *Daniel.*

Daniel also is a mighty prophet, whose vision is of still ampler sweep, and longer range. For it embraces nations more widely spread, and opens down even to Macedon, Greece and Rome. But nothing does he see of endless punishment, unless it is recorded in the twelfth chapter of his prophecy, where he says, (xii. 1,) "And at that time shall Michael stand up, the great prince which standeth for the children of my people; and there shall be a time of trouble, such as never was since there was a nation, even to that same time. And at that time, thy people shall be delivered, every one that shall be found written in the book. And many of them that sleep in the dust of the earth shall awake, some to everlasting life, and some to shame and everlasting contempt." But I think intelligent Christians, at this late day, will hardly attempt to raise an argument for endless woe upon this solitary text, for the following among other reasons.

1. Because the prophecy of Daniel, being almost exclusively symbolical, it were quite unnatural to understand this text of it, *literally.*

2. Because the very same resurrection symbol is employed by Ezekiel, who explains himself to have reference exclusively to *scenes of time.* Ez. xxxvii. 1, 14. Why shall it be otherwise with Daniel?

3. Because the words "*shame*" and "*contempt,*" seem quite too common-place to be dictated by the Spirit, to express the awful doctrine of endless punishment, to a people to whom that doctrine had been before unrevealed.

4. Because the language employed, *if* taken *literally*, does not express a *general* resurrection, but only *partial.* "*Many* of them that sleep," &c. Why did the prophet not say *all?* Evidently, because it was not intended to embrace all, but only a part; nor yet to embrace the righteous only, for it embraces both good and bad. A state of sin and apathy is in Scripture language, a state of sleep and death. The arousal from this state, may well be called a resurrection, and Paul so calls it when he says, "Awake thou that sleepest, arise from the dead, and Christ shall give thee light." The spirit foresaw that many who were in a state of sin and apathy would be aroused, and therefore he speaks partitively, "*many* of them that sleep," &c.

5. Because, finally, and conclusively, it is plain, that whatever event was meant, has already taken place. The prophet tells us *when* it was to be, as exactly as he does when "Messias should be cut off." And,

First, it was to be when there should "be a time of trouble such as never was since there was a nation, even to that same time," xii. 1. In Matt., (xxiv. 21,) Jesus, speaking of the destruction of the Jewish state, says, "For there shall be great tribulation, such as was not since the beginning of the world, no, nor yet shall be." The events are *one*. *Jesus* thus explains *Daniel*. Could he have a better expositor. Jesus *is* Daniel's "Michael." But,

Second, Daniel was told, in language which events have clearly interpreted, when the time should be. "Then I, Daniel, looked, and behold there stood other two, the one on this side of the bank of the river, and the other on that side of the bank of the river. And one said to the man clothed in linen, which was upon the waters of the river, How long shall it be to the end of these wonders? And I heard the man clothed in linen which was upon the waters of the river, when he lifted his right hand and his left hand unto heaven, and sware by him that liveth forever and ever, that it shall be for a time, times and an half. And when he shall have accomplished to scatter the power of the holy people, all these things shall be finished." xii. 7.

Here then we have definiteness. For we know what the scattering of the holy people was. It was the scattering of the Jews, prophecied as we have seen,* and largely dwelt upon by Daniel's brother seers. And *when* that occurred, is matter of simple history — as well known as the time of the sacking of Rome by the Goths and Vandals, if not indeed better. It occurred nearly two thousand years ago. And then "all these things should be *finished*." To prove that the resurrection spoken of by Daniel is yet future, were, therefore, to prove that the dispersion of the Jews is yet future! That that resurrection, mean it what it may, is past, we have then the exposition of Jesus, and the oath of the angel of God. Unless it *is* past, Daniel made a mistake. But no, we trust him for the event, and not less for the time when it should take place.

As to the word everlasting, we have seen how the prophets apply the Hebrew it covers up to the duration of temporal calamities. It will be critically examined in a future letter.

And now leaving Daniel, with endless misery still undiscovered, we come to the *minor Prophets*; but still discover nothing of that fearful doom. Not a glimpse of it appears among all the hot curses which they hurl at wicked men and nations in the name of God. To affirm this, is not assumption, seeing that we know not whether any intelligent Bible reader denies it.

Thus ends our review of the Old Testament.

* See Ez. xx. 23. v. 10. Deut. xxxii. 36. Jer. xviii. 17. Ez. xii 15.

Thus we bid adieu to the prophets. "Munificent and modest benefactors, they knocked at the door of the human family at night, threw in inestimable wealth, fled, and the sound of their feet dying away in the distance, is all the tidings they have given of themselves." But they threw in no torch of *endless death!* And if it be said, neither did they of endless life, we shall not stop to dispute it; because it is in perfect keeping with Jehovah's character, to surprise his children with blessings unforetold,—a very different thing indeed from surprising them with *endless* misery unforetold, and against which they must, of course, have been unadmonished. I may, for pleasing effect, withhold, for a little time, good tidings from my neighbor. Who will say that it follows, therefore, that I may withhold alarm, when at dead midnight, I see his house in flames over his head and the heads of his sleeping family? Who?

It is easily reconcilable with goodness, too, that creatures like men, profiting from experience, should not always be *at once* admonished, of their exposure to certain *temporal* evils. For there is an "afterwards" in which they may profit from the *experience* of them. But not so, eternal evil. And here, before proceeding to the New Testament, a few reflections, similar to previous ones, seem called for. And,

1. At least, *until* Christ came,—that is, for four

thousand years—the Father gave to his children upon earth, no intimation that he intended to punish them forever. Can it be, that he was all that time, sending them "away into everlasting punishment?" What a charge to bring against the Judge of all the earth. A word and *such* a blow, and the blow first! Think of it, brother.

2. This silence of the Old Testament seems the more remarkable, because made up of every variety of composition — historical, legal, prophetic, experimental. Especially do the Psalms draw aside the vail from the pious heart, and reveal its workings; yet no suspicion of endless woe appears. Jeremiah wept in Zion, as it would seem no other person ever did. Yet is he farthest from any *intimation* of endless woe. Even he assures us, withal, that "The Lord will not cast off forever. But though he cause grief, yet will he have compassion, according to the multitude of his mercies." *

3. The heathen, during all this long period, or rather as far back as their history carries us, were in full possession of this dread dogma; though "without God and without hope in the world." Now, how is it that the poets of the heathen should, in the discovery of divine truth, so steal the march upon the prophets of God? — how is it that the heathen should gather higher knowledge at the cave

* Lam iii. 32.

of the *Sybils*, than God's people at "*the holy of holies*"— how is it that heathen priests should learn higher wisdom at the shrines of their Apollos, than Moses in the holy mount where he talked face to face with the living God? Is mythology so much wiser than theology? Or is the dogma in review, only a myth, a mere heathen *ism?*

4. May we not well here ask, how this silence of four thousand years of inspiration upon the doctrine in question, comports with the modern notion that without that doctrine, little can be done to save souls. Evidently, the two things do not quadrate at all. Either the church has made a mistake for the last thousand years, or else Jehovah made a mistake for the first four thousand years. For he did not see fit to suffer that doctrine to be *revealed* by the prophets and wise men whom he sent to instruct and save his people, for at least so long a time. Was Jehovah so long *experimenting* upon means of salvation? and was it only after so long a *trial*, that he discovered that it was of no use to belabor men with the means which he had so long been employing, and that the threat of endless misery was the effective saving agency? Nay, for Jehovah never experiments upon the immortal destiny of his trembling ones!

Divine revelation *is* indeed *progressive*,—first the blade, then the ear, then the full corn in the ear, (not first the full corn in the ear, then the ear, then the blade, and then the dead germ.) And this progressiveness of revelation is perfectly consistent with Universalist ideas of human discipline and growth.* But, viewing the present as man's *only* state in which to fit himself for heaven, *then* the notion that Jehovah had a mighty saving means which, for four thousand years he would not employ, though for the want of it he saw unnumbered multitudes of his creatures sinking into hopeless perdition! — well, brother, think of it!

5. If the individual man lived through the thousands of earth's years, with faculties unimpaired, it would seem less unreasonable, that the doctrine of such a punishment should be withholden for the earlier thousands of these years. But it is not so. "Throughout all ranks and conditions one generation passeth and another generation cometh; and this great inn is by turns evacuated and replenished, by troops of succeeding pilgrims." The individual lives his short day, dies, and is thereby carried quite beyond the reach of whatever means of grace may be vouchsafed to his posterity. To him, born under Moses, and a thousand years *lost*

* "What hinders, therefore, but that mankind may draw lots for their conditions? They take their portion of faculties and opportunities, as any unknown cause, or concourse of causes, or as causes acting for other purposes, may happen to set them out; but the event is governed by that which depends upon themselves, the application of what they have received."— Paley's Nat. Theolo. p. 290.

before Jesus *comes* (with the saving grace of endless woe?) the gospel is to him, indeed, an idle tale. Said a prince of one of the South Sea Islands, who had religiously devoted all his sons to death, before the Gospel reached him, "*it comes fifteen years too late.*" And, as the Gospel could not bring back to life again, the children whom he had idolatrously sacrificed, so it can no more bring again into the region of hope, those whom the law consigned to despair, thousands of years before the Gospel was proclaimed.

In conclusion, if all this be so, may we not well ask, "Who is the Lord?" And now, brother, leaving you to ponder the foregoing, let me pass on to the New Testament, to see what light that throws upon the question in discussion.

Yours truly.

LETTER V.

NEW TESTAMENT EXAMINED.

Positive evidence demanded, and five reasons why—Symbols of New Testament and Old—Precise question in debate—Key-texts—*Aionion* supposed to be untranslated—What does it mean?—Appeal, 1st, to *classical usage*—Authorities—Origin—How Inspiration employs words—Bible usage inferrable from classical—2, Appeal to *Bible usage*; *First*, Old Testament—Quotations—Syllogism—Further quotations; *Second*, New Testament—Quotations—Clarke—"*Eternal fire*" of Sodom considered at length—Summary—*Specific* meaning of Aionion in our own key-text, not *endless*—Such a meaning forbidden, 1, By the spirit of its Author; 2, by its substantive; 3, by the character of the discourse; 4, by God's *elder* Scriptures; 5, such meaning for it finds no support in other *written* Scriptures—Texts examined—"*Wrath to come*," "*unquenchable fire*,"—Clarke—Connexion between the Old Testament and New—Quotations from Eusebius—"*Worm that dieth not*,"—Origin of the figure, where Jesus got it—Meaning of Isaiah lxvi. 23, 24—"*Hell* (gehenna) *fire*"—(*Hades—Hell*, considered in a note)—Eight considerations about it—Preachers unapostolic?—"*He that believeth not shall be damned*"—"*Lose his own soul*"—"*The rich man and Lazarus*"—"*Whither I go ye cannot come*," considered at length;—6, *Endless*, *forbidden*, as the meaning of aionion, (note on the words, *life eternal*) by other Scriptures,—1, By those which set forth the character of God—Woods and Finney—Endless punishment useless—Stuart—Hopkins—Saints *petrified*—2, By those Scriptures which speak of punishment according *to works*; 3, By the spirit of certain parables; 4, By Matt. v. 43-48, &c., Lam. iii. 32, Isaiah lvii. 16, &c.; 5, By the promise in the garden; 6, By God's revealed purpose; 7, By His plan; 8, By the completion of Christ's work; 9, By the shout of the apostle Paul—Summary—Conclusion.

Dear Brother,—

We have now passed over forty of the less than sixty centuries of time, without discovering the least trace of the doctrine of endless punishment among the authoritative revelations of Jehovah.

We have also seen that the absurdities, which, to human reason, are involved in that doctrine, are great, numerous and both multiplied and intensified by the increase of light.

From what we have seen, therefore, we conclude that the evidence now necessary to establish that doctrine, must be most positive and absolute. For, to do so, were to establish,

1. That the chief of penalties was carefully excluded from the *special dispensation* of penalties,—that is, from the *legal.*

2. That in the dispensation, *not* legal, but so much *better* than the legal, that the latter, compared with it, " hath no glory by reason of the glory that excelleth," * this hitherto hidden hydra of everlasting pain, is brought forth to the light and let loose before the eyes of men ; — and all this, just at the moment when wakes from overhead, the song,

*But if the ministration of death, written and engraven in stones, was glorious, so that the children of Israel could not steadfastly behold the face of Moses for the glory of his countenance; which glory was to be done away:

How shall not the ministration of the Spirit be rather glorious?

For if the ministration of condemnation be glory, much more doth the ministration of righteousness exceed in glory.

For even that which was made glorious had no glory in this respect, by reason of the glory that excelleth.

For if that which is done away was glorious, much more that which remaineth is glorious.—2 Cor. iii. 7—11.

"Glory to God in the highest; on earth peace, good will to men!"

3. It were to prove that the Father, for four thousand years, scrupulously withheld from the millions of his tempted children, while alive, all knowledge of a woe into which he forever plunges them, now they are dead.

4. It were to prove that heathenism long stole the march upon true religion. For, as we have seen, *it* had the doctrine in question, as a saving agency (?) long before Bible religionists gained a glimpse of it!

5. It were to prove a point, as we have seen, in the teeth of the most appalling absurdities.

Now we submit whether, to prove so much in favor of heathenism, and against common sense, consciousness, humanity and God, the evidence should not be the most positive and absolute?— whether, if the evidence leave a doubt, common sense, consciousness, humanity and God, should not have the benefit of it?

These preliminary remarks are dropped, merely that we may see just where we are, and not because we anticipate any formidable difficulty in what remains of our Bible examination.

We now enter a Dispensation, whose symbol is not *Sinai*, with its rumbling thunderbolts, but *Calvary*, with its soft whisperings of mercy, and the cross from which the dying prayer of the Crucified floats up towards heaven. We may therefore well enter it *hopefully*. And as we do so, let us note,

1. That we have no controversy about any *place* of punishment.

2. About any *time* of punishment, but,

3. Only about the endless *duration* of punishment. And that, therefore,

No reasoning is relevant to our present discussion, unless it bear upon the last of these three points. By carefully marking this consideration, we may avoid confusion, and prolixity. *

Does the New Testament teach the doctrine of endless punishment? This is the question. And the most natural key to its solution, would seem to be the text,—

"*These shall go away into everlasting punishment.*" Matt. xxv. 46.

And, therefore, this text shall be the rallying point of our argument.

What then does it mean? — or, rather, what does its word *everlasting* mean? or, still rather, what does the word *aionion* mean, which the word everlasting covers up? For the word which fell from the Saviour's lips, may be quite as reliable as that which fell from the translator's pen.

We have some words, as "*rabbi*," and "*baptizo*,"

* As the author, with printing and writing going on together, has already reached the limits he assigned his letters, he feels quite embarrassed at the necessity of severe condensation.

taken into the English version of the Greek and Hebrew Scriptures, untranslated. Let us now suppose the word *aionion* so taken into our key-text. It would then read, "These shall go away into *aionion* punishment." Most readers would then be obliged to say, we do not know the meaning of this foreign word, and therefore cannot understand the punishment. And now, as though you and I did not know its meaning, let us proceed to ascertain it. And,

1. As it is a Greek word, we will proceed to take the testimony of the Greeks themselves. Certainly, they must have understood their own language. How they understood this *word* of it, we may learn from dictionaries of their language, compiled, not, generally, by theologians who had a creed to save, but by critical linguists who had a classical reputation at stake.

Aion and *aionion* have the same general signification, the latter being the adjective of the former and drawing its meaning from it. The same Hebrew word, *gnolem*, being translated, sometimes by the one, and sometimes by the other. * Of course, it is *aion*, the *noun* that lexicographers chiefly define. And how do they define it.

Schrevelius says it means, "time, whether longer or shorter, past, present, or future; the life of man."

* The Hebrew has no formal adjectives.

Schleusner says — " Any space of time, whether longer or shorter, past, present or future, to be determined by the person or things spoken of, and the scope of the subject."

Parkhurst.— " Duration of time with great variety."

Donnegan.—" Time; a space of time; life-time and life; the ordinary period of man's life; the age of man; man's estate; a long period of time; eternity."

Pickering. — " An age, a long period of time, indefinite duration, eternity, * * * * time whether longer of shorter, past, present or future."

Such is the Greek usage of the Greek word in question. The celebrated Origen, the earliest of Christian scholars, writing in Greek, therefore affirmed *aionion* punishment, while stoutly arguing against *everlasting* punishment. It was perfectly consistent for ancient Universalists to believe in *aionion* punishment. Why not then for modern ones? And now, the term in question being of such variable signification, and, as we have seen, involving the notion of eternity, only in its *remote definition*, by what authority has it been made to mean *endless*, when it defines the punishment which " the God of all grace " inflicts upon his tempted offspring?

But you will perhaps say that our present business is with the *Bible*-usage of the term in question.

And it certainly is. But we must bear in mind, that Inspiration, ordinarily, uses the language it finds in the world, rather than constructs a new one; and, that, therefore, the presumption ever is, that it employs words as they are understood by the people to whom it immediately addresses them. Otherwise how could it be understood at all? However, we will not merely *infer* Bible-usage from popular usage, but listen to a plea of the *Book* in its own cause.

2. Bible-usage. And

First, The Old Testament.

In the Septuagint, (Greek version of the Old Testament) the word *gnolem* is, as we have before intimated, rendered by *aion* when used as a noun and by *aionion*, when used as an adjective; while these *Greek* terms are rendered, in our English version of the Old Testament, by the words, "*forever*," "*everlasting*," "*never*," "*of old*," &c. They are the original Greek, in the following texts:

"For all the land which thou seest, to thee [Abraham] will I give it, and to thy seed *forever*." Gen. xiii. 15.

"And all this land that I have spoken of, I will give unto your seed, and they shall inherit it *forever*." Ex. xxii. 13.

"Surely the land whereon thy feet have trodden, shall be thine inheritence, and thy children's forever." Josh. xiv. 9.

Now suppose I take these three texts and argue thus:

1. What is to be possessed *forever*, can never be lost.

2. Abraham and his seed were to possess Canaan *forever*.

3. Therefore, they possess it still.

Thus do I *prove*, by the word of God, that the Jews can never have been, and shall never be, driven from Canaan. Do you dispute my reasoning? Well you may! But mark, it is precisely the reasoning by which you prove that the sinner shall never be delivered from punishment! So I have only to ask you, either to admit my reasoning, or to abandon your own. But let us note other instances to our purpose.

"Thou shalt take an awl and thrust it through his ear unto the door, and he shall be thy servant forever." Deut. xv. 17.

"They shall be your bondmen forever." Lev. xxv. 46.

How idle then to talk of slavery, or servitudes ever being abolished! Just so idle is it, to talk of sinners ever being delivered from punishment!

"The leprosy therefore, of Naaman shall cleave unto thee, [Gehazi,] and unto they seed forever." 2 Kings v. 27. Is Gehazi a leper still in eternity? He was to have an *aionion leprosy*, just as sinners are to have an *aionion punishment!*

"And this city [Jerusalem] shall remain forever." Jer. xvii. 25.

"God will establish it forever." Ps. xlviii. 8.

"It shall not be plucked up, nor thrown down any more forever." Jer. xxxi. 40.

Does Jerusalem still *remain unplucked up and stable?*

"It shall not be quenched night nor day; the smoke thereof shall go up *forever.*" Isa. xxxiv. 10.

This is the fire that burned up Idumea. Do you say it is still burning! Why then do not travellers give some account of it?

In Leviticus vi. 15, it is said of the fire upon the altar, "It shall *never* go out." Does it burn there still? Texts like the above, illustrating the Bible use of the terms in question, might be multiplied. But these sufficiently show that, in the Bible, as in the classics, it is used as an indefinite term, signifying "time, whether longer or shorter," duration of time with great variety.

But perhaps you will further say, it is the *New* Testament usage that we need to know. Very well. Let us turn to *that,* and ask,

Secondly, What is the usage of the term in question in the New Testament? Its usage, where it comes directly from the lips of *Jesus,* and *not* through the *Hebrew?* Is it there used with a strict reference to eternity, or *indefinitely,* as in the classics and Old Testament? In the following texts, it is the original for the word *world.* The harvest is the end of the *world.** Matt. xiii. 39.

"What shall be the sign of thy coming, and of the end of the *world?*" Matt. xxiv. 3.

"Lo I am with you always, even unto the end of the *world.*" Matt. xxviii. 20.

"And they are written for our admonition, upon whom the ends of the *world* are come." 1 Cor. x. 11.

"And now once in the end of the *world,* hath he appeared to put away sin by the sacrifice of himself." Heb. xix. 26.

Now whatever is meant by the term *aion,* (translated world, in these texts,) it means a period that *ends.* And what ends, not to say, what ended long ago, is not endless! *That's certain!*

In Matt. xii. 32, we have aion *upon* aion. "It shall not be forgiven him, neither in this *world,* neither in the *world* to come." Certainly one *eternity* never *ends* to give place to *another!* The meaning evidently is, "neither in this age or dispensation, nor the age or dispensation to come.†"

* In this and similar texts, it is certain that the word should have been translated *age* or *dispensation;* and here mark, that "the field is the *kosmos,*" while the "harvest is the end (not of the *kosmos,* but) of the *aion.*"

†Dr. Clark says on this phrase, "Though I follow the common translation, yet I am fully satisfied the meaning of the words is, neither in this dispensation, (viz., the Jewish), nor in that which is to come, viz., the Christian. *See Commentary.*

The word *aionion* is *translated,* "*ages*" in the following texts. And when used in the plural, the ages it groups, must, of course, be each *limited.* There cannot be a plurality of *eternities!*

"That in the *ages* to come, he might show the exceeding riches of his grace." Eph. ii. 7.

"Even the mystery which has been hid from *ages* and from generations." Col. i. 6.

These references sufficiently show, that the New Testament usage of the term in question differs not from that of the Old Testament, and the classics. As to the adjective *aionios,* it is applied to punishment only five times, and, strictly speaking, only four; twice by Matthew, once by Paul, and once by Jude. And in one of these instances, it is plainly used to express limited, very limited duration. For what fire it was that burned up *Sodom* and *Gomorrah* is just as obvious as is what fire burned up *Moscow,* yet it is called *aionion* fire.

We have heard David say, the "Lord is *known* by the judgments he executeth." So Jude sets forth the destruction of the cities of the plain, as a judgment by which the Lord is *known* — as an *example.** But a fire out of sight, in eternity, cannot be an *example* to *mortals.* How strange the theo-

*Even as Sodom and Gomorrah * * * * are set forth as an *example*, suffering the vengeance of eternal fire. Jude 7.

logical hallucination that should attempt to make it so.

How did *Jeremiah* understand the punishment of Sodom? He regarded it as *less* than the punishment of *Jerusalem*, while, as we have seen, for Jerusalem he intimates no punishment in the future world. Thus he cries, "For the punishment of the iniquity of the daughter of my people is greater than the punishment of the sin of Sodom, that was overthrown as in a *moment*, and no hands stayed on her." Lam. iv. 6.

How did *Peter* understand the destruction of Sodom? He says, "And turning the cities of Sodom and Gomorrah into ashes, [God] condemned them with an overthrow, making them an ensample to those that afterwards should live ungodly." 2 Peter ii. 6. This quotation from Peter is obviously parallel to that from Jude. Both speak of the punishment as an *example*, and both as by *fire*. Of course, both mean the same fire; only one calls it "*aionion* fire," and the other, the fire that turned the "cities into ashes."

But it seems idle to spend time on a point so plain as this. Barnes, who does not wholly give up the passage to Universalists, says: "It cannot be used to prove that the particular dwellers in Sodom will be punished forever;" and that, "the meaning is, that the case was one which furnished demonstration of the fact that God will punish sin; that this was an example of the punishment which God sometimes inflicts on sinners in '*this* world,"—which is all exactly to our point. But when he adds, "and a *type* of that eternal punishment which will be inflicted in the *next*," he travels completely out of the record. For there is nothing intimated about a *type*. The *type* was in his own brain, and he must needs make this reputed orthodox text its *anti*-type. If it is a type of anything spiritual, it is of *annihilation*. But all this orthodox manœuvring about this text of Jude, would be amusing, were it not lamentable! Sodom and Gomorrah were an example to which the prophets and Jesus often referred, but never as suffering in the future world. Why, we hear Jesus say, (Matt. xi. 23,) that if the mighty works which were done in Capernaum had been done in Sodom, "it would have remained until this day;" which is equivalent to making its punishment, its being swept away, (brought down to hell— *hades* — *sheol*,) as a city, without the least allusion to fire in the future world!

But enough, — too much, only that theological times are strange. The fire that burned Sodom is called *aionion* fire, and we know that that went out. And now, brother, I submit, whether we are not prepared to say from actual examination, that the Greek word *aion*, with its adjective, *aionion*, is used scripturally as well as classically, as an indefinite term, frequently expressing indefinite periods of limited duration.* *I think nothing can be plainer.*

Under the light of the preceding remarks, let us return again to our key-text, "*These shall go away into aionion punishment.*" But still we are in the dark about its meaning. We have only learned that it may mean any one of a great variety of durations, according to the subject to which it is applied. We have seen it applied to nationalities, which long ago expired; to cities, which long ago came to nought; to priesthoods which long since ended, and to fires which long since went out. We have only ascertained its general meaning, without reaching its specific meaning in our key-text. *That* meaning can be ascertained only by specific examination of the circumstances under which it is therein used. To that examination, then, let us now turn our attention. The term *aionion*, *sometimes*, (by virtue of its object,) means *endless*. Does it so mean here? You affirm — I deny; and this, for reasons among which are the following:

1. *Such a meaning of the word would seem to be forbidden by the Spirit of Him who uttered it.*

*It is said that, owing to the bituminous deposites of the vale of Sodom, it burned very long, and even tradition has made it burn for thousands of years—a tradition of no small moment in this discussion.

And we know that *his* spirit was the spirit of the *Father*. Surely, from the same immaculate lips proceed not both the prayer, "Father, forgive them," and the affirmation, "I will curse them with endless despair." As it were not like Washington, to doom prisoners taken in war to the slow fire of the most lingering torture, so, and infinitely more, it were not like Jesus to draw out the human soul in suffering to all eternity.

2. *Such a meaning seems forbidden by the substantive to which the adjective is applied.* That substantive is *kolasis*. What does it mean? I have before me, Pickering's Comprehensive Dictionary of the Greek language, published as late as 1846. And thus he defines *kolasis*, "the pruning of trees; in the New Testament, punishment, chastisement, correction; a hindrance, an obstacle; reproof, restraint, check." Of course, the noun, *kolasis*, draws its meaning from its root, which is *kolazo*, and which is thus defined; "to lop off, to check, to prune, or curtail anything." And from the same root comes *kolasma*, which is defined, a punishment, chastisement, correction," &c. The leading idea of the word *kolasis* is, then, that of pruning, correction. And I submit whether, to speak of endless *pruning* or endless *correction* of a *hopeless* soul, at the hands of the perfect God, were not *absurd* — a solecism in *idea* if not in *terms*. Certainly, the punishment which is *corrective* cannot

be *endless.* The word *kolasis* is used to express punishment, nowhere else in the New Testament. Under the definition above given, it takes the adjective, *aionion*, most naturally, as an indefinite modifier, merely expressing the fact that the punishment will continue, till its object is fully gained.* But,

3. We object to giving the *aionion* of our text its extreme meaning, *because it occurs in one of the most highly wrought figurative discourses ever uttered.* The whole of it is in the loftiest strain of Oriental imagery. Now, plainly, to take the particular words of such a discourse, and subject them to the plummet and square of prosaic, literal criticism, were simply ridiculous. As well attempt to literalize the language of Isaiah,† in describing the downfall of Babylon,—language, of which that of Jesus, in describing the downfall of the Jewish state, is, in many respects, almost a copy. So that, if *aionion*, did prosaically mean endless, it were contrary to all rules of *literalizing* figurative words, to make it mean that in this place. A word only is needed to uncloak the folly of attempting to make it do so. And so we pass on to say, further, that,

4. We object to forcing the extreme meaning upon the word in question, *because such a meaning finds no support in God's elder Scripture,*—no sup-

*The reformatory object of punishment is clearly set forth in other Scriptures, such as Ez. xiv. 10. How say some that there is no pun ishment in this life! See Jer. iv. 6; Lev. xxvi. 24-28.

† See Isaiah xiii.

port, in all which man reads, and from which he reasons, (Scripture aside,) both within and without himself. This is sufficiently seen in the numerous and cruel absurdities, involved in the doctrine of endless punishment, in part set forth in the first series of these letters. If the reader will reconsider *them*, we have no need to dwell further upon the point here. And let him all the while bear in mind that we are not arguing against giving *aionion* its *ordinary* meaning as applied to suffering, but only against *forcing* upon it, as thus applied, a meaning *unnatural* and *extreme*. But still further,

5. We object to giving the text so extreme a meaning, *because such meaning finds no support in other written Scriptures.*

We have fully seen that such a definition of the punishment which God inflicts, finds no support in the revelations of the *first four thousand* years of time. Does it in the revelations of the *last two thousand?* Of course, you will say it does, and, perhaps, quote in proof, Matt. iii. 12.

"Whose fan is in his hand, and he will thoroughly purge his floor, and gather his wheat into his garner, but he will burn up the chaff with unquenchable fire."

Let us examine this text a little carefully, inasmuch as the settlement of *its* import, must substantially settle that of several other similar ones, varying but a little with it in phraseology, and evidently the same in meaning.

And to begin, let us notice "the wrath to come," spoken of by John the Baptist, in verse 7th. What that wrath was, we have seen all along the way of "Moses and the prophets" down to the closing up of the Old Testament canon, where it is graphically set forth by Malachi. That prophet proclaimed it, as a thing to occur *in close connexion with the rising of the "Sun of Righteousness,"* that is, with the *advent of Christ.** He also mentioned it as "the great and terrible day of the Lord," of which Elias, (John the Baptist) should be the forerunner. When John the Baptist came, therefore, this woe, smiting, "wrath to come," so long the subject of prophecy, was immediately before him. And as his mission had reference to it, it was natural that he should speak of it. And, mark, he does not speak of it as a *new* revelation by him *made*, but as one of which the people had been already warned. It was, therefore, upon his lips, but the reiteration of an *old* revelation, under which many of God's ancient prophets had been bowed down. For they, many of them, had "spoken of these things." But let us hear Adam Clarke.

"'*Wrath to come!*' The desolation which was to fall on the Jewish nation for their wickedness, and threatened in the last words of their own Scriptures.

* Malachi iv. 1, 2, etc.

See Malachi iv. 6. 'Lest I come and smite the earth (את הארץ *et ha arets*,—this very land,) with a curse. This wrath or curse was coming,'" &c.

The "wrath to come," then, was an *Old Testament* threatening, announced by John, to be *executed* under the *New*. But we have seen that the Old Testament is silent about *endless* wrath.

And here let it be said, that this connexion between the closing up of the old dispensation, and the opening of the new, is exceedingly important to be well understood, and, to the unprejudiced mind, is *easily* understood. Such a mind, stepping from Malachi to the Baptist, will see that the latter makes no new revelation of woe, but is only the prophetic harbinger of one already proclaimed. But Clarke, proceeding, makes the tree, the Jewish nation, and the "axe laid at the root" of it, and the "fan," the Roman armies. From his remarks on verse 12, we quote as follows:

"*His floor.* Does not this mean the land of Judah, which had been long, as it were, the threshing-floor of the Lord? God says, he will now, by the winnowing "fan" (the Romans,) thoroughly cleanse his floor,—the wheat, those who believe in the Lord Jesus, he will gather into his garners,—either take them to heaven from the evil to come, or put them into a place of safety, by sending them to Pella, in Caelosyria, previously to the destruction of Jerusalem. But he will burn up the chaff—the disobedient and rebellious Jews, who would not come to Christ that they might have life."

So speaks Clarke, while in the presence of the immediate connexion between the Old Testament and the New. Nor could he speak otherwise, till removed from that presence, he became forgetful of it, and fell more fully under the influence of scholastic theology.

But you say, these wicked Jews, or whoever may be meant, were to be burned with "*unquenchable fire.*" Certainly, they were to be burned up with "*puri asbesto.*" And what does this mean. Clarke shall answer. On this text he says:

"'*Unquenchable fire.*' That cannot be quenched by *man.*"

The simple idea is, that the fire would do its work. The tree being, as Clarke says, the Jewish nation, the fire of judgment, spoken of, of old, would burn till it should be consumed — or whatever its fuel, it would burn till its end should be accomplished. A very clear illustration of this, is found in the Septuagint version of Ezekiel. "I will kindle a fire in thee [Judea], and it shall devour every green tree in thee, and every dry tree; the flaming flame shall not be quenched, and all faces from north to south shall be burned therein. And all flesh shall see that I the Lord have kindled it: it *shall not be quenched*, [that is, it shall be unquenchable.] Ez. xx. 47. Jeremiah uses the phrase in the same way in his prophecy, vii. 20, and xvii. 27. So also Isaiah lxvi. 23, 24.

But, brother, my limits forbid that I should dwell on all these points. The classical use of the terms now in question (*asbestos pur*) is the same as the prophetic. Eusebius, as quoted by Thayer, speaking of several Christian martyrs, says, "They were carried on camels through the city, and in this elevated position were scourged, and finally consumed or burned in unquenchable fire, (*puri asbesto*,) the very phrase employed by our Lord, and by our translators rendered by the words *unquenchable fire.* So those martyrs suffered *unquenchable* fire, but did they suffer, or rather are they *suffering*, forever! Then why the million ignorant Jews who sank down in the flames of Jerusalem! Who believes that they are still burning? Whoever he be, he should have some better proof than the Bible phrase, *unquenchable fire*, affords. For that phrase affords *no* support to the extreme meaning of *aionion*, in the key-text of our discussion.

But, perhaps, you will say, Mark speaks, not only of "the fire that shall never be quenched,"* but of fire "*where their worm dieth not.*"† He does, indeed, but what does he mean? The figure he em-

* The phrase "the fire that never shall be quenched" is in the original (Mark xi. 45,) the same as in the text we have considered, —"*pur to asbestos.*" The only real difference is in the translation.

†Mark xi. 44.

ploys was familiar to the Jews, and had its origin in the seething corruption of the valley of Hinnom—*gehenna*—(translated hell,)—a valley under the walls of Jerusalem, which received all its filth, and where, therefore, notwithstanding fires are said to have been constantly burning, worms were ever breeding in the unconsumed putrefaction. This valley is used thus figuratively by Jeremiah, to represent, fearful overwhelming judgments. So much is plain.

But never mind the origin of the language "*where their worm dieth not.*" Where did our Saviour get it? If we turn back to Isaiah lxvi. 23, 24, we read, "And it shall come to pass from one new moon to another, and from one Sabbath to another, shall all flesh come to worship before me, saith the Lord. And they shall go forth and look upon the carcasses of the men that have transgressed against me; for their worm shall not die, neither shall their fire be quenched; and they shall be an abhorring unto all flesh."

We have spoken of the importance of marking well the connexion between the Old and New Testament. The above is another of those texts which link them together, and make them mutually expound each other. Let us look at it.

1. Whatever it mean, it is past all question, that the scene of it is set in time. "New moons" and "carcasses" and "flesh," do not quadrate with our

notions of the world beyond the grave — spiritual world. So much then is *fact*. The scene is set in time.

2. The coming of all flesh to worship before God, is obviously the coming of the Gentiles, into the church, when the middle wall of partition is broken down, and the Gospel invitation is extended to all. Says this same prophet, speaking of Christ, "to him shall the *Gentiles* seek, and his rest shall be glorious."

3. The men who have transgressed, and upon whose carcasses the Gentiles look, are, plainly, the Jews, who, for their disobedience are, as a nation, miserably destroyed, by war, pestilence and famine. For in *fact*, the very atmosphere *was* defiled about Jerusalem, by their unburied carcasses, when Titus ran his plough share through it.

4. The destructive part of the scene, therefore, is just that bitter "latter end" which Moses foresaw, and upon which later prophets dwelt — that very "curse" which Malachi threatened,— that "wrath to come," of which John the Baptist was the immediate harbinger. See Jer. vii. 33 ; xix. 7, etc. Thus do we evidently get at the exact meaning of the prophet when he says, "for their worm dieth not, neither shall their fire be quenched." Jesus, addressing Jews, links the Old Testament with the New, by copying Isaiah's *words* —words familiar to the Jew,— how shall he not copy his *meaning* also.

Or in case he does not do so, how, pray, should his Jewish hearer understand him? Certainly he could not, unless Jesus explained himself, as using language in a *new sense.* But he made *no* explanation. When he quotes Isaiah, therefore, it is equivalent to saying, "*As saith the prophet Isaiah,* so I say," &c. And I am bound to interpret his meaning in the text under review, according to the known and obvious Bible-usage of the figure he employs.

Thus does neither the word "*unquenchable*" nor the phrase "*their worm shall not die,*" afford the least support to the severe interpretation of our leading text,—or even *suggest* that "*aionion*" should mean endless, when applied to punishment.

But, perhaps, you will further say that, whatever "*unquenchable*" may mean, and whatever, "*their worm shall not die*" may mean," the "*hell-fire*" with which Jesus threatened, necessarily preys upon its victims forever! So have many said, and so it is easy to say. But to say so is, simply, to beg the question, as thousands have unwittingly done before you. But we will give it a passing notice; and, as the question, *what* or *where* is hell (*gehenna,* not *hades* *) is not properly involved in a discussion

* We no where read of *hades-fire.* Hades is found in the New Testament eleven times, in ten of which it is translated *hell.* As we have before said, it is equivalent to the word *sheol,* and appropriately translated *grave,* when not used more figuratively.

In Matt. xi. 23, and xvi. 18, and in Luke x. 15, it represents the *grave-like* desolation, predicted of certain cities, and, as we hav which has reference only to the *duration* of punishment, it shall have *only* a passing one.

1. We have no instance on record of the use of the term hell, (gehenna) *outside the Bible*, to signify a place of punishment in the future world, till about one hundred and fifty years after Christ, when it appears in the language of a converted heathen philosopher, Justin Martyr. *

2. The word Gehenna, as all agree is compounded of "*ge*," and "*hinnom*," (that is, *valley of Hinnom*), and that valley, with its fire and corruption, is, in the Old Testament made a symbol of temporal calamity. Jer. vii. and xix.

shown from the highest orthodox authority, has no reference to punishment in the future world.†

In Acts ii. 27, 31, it represents the place where the soul of Jesus was — and I think nobody believes he was in the popular hell. He was only in *hades*, the grave —place of the dead.

In Revelation i. 18, and vi. 8, it is associated as the grave with death, while,

In Rev. xx. 13, it is said to deliver up the dead that are in it, and

In Rev. xx. 14, it is represented as being itself destroyed, together with death. And hence,

In 1 Cor. xv. 55, Paul shouts "O hades [translated grave] where is thy victory !" Hades is emptied completely by the resurrection. The rich man, Luke xvi. 23, can no longer be therein, *certainly!*

And these are all the instances of the use of *Hades* in the New Testament. If you ask *why* it should have been translated hell in every case, except in that of the apostolic shout, I can only answer, *The Lord knows*—I don't. The translators are gone, where they can't be questioned.

* It is now well understood that the Targums in which this word is thus used, belong to a much later age.

† See page 293.

3. Our Saviour gives us no intimation that he uses it in any new or more extended sense.

4. The first instance in which he uses it, is in a way forbidding to the idea of endless misery. See Matt. v. 22. For the difference between the offences mentioned, is not so great, that the committer of either of the two former should be merely punished temporally, stoned, perhaps, and the committer of the last, handed over into the future world to be plunged into everlasting misery. Such an idea were too absurd. Especially, while, as we have seen, the term gehenna (hell) had never before been used with such a meaning, and even endless misery itself had never before appeared among the revelations of God. If our Saviour had here meant to give it a new meaning, he would have said so.

5. The only instance of its Bible use,* in which the context clearly and explicitly lays open its meaning, obviously makes it express merely temporal miseries — the very miseries predicted by Jeremiah when he says, "And I will make void the counsel of Judah and Jerusalem in this place, and I will

* Matt. xxiii. 33. By reading right on from this text, its meaning is clearly seen, and that Jesus in weeping over Jerusalem, wept over just what the prophet Jeremiah and others foresaw. Nor does Jesus give the least intimation that he means any thing more. His language is no bolder than Isaiah uses, prophetic of the downfall of Babylon,—(which see Isaiah xiii,) and he declares that all over which he weeps shall be fulfilled *upon* (v. 36) and *during*, (xxiv. 34) that "generation." What can be more definite!

cause them to fall by the sword before their enemies, and by the hands of them that seek their lives ; and their carcasses will I give to be meat for the fowls of heaven and for the beasts of the earth. . . . And I will cause them to eat the flesh of their sons and the flesh of their daughters, and they shall eat every one the flesh of his friend in the siege and straitness, wherewith their enemies, and they that seek their lives shall straiten them." "For they shall bury in Tophet [that is, Valley of Hinnom — gehenna — hell] till there be no place." * And we know how this was literally fulfilled when Jerusalem fell, — when the Jewish state was overthrown, and the "holy people" scattered.

6. The term hell (gehenna) is not mentioned at all by John in his Gospel; nor does he make any allusion to the general tribulation of which the other Evangelists so freely speak. Why may not this silence be, for the reason that, writing *after* the ancient prophecies had been fulfilled in the destruction of the city over which Jesus wept, the special bolt of gehenna-fire (hell-fire), had already expended its force?

7. The word hell (gehenna) is not mentioned in the "Acts of the Apostles," with all its recorded sermons of the apostles, nor in all the apostolic writings, save once: and that by James, * in a way

* Jer. xix. 7, 9. vii. 32. * James iii. 6.

to make nothing for it as a place of *post mortem* punishment, but the contrary.

8. The Saviour threatens the unbelieving Jews with it but once.* Matt. xxiii. 33. In the other instances of its use he is addressing the disciples, whom he is ever guarding against being involved in the approaching ruin — "the wrath to come" — that wrath of which the prophets spake, who spake *not* of eternal wrath, — that wrath which had been so long accumulating, (verse 34), and which should come on that generation, (verse 36,) and which Jesus more fully sets forth in the chapters following, and all of which should be fulfilled before that generation should pass away, (xxiv. 34.)

9. Hell, (gehenna) is no where mentioned in connexion with the resurrection of the dead, or as among its consequences. How significant!

The above are among the considerations which perfectly satisfy me, that our Saviour did not use the word gehenna (hell), to express a place of endless misery. Certainly, it would seem that his disciples could not have so understood him, seeing that they make no use of the term, (save in the solitary instance mentioned), in all their writings and recorded discourses. For how could *such* a word, conveying *such* a sense, have been so *soon* and *easily* forgotten by them? Were they re-

* The Gentiles are *never* threatened with it—a very significant fact.

creant? And if they were not recreant in their neglect to use that word, it may well be asked, by what authority it so interlards modern sermons?—by what authority are pulpits now so *un*apostolic?* But I must hasten away from this point, with the single remark that we still find nothing to support the terrific meaning which the church has given to the *aionion* punishment of our key-text.

But, perhaps, you will say, "the Scriptures read that, '*he that believeth not shall be damned.*' And to be damned means to be forever miserable." To this, it is only necessary to say that the word here translated damned, is the same that is translated condemned in Matt. xx. 18, "and they shall *condemn* him [Jesus] to death." Also in John viii. 10, "hath no man *condemned* thee, . . . neither do I *condemn* thee." Also in Romans ii. 1, "thou *condemnest* thyself." Also in Mark xiv. 64,—"and they condemned him to be guilty of death." Now, would it alter the meaning of these Scriptures, to substitute the word *damned* for the word condemned? Certainly not. And so also, the saying, "he that believeth not shall be damned," means only what it would have meant if the word *katakrithesetai*, (translated damned) had been translated *con-*

* And here it may be said that in all the sermons of Peter, Paul and Stephen, and others, recorded by Luke in The Acts of the Apostles, *no language is used which is capable of being* TORTURED *into an equivalent to this word hell as popularly construed.* Read and see.

demned as elsewhere. Its true meaning is, indeed, important. But it is the mere form of its translation that invests it with such *boundless* terror. To be damned then, is the same as to be condemned. And this condemnation may be to suffer little or much. There is nothing in the word to indicate which. *

Do you say, the Bible asks, "For what is a man profited if he shall gain the whole world and lose his own soul?" And certainly it does. And to dispose of this matter in a word, let us quote with the word *psyken* (soul) untranslated; thus—"For whosoever will save his *psyken* shall lose it, and whosoever will lose his *psyken* for my sake, shall find it. For what shall a man be profited, if he shall gain the whole world and lose his own *psyken?* or what shall a man give in exchange for his *pyskes*. Matt. xvi. 25, 26. Now, plainly, whatever this Greek word means in any *one* of these places, it means in the *others*. But I will leave this matter with Dr. Clarke, who frankly and truly says,

"'*Lose his own soul.*' Or, lose his life, την ψῦχην αυτου. On what authority many have translated the word ψυχη, in the twenty-fifth verse, *life*, and in this verse, *soul*, I know not; but am certain it means *life* in both places. If a man should gain the whole world, its riches, honors and pleasures,

* The words damnation and condemnation following the same aw, to them also the above remarks are applicable.

and lose his *life*, what would all that profit him, seeing they can only be enjoyed during *life?*" So Clarke; and the seminary school boy is to be pitied, who cannot see the justness of his criticism.

Am I pointed to the parable of the rich man and Lazarus? Then I have to say that it is doubtless a highly wrought allegorical representation of the wretchedness of the Jewish Nation, as the fulness of the Gentiles should be coming in. But be it what it may, one thing is clear, the misery it involves is that of which Moses and the prophets spake. For when the rich man in hell (*hades**—*sheol*—*not* gehenna) would send to his brethren from the dead, lest they come to that place of torment, the answer given by Abraham is, "they have Moses, and the prophets, let them hear them." And this is certainly equivalent to saying that Moses and the prophets wrote about that dreadful place. For, otherwise, why should the brethren of the rich man be referred to *them for admonition against coming into it*. But, as we have seen, Moses and the prophets make not the least allusion to a place of punishment, not to say of endless punishment, in the future world. The argument then may stand thus,

1. The miseries of the rich man are spoken of by Moses and the prophets.

* See note on page 340. See also towards close of letter.

2. Moses and the prophets speak only of temporal miseries.

3. Therefore, the miseries of the rich man must have been temporal.

I see not how any one can call in question either the soundness of the premises of this syllogism, or the justness of its conclusion. And, therefore, I am not surprised at the remark of a late and able clergyman,* of acknowledged evangelical faith: "When I would prove endless punishment, I do not go to the parable of the rich man and Lazarus.

But perhaps you will quote the text, — "Whither I go ye cannot come," as supporting the notion that *aionion* should be translated extremely —a text which is, by many, deemed the Malakoff of anti-Universalism. Let us briefly consider it, with the three following passages in which it occurs, before our eyes.

"Then said Jesus unto them, Yet a little while am I with you, and *then* I go unto him that sent me.

"Ye shall seek me, and shall not find *me*: and where I am *thither* ye cannot come." John vii. 33, 34.

"Then said Jesus again unto them, I go my way, and ye shall seek me, and shall die in your sins; whither I go ye cannot come."† John viii. 21.

"Little children, yet a little while I am with you. Ye shall seek me: and, as I said unto the Jews, Whither I go ye cannot come. so now I say to you." John xiii. 33.

* Rev. Martin Cheney.

† The two propositions, "*Ye shall die in your sins*," and "Whither I go ye cannot come," stand perfectly distinct in the record. Not, *if* ye shall die, &c. Mark well!

The second of these texts is but a substantial repetition of the first, as the evangelist would have us understand from the use of the word "*again.*" Do they teach the endless exclusion of the Jews from the Saviour's presence in heaven? I think not for a number of reasons, among which are the following:

1. Because the seeking mentioned, obviously has no reference to individual, spiritual salvation—salvation in the future world. Our limits forbid that we should more than hear *Barnes* on this point. And he, being purely Orthodox, his testimony is sufficient. On John vii. 34, he says: "The meaning is, where I shall be, you will not be able to come; that is, the Messiah would be in heaven, and though they would earnestly desire his presence and aid, to *save their city and nation from the Romans*, yet they would not be able to obtain it, represented here, by their not being able to come to him. This does *not refer to their individual salvation*, but to the deliverance of their nation. It is not true of individual sinners that they seek Christ in a proper manner, and are not able to find him. But it was true of the Jewish nation that they looked for the Messiah, and sought his coming to deliver them, but he did not do it." So *Barnes*, and, substantially, so *Clarke* and *Bloomfield*. And surely, such testimony, coming from men of such depth of theological

research, and wealth of erudition, and critical exactness, and withal, so purely Orthodox, is not easily set aside, especially when so plainly just and true. But,

2. I object to the popular view of the text in question, because no such impression was left upon the minds of the Jews to whom it was addressed, as that view would be likely to produce. It only made them ask, "Whither will he go, that we shall not find him? Will he go to the dispersed among the Gentiles, and teach the Gentiles?" John vii. 35.

Now we submit, whether, if Jesus had intended by these texts, to teach the doctrine of endless woe, he would not have made his hearers, who were so in danger of sinking into it, understand *something* about it. But he does not make them even *suspect* any reference to scenes beyond time. True, indeed, he did not always make himself *immediately* understood. But in a matter of such awful and decisive importance, as endless weal and woe, dependent on a moment, we cannot believe that he would speak in clueless enigmas. The meaning of a dark parable spoken to-day, he might clear up to-morrow. But that he should speak dark parables and blind words to the Jews, to be understood by them, only when, in some far-off region of eternity, where there is, "to pain no pause, to guilt no plea," were too much to believe of him, as the lovable and sympathetic Son of God. But,

3. I object to the popular view of the first two of these texts, because, to adopt it, were *to make all the promises of God of no effect.* Let us carefully look at the three texts recorded by John. Of these, the first two are, as we have said, parallel; the second being connected with the first by the word "*again,*" and so evidently meaning the same things, that Dr. Clarke makes his comment on the one answer for both. And *both, you* say, mean that the Jews can never enter heaven. Perhaps our Lord foreknew that you would say so, and, *therefore,* gave us the third, which I requote;—"Little children, yet a little while I am with you. Ye shall seek me, and as I said unto the Jews, whither I go ye cannot come; so now I say unto you." And here mark,

First, That Jesus, lest he should be misapprehended when addressing his disciples, quotes the exact words which they had heard him address to the Jews—"*Whither I go ye cannot come.*" And,

Second, Mark the "*as,*" and "*so.*" "AS I said unto the Jews, SO I say unto you;" that is, I use towards you, the same words, with the same signification. Surely, nothing can be more definite — nothing in logic can approach nearer to the absolute exactness of mathematical demonstration.

Now do you say that the words, "whither I go ye cannot come," when addressed to the *Jews,* signify *their* final exclusion from Heaven? Then you must also say that the same words, addressed to the *disciples*, signify *their* final exclusion from heaven. For, as we have seen, "*as*" the Saviour addressed those words to the one, "*so*" he addressed them to the other. The sword you plate is double-edged, cutting both ways. It visits the good and the bad,—those who sought Christ's life, and those who sought his salvation,—with a common doom. To both, it says, "*Whither I go ye cannot come.*" But you say, "the disciples would go to Heaven;—I do not *mean* to exclude *them.*" I know you do not. But the mischief is that you cannot help it, so long as you cling to your chosen exposition of the texts in review! Your argument is good for the endless destruction of *all*, or else it is good for *nothing*. You must either abandon it, in a complete *reductio ad absurdum*, or else abandon all hope for your race,—not excepting the very body disciples of Jesus himself! Such are your alternatives.

Or, if, struggling in the meshes of logical difficulty, you shall say, "there are *other* Scriptures which show that the true disciples would be saved," you thereby admit what is fatal to your cause—that is, you admit that there is nothing in *this text forbidding* their salvation. And if there is nothing in this text forbidding the *disciples'* salvation, then, there can be nothing in the former two texts, forbidding the salvation of the *Jews*. And so, what you impliedly admit, is all that our argument requires. That third text so clearly interpreting the first two, enables us to conclude this argument in a moral certainty. Jesus knew that that text would be needed, and gave it. Let us be grateful to Him for it.

Do you ask what these texts *do* mean? I answer, (though not necessary to the argument) they mean that, in the coming calamities, of which we have heard Barnes speak, Jesus would be alike personally absent, both from the Jews and from his disciples, without reference to any relation which they should sustain to him, in the vast ages of Eternity. And thus, even these texts, deemed so formidable to Universalism, are the farthest from affording support to the notion that an extreme sense should be forced upon *aionion* when applied to the punishment of mortals.

But we cannot dwell longer upon this fifth proposition. What we have said, far from being exhaustive, may, however, well suffice, upon the principle that the greater contains the less — the greater difficulties being removed, the smaller, involved in *the greater*, take the same way. We pass then, to say,

6. That the popular exposition of *aionion* pun-

ishment, is not only *unsupported* by other Scriptures, but *forbidden* by them.* And,

First, forbidden, indirectly, by those Scriptures which set forth the attributes of God. These attributes constitute a perfectly harmonious family, with *Love* at its head. Justice and mercy have, therein, no quarrel. Jehovah cannot do an *unmerciful* thing because he is *just*, even as he cannot do an

* It may be said that if *aionion* does not mean endless when applied to *punishment*, it does not when applied to "*life.*" And so, as the Jews have been driven out of Canaan, the Saints may yet be driven out of heaven. Or that, if sinners get out of hell in spite of *aionion*, so may also saints get out of heaven in spite of it. To this we have to say,

1. That we cannot help the consequences of a fair, honest exposition of *aionion*. Whatever be the effect on the Christian's heaven, we cannot put the Jews back into Canaan, or restore the ancient glory of Jerusalem, or show that the fires of Idumea, Judea, and Sodom are still burning. Nor can we, even to save *heaven itself*, alter the classical or Bible-usage of the original Greek. Facts are facts. We cannot ignore them. Nor can any *heaven*, built up upon their ruins, be more substantial than castles in the air. But I remark,

2. That *aionion* being an indefinite term, and as such, of course, not marking anything like specific duration, as *just* so many months, years, &c., but dependent for its signification upon the subject to which it is applied, and the circumstances under which it is used, may well mean differently, when applied to a punishment which, as we have seen, the attributes of God naturally limit, from what it does, when applied to benefits, which, it would seem quite natural that the being *possessed* of those attributes, should everlastingly bestow upon his intelligent, accountable, progressive offspring. So that any limitation of *aionion*, as applied to *punishment*, by no

unjust thing, because he is *merciful.* There is no truth, therefore, in the couplet,

> "Thy justice might have struck me dead,
> But mercy held thine arm."

Does mercy hold back God from being *just?* Then does it make him unjust! Or does Justice hold back God from being merciful? Then does it make him unmerciful! But no, all the Divine attributes are in harmony, ever acquitting or condemning by unanimity. The voice of one is the voice of all. And now, if we question *Justice* about endless punishment, what is the response?

Jehovah implanted in man an idea of Justice, which man can no more alienate, than he can alienate

means necessarily belongs to it, as applied to blessing, but rather the contrary. However,

3. It is indeed true, that if our *only* hope of immortal life rested upon the word in review, we should feel that it was *liable* to fail. How could we then avoid some suspicion, whether, as the Jews were scattered from their *aionion* Canaan, two thousand years ago, so we *might* yet be scattered from our *aionion* heaven. If in God's covenant with *them*, it meant limited duration, why not in his covenant with *us*. And thus, though, as we have said, *there are strong reasons for construing* this indefinite term, when applied to the *blessing* of a God of infinite goodness, as we should *not*, when applied to his *cursing*, still, it were of itself but an imperfect support for our hope of endless life. But,

4. There are other Scriptures which either by themselves, or in combination with the revealed character of God, and man's instinct of endless existence, put the fact of that existence for man, beyond all question.

his consciousness of his own existence. And, under that idea, he *feels* that, if Justice means *anything*, it means *some* proportion between crime and punishment. But endless punishment recognizes no such proportion. It is therefore unjust, and because unjust, not of God. Justice sets bounds to the punishment of limited transgression, which no presumption can overleap, no councils vote away. And so does every other moral attribute of Jehovah.

To set this matter in a clearer and more practical light, let us further say, that, if, from Jehovah's character, *anything* is inferrible, as to what he will or will not do, then, is it obviously inferrible, that he will not punish his own tempted children forever. Or, if such punishment *is* consistent with his attributes, *then*, who can conceive what would *not be*. *Then*, we may never say, "the Lord is *good*, or *just*, and *therefore*, he will, or will not, do this or that; — *then* do we find in his *character*, no ground of hope; — *then* have we lost our Father! This is a point on which we will not dwell, as it was incidentally considered in the first series of these letters, and, especially in those of them devoted to exposing absurdities. And yet, we wish to add that,

The only ground on which endless punishment can be justified to reason, is the ground that *a single sin deserves it*. For, if a single sin does not deserve it, no conceivable number can. For no finite number bears *any* relation to infinite duration, which is not borne by a single unit. This is seen and confessed by the more consistent and hardier theologians of the orthodox school, such as Woods and Finney.

Dr. Woods says, "We hold that sin, wherever found, and whether continued for a longer or shorter time — that *sin itself*, is so great an evil, that it does, according to God's holy law, deprive the sinner of all good, and plunge him into a state of endless misery." And again, "sin, here committed, even one sin, has such hatefulness, malignity, and destructiveness, that it does justly bring the sinner into a state of never ending perdition." * And yet again he says, "the justice of that penal consequence of sin [endless punishment] which is set forth in the Scripture, results, essentially from the intrinsic evil of sin." So the Doctor, and so we have it, that the most trifling single sin, committed under the most trifling circumstances, possesses in *itself* the *essence* of endless damnation,— so that every child, of just a few years, even though born in heathenism, has already secreted in his young heart, the moral virus, the quintescence, the black bile of a *thousand* endless damnations! Now I will not say that this is a damnable heresy! But I will say, that, if it is *not*, then, reason is a dolt, con-

* Woods' Works, vol. iii. p. 288, 291.

sciousness a lie, and the doctrine of a Good God, a myth!

But as Woods, so Finney, who says, "one breach of the precept always incurs the penalty of the law, whatever that penalty is;"—and he holds it to be endless woe. Nor is this all; for, arguing his point in a way, practically to illustrate the infinite divisibility of propositions, his metaphysics eke out the conclusion that they "who deny endless punishment, *manifestly consider the guilt of sin as a mere trifle*," "that sin *deserves* endless punishment, just as much as it deserves *any* punishment;" and, finally, that a threatening of limited punishment would "be, after all, *offering a reward for sin*." *

What a *descending* climax is here! capable of being reached only by Finney's accustomed infinite series of propositions; and, when reached, a most miserable absurdity, and every step towards it, an absurdity! To punish an offender for only *years*, though reckoned by *billions*, "offering a reward for sin!!! † But such are the insanities of even wise and good men, long bewildered in the maze of speculative theology. It is not strange that men thus bewildered, should see eternity in the *aionion* of the punishment of sin.

* Systematic Theology, p. 215, 317.

† I would not be satirical. But if Juvenal were here, would not Finney afford him a worthy subject? Yes, even Finney, the excellent, in spite of all his excellences.

Another word seems to be needed here. For if anything is plain, it is that the Bible character of Jehovah forbids that he inflict a useless, and because useless, vindictive punishment. But endless punishment is thus useless.

1. It must be useless to the *sufferer*. That he should profit from his sufferings, is forbidden by the very nature of his sentence. All "*afterwards*" for reformation is thereby denied him; and this, equally, whether his anguish is made endless by direct judicial decision, or by the withdrawal from him, of all means of grace. To him, only, remains the fatal alternative of hardening himself in sorrow, saying, "evil, be thou my good," to all eternity. Eternal suffering, then, must be useless to the sufferer, and, in reference to him, therefore, its infliction can be underlaid with no benevolent intent.* And,

2. It must be worse than useless to others. If a portion of our race are to lie forever under suffering, that suffering must be either known or unknown to the saved. If *unknown*, it can be of no benefit to them. It will then be to them, only as though it were not, and therefore, so far as they are concerned, might as well not be; whereas, if *known* to them, it must be to them, worse than useless. This seems quite obvious. And yet Orthodoxy has attempted to conceive the contrary.

*Not so, *temporal* punishment. See Letter xxv.

Professor Stuart says, "That the blessed in heaven have some cognizance of the wicked and their sufferings, seems to be plainly disclosed in Luke xvi. 26." The only use, however, which he finds for this, is to aggravate the sufferings of the *lost.* With regard to the *saved*, he finds some difficulty, arising from their proximity to hell, but concludes, as we have seen,* that Heaven in mercy, may either extinguish their "social susceptibilities," "or so overwhelm them with a sense of the Divine goodness, that they will not be disturbed by sights and sounds of woe—woe, which the Professor likens to a perpetual death-agony. For he says, (as quoted by Barnes, on Rev. xx. 14.) The "second death differs from the first, in the fact that it is not a separation of the soul and body, but a state of *continual agony* like that which the first death inflicts—like that in intensity, but not in kind." Well may the social susceptibilities of saints who are to witness it forever, be forever extinguished.

So Stuart. Not so the excellent Dr. Hopkins, who figured so largely in New England orthodoxy, a little longer ago. He is very bold, and says of the lost, (as quoted by C. F. Hudson,) "The smoke of their torment shall ascend up in the sight of the blessed forever and ever, and serve as a most clear glass, always before their eyes, to give them a

* Letter xxii.

constant, bright, and most affecting view. . . . This display of the Divine glory will be in favor of the redeemed, and most entertaining, and give the highest pleasure to those who love God, and raise their happiness to ineffable heights." Should this eternal punishment "cease, and this fire be extinguished, it would in a great measure obscure the light of heaven, and put an end to a great part of the happiness and glory of the blessed."

This is, indeed finding a use for endless punishment with a vengeance. But as nothing is made in vain, and this seems its only *possible* use, the doctor was consistent in thus appropriating it. And we have a sort of respect for that sternness of Calvinism which shrunk not before so terrible a necessity. But what a horrid conception! Saints in the galleries of heaven, so petrified into savageness, that they can draw sweet satisfaction from looking down upon the endless suffering of their *friends* in hell! Such is Hopkinsianism, a natural wild of so-called Orthodoxy, from which we hasten away, and proceed to say,

3. That, as endless punishment is of necessity, worse than useless to both the lost and the saved, (saying nothing of angels,) it must be *vindictive*, or something as bad; that is, God must inflict it, if at all, merely because he finds pleasure in seeing his creatures suffer forever. For no other conceivable

reason can he keep sinners *alive* in endless suffering. And can all this be true of an Infinite Being, whose attributes all blend into perfect *Love*, as all the colors of the rainbow blend into the purest white? No! God's *character* forbids that he punish vindictively—that he draw out a useless punishment forever. And so we come again to the conclusion that the *aionion* punishment of the Bible is not endless. But we hasten to say,

Secondly, What is worthy to stand in a distinct proposition, though the spirit of it is involved above,—that endless punishment is forbidden by all that class of Scriptures which speak of man's being rewarded "according to his works;" for, *certainly*, his *works* are *limited*, and,

Third, By the spirit of such parables as that of the "*Prodigal Son*," the "*Pieces of Silver*," and the "*Lost Sheep*." The woman sweeps till she finds her lost piece of silver, the shepherd goes "into the mountains" till he finds his lost sheep, and the results of sin work the reformation of the prodigal, whom his father welcomes back again to his heart of undying love. And,

Fourth, Endless punishment is forbidden by all that class of Scriptures to which belong the words of our Lord,

"Ye have heard that it hath been said, Thou shalt love thy neighbor and hate thine enemy:

"But I say unto you, Love your enemies, bless them that curse you, do good to them that hate you, and pray for them which despitefully use you and persecute you;

"That ye may be the children of your Father which is in heaven: for he maketh his sun to rise on the evil and on the good, and sendeth rain on the just and on the unjust.

"For if ye love them which love you, what reward have ye? do not even the publicans the same?

"And if ye salute your brethren only, what do you more *than others?* do not even the publicans so?

"Be ye therefore perfect, even as your Father which is in heaven is perfect." Matt. v. 43–48.

Now, if we are like God when we love *our* enemies, then he loves *his.* And certainly, if he loves his enemies, as he surely does, the punishing them to all eternity, — inflicting upon them an eternally *useless* punishment,—were, certainly, a queer way of showing it. Moreover, if he loves his *enemies at all*, as he is unchangeable, he must *always* love them, Or, if he ceases to love *his* enemies, then, just in proportion as we are brought into his likeness, we shall cease to love *ours.* But no; "his tender mercies are over *all* his works"—that is, his works, in all worlds, and in all duration. And so it comes to be true, that he "will not cast off forever; but though he cause grief, yet will he have compassion, according to the multitude of his mercies." Lam. iii. 31, 32. That I, [Jehovah] "will not contend forever, neither will I be always wroth! for the spirits should fail before me, and the souls which

I have made." Isaiah lvii. 16. How tenderly does Jehovah here speak. "*The souls which I have made!!*" As much as to say, "*Impossible that I should punish my own dear offspring forever!*" And so does it seem impossible that the *aionion* of our key text should mean *endless.*

And here let it be remarked, that this *indirect* argument, going down, as it does, into the deeps of the Divine *character*, is fundamental, affording the only true key to what would, otherwise, be the dead locks of textual difficulty. The character of God is, to the details of his government, what our *Declaration of Independence* would be, to the details of ours, were we true to its spirit. But,

Fifth. Such a construction of *aionion* is indirectly forbidden by the garden promise that, "the seed of the woman shall 'bruise' the serpent's 'head.'" Gen. iii. 15.

The serpent is the devil. Christ the seed. And Paul tells us, (Heb. ii. 14,) that Christ's mission to this world was, "that, through death, he might destroy him that had the power of death, that is, the devil." And now, where can any death reign, when he who has the power of it is destroyed?

And, too, all moral evils are represented as the *works* of the devil. Where then, can all these be, when their Satanic *author* is destroyed? Will there be other Satans raised up to take them in charge, or will the Father, who destroys the *devil*, carefully protect and perpetuate his *works of misery?*

On the text, "thou shalt bruise his head," the orthodox Henry well says, "He [Christ] shall bruise his head; that is, give a total overthrow to his kingdom and interest." But no, says our objector, The seed of the woman shall only bruise the serpent's *tail*. The serpent shall triumphantly live and reign forever in hell, over the masses of adult humanity, while the seed of the woman — *Jesus* — shall find his enterprise of salvation, relatively to the devil's success, a most splendid failure! But we know the contrary, for the prophet assures us, that Jesus shall "see of the travail of his soul and be satisfied." * And surely he can never be satisfied, while millions, nay, while a *single soul*, for whom he spilt his blood, is in sin and misery. But

Sixth, So dreadful a meaning for the *aionion* of our key-text, is forbidden by those Scriptures which set forth the *comprehensiveness* of God's saving *purpose*. And what is that purpose? Paul shall answer. "Having made known unto us the mystery of his will, according to his good pleasure which he hath purposed in himself, that in the dispensation of times, he might gather together in one, all things in Christ, both which are in heaven and which are on

*Isaiah liii. 11.

earth, even in him." Eph. i. 9, 10. And what is intended by this universal gathering, can hardly be mistaken, after hearing the same apostle say to the Colossians, "For it pleased the Father that in him should all fulness dwell; And having made peace by the blood of his cross, by him to reconcile all things unto himself: by him, I say, whether they be things on earth, or things in heaven." Col. i. 19, 20. If we turn to Phillipians ii. 5-8, we find the same general sentiment expressed.

And now, when it is understood that these several texts are but a sort of formal statement of the radical design of the Father, in sending his Son into the world, how plain it seems that, in the "dispensation of the fullness of times," no soul shall be left ungathered, unreconciled, unsubmissive, and that, therefore, *aionion* punishment must have an end. And further,

Seventh. According to Jehovah's *purpose*, is his *plan for accomplishing it.* For he makes the sacrifice of his Son a propitiation "for the sins of the *whole world.*" 1 John ii. 2. And again, "we have seen and do testify, that he sent the Son to be the Saviour of the world." Surely Jesus is not the Saviour of those whom he does not save. And again, "For there is one God and one Mediator between God and men, the man Christ Jesus, who gave himself a ransom for all *to be testified in due time.*" 1 Tim. ii. 6. And *how* testified? Evidently *practically*. For it had been *theoretically* testified already, by the apostles. In due time, or, as Paul has it elsewhere, in "the dispensation of the fulness of times," that Christ *died* for all, would be testified by the actual *salvation* of all. And all of this is in perfect keeping with the words of the same apostle, when he says, "But where sin abounded grace did much more abound, that as sin hath reigned unto death, even so might grace reign, through righteousness unto eternal life, by Jesus Christ our Lord." Rom. v. 20, 21. And so shall the promise made to Abraham be fulfilled, that in his seed, all the families of the earth should be blest. So shall Jesus "draw all men" to himself, even as the Father "will have all men to be saved and come to [or by coming to] the knowledge of the truth."

Eighth. And thus is it just in keeping with the Father's purpose, and the comprehensiveness of his Son's mission, that the latter should reign till all "things shall be subdued unto him." "For he must reign till he hath put all enemies under his feet. The last enemy, death, shall be destroyed. For he hath put all things under his feet. But when he saith all things are put under him, it is manifest that he is excepted that did put all things under him. And when all things shall be subdued unto him, then shall the Son, also, himself be subject unto him that put all things under him, that God may be all in all." (1 Cor. xv. 25–28.) And here mark, that the very same word, *hupotasso*, which is in the 27th verse rendered by "*put under*," and in the 28th by "*subdued unto*," as expressing the subjection of all to Christ, is used in the 28th verse, and there rendered by the words "*be subject to*," as expressing the subjection of Christ to the Father; thus showing, as clearly as language can, that the subjection of all to Christ is of the same nature as that of Christ to the Father,—that is, *voluntary*. And, indeed, in no other sense can God's creatures ever be more subject to him than they now are, have always been, and must necessarily ever be. They are as much shut up by his power *now*, as they would be if swept into a flaming subterranean prison, and the gate barred down upon them forever. And is *such* the victory of the gospel? Are such the *spoils* of the *Redeemer's war*? Nay, were not such, rather the victory of that very devil, whom Jesus came into the world to *destroy?* But not thus does the Gospel subjugate sinners. Such a subjugation of them could bring no glory to Jesus. But,

Ninth. The hitherto popular view of the duration of *aionion* punishment, seems forbidden by the exultation of the Apostle Paul. That great Apostle as, turning away to the Gentiles, he contemplated the sin, the wretchedness, and the approaching calamities of the Jewish nation, had "great heaviness and continual sorrow of heart." So we find him in the opening of the ninth chapter to the Romans. But as he reasons his way along the ninth, tenth, and eleventh chapters, his sorrow is gradually turned into joy. For thus he soars in his conclusion:

"For I would not, brethren, that ye should be ignorant of this mystery, (lest ye should be wise in your conceits,) that blindness in part is happened to Israel, until the fulness of the Gentiles be come in.

"And so all Israel shall be saved: as it is written, There shall come out of Sion the Deliverer, and shall turn away ungodliness from Jacob:

"For this is my covenant unto them, when I shall take away their sins.

"As concerning the gospel, they are enemies for your sakes: but as touching the election, they are beloved for the fathers' sakes.

"For the gifts and calling of God are without repentance.

"For as ye in times past have not believed God, yet have now obtained mercy through their unbelief;

"Even so have these also now not believed, that through your mercy they also may obtain mercy.

"For God hath concluded them all in unbelief, that he might have mercy upon all.

"O the depth of the riches both of the wisdom and knowledge of God! how unsearchable are his judgments, and his ways past finding out!

"For who hath known the mind of the Lord? or who hath been his counsellor?

"Or who hath first given to him, and it shall be recompensed unto him again?

"For of him, and through him, and to him, are all things: to whom be glory for ever. Amen." *Rom.* xi. 25—36.

And what mean these exultant words of him who,

just now, was so heavy-hearted. Why, he had been looking, chiefly, upon the *darkness of the present;* he has now come to contemplate the *brightness of the distant future.* He had been thinking of Israel *lost*, and was sad. But now his inspired reasoning, culminating in, "*So all Israel shall be saved,*" he emerges from his sadness, and his exultation knows no bounds. "O, THE DEPTH OF THE RICHES!!" &c.

Turn to the fifteenth of first Corinthians. There, again, we find him filled with exultation,—and that, too, just at the time when, had he believed in the since popular doctrine of endless woe, it must have most painfully weighed down his spirits. For he is there expounding the "*resurrection of the dead*"—of all the dead. The question he raises is, simply—"*How are the dead raised up?*" In Christ, he assures us, *all shall be made alive,*" and proceeds to notice *how.* And here, without touching any nice points about the *resurrection*, it is enough to say, that Paul contemplates, in his description of it, certain final results; and that these are such as fill him with unmingled exultation. For thus he concludes his exposition:

"Behold, I show you a mystery: We shall not all sleep, but we shall all be changed.

"In a moment, in the twinkling of an eye, at the last trump: for the trumpet shall sound, and the dead shall be raised incorruptible, and we shall be changed.

"For this corruptible must put on incorruption, and this mortal must put on immortality.

"So when this corruptible shall have put on incorruption, and this mortal shall have put on immortality, then shall be brought to pass the saying that is written, Death is swallowed up in victory.

"O death, where is thy sting? O grave, where is thy victory?

"The sting of death is sin; and the strength of sin is the law.

"But thanks be to God, which giveth us the victory through our Lord Jesus Christ.

"Therefore, my beloved brethren, be ye steadfast, unmoveable, always abounding in the work of the Lord, forasmuch as ye know that your labor is not in vain in the Lord."—1 *Cor.* xv. 51–58.

Now, I ask, what means this resurrection shout of the apostle, if he believed that all who had died unfit for heaven,—and among them, of course, the masses of his Jewish brethren, must, at the sound of the "trump," come up out of gloomy *hades*, receive their sentence, and go down with weeping and wailing, into fiery *gehenna*, for safer and severer keeping, forever! Ought he not, *then*, rather to be filled with his "great heaviness and continual sorrow of heart?" But no; the eye of the apostle is now upon *ultimate results.* He now sees that, though "the creature," (Rom. viii.) or rather *creation*, "is made subject to vanity, not willingly, but by reason of him who hath subjected the same in hope." Yet, it "shall be delivered from the bondage of corruption into the glorious liberty of the children of God." Carried forward into eternity, and viewing all things from the height of the immortal resurrection, he sees *no gehenna*, nothing to *deplore*, nothing to *damp his spirits*; but filled with necessary rapture, his exultation *again* knows no bound! Then, though contemplating the worst for his nation and race, he can well exclaim, "through the thick gloom of the present, I behold the brightness of the future, as the sun in the heavens!"

We have seen Stuart suppose that social susceptibilities shall be extinguished in heaven, to prevent the songs of the redeemed from being interrupted by sights and sounds of woe. But no one supposes those most Christian attributes to be extinguished in *this* world, that men should look without sad emotion, and even with *jubilant exultation*, upon the prospective endless pain of the "bone of their bone, and flesh of their flesh." The soul of Paul had not been thus blighted *yet*—he was *yet* capable of *sympathetic "sorrow" and "heaviness of heart."*

How then, I again ask, could he exult over the resurrection, if the masses of adult humanity, awakened by the Archangel's trump, were to be cursed out of the grave (hades) into endless woe! How then, as the heart of affection throbbed his breast, and as he had well learned the lesson of loving his enemies, must he not have rather exclaimed, "*Lord, rather let us all be annihilated together!!!*"

The rich man in the parable is represented as being in *hades* (hell,) and now Paul sings complete victory over (hades) hell. For he exclaims, "O grave," (original, "hades")—"O grave"—or, to translate as the word *hades* is translated in every other place in the New Testament—"O *hell*, where is thy victory!" Hell, (hades—*the grave*) is conquered, *emptied!* all have come up from it,—"*raised in glory*." In the language of Dr. Clarke in another connexion:—"The salvation from sin here, is as extensive and complete as the guilt and condemnation of sin. Death is conquered, hell disappointed, the Devil confounded, and sin totally destroyed! Here is glorying, *to Him that loved us and washed us from our sins in his own blood, and has made us kings and priests to God and the Father, to glory and dominion forever and ever—Amen!* HALLELUJAH! THE LORD GOD OMNIPOTENT REIGNETH! AMEN AND AMEN."* So Clark and so we.

It was with Paul, not altogether unlike as with other Christians. In the midst of strife, and sur-

*Com. on Rom. v. 21.

rounded by clouds and darkness, the glories of the far distant future, were not always present to his mind. But when, enraptured with *ultimate results*, as seen through the golden vista of the resurrection, these glories *are present* to his mind, *then*, sin, death, and hell are *absent*, and he exclaims, "O THE DEPTH OF THE RICHES!!" And this, his exultation, forbids the idea that he regarded the punishment of sin as *endless*. And if not *he*, then certainly not *we*. And our key text must be expounded accordingly.

Thus have we shown in this long letter,

1. That according to both classical and Bible usage, it is perfectly fitting to apply the word *aionion* to punishment of limited duration, and that, therefore, its specific meaning must be determined by an examination of its specific use. And,

2. We have shown that to make it mean *endless*, in Matt. xxv. 46, were to commit violence upon it.

1. Because such definition is forbidden by the spirit of him who uttered it.

2. Because forbidden by the substantive to which it is applied.

3. Because used in highly wrought figure.

4. Because forbidden by Jehovah's elder Scriptures.

5. Because such an extreme definition of the

term finds no support from *other* written Scriptures. (Under this head, we have examined the texts supposed most formidable to Universalism.)

6. Because *forbidden* by other Scriptures. (Under this head, we have examined some of the Scriptures which, either directly, or by implication, prove the contrary, that, is prove Universalism.)

7. Because inconsistent with the exultation, and, especially, the *resurrection*-exultation, of the Apostle Paul.

Our attempt at brevity *and* comprehensiveness, has, of course, left many things unsaid. No doubt you will find difficulties unsolved, and even unnoticed. But you do well to bear in mind, that that system of doctrine which presents *no* unsolved difficulties, even its most ardent abettors being judge, has hitherto found no place among men. Nor should you forget that the doctrine, over against which, the doctrine of these letters is set, not only involves difficulties unsolved, but also so great, so numerous, and so increasing with the increase of light, that, as we have seen in the opening of this letter, it can be received only upon evidence, the most *positive* and *absolute.*

And now, I submit to you, brother, whether such evidence for it is not *absolutely wanting;* and whether the argument we have indirectly presented for the ultimate well-being of the whole human family, does not seem, even to *you*, to afford strong ground for so glorious a hope. And, bearing in mind that the letters of this last series, are little more than suggestive, (far from being *exhaustive*), and that, as such, they are designed, not so much to convince, as to arouse to the thorough search which shall result in *self*-conviction, I trust you will prosecute the inquiry they institute, till, in your mind, it is fully *settled—practically* settled—either that God *will* "cast *off forever*," or that he will "*not.*" Nor, if you prosecute such inquiry with the earnestness and impartiality which its supreme importance demands, can I have any possible doubt of the result. Then am I confident that, *you*, too, shall yet see creation fraught with richer and higher glories, and that He, who nightly hangs out the stars "to tell us he resides above them all," can have no disposition to punish forever the children of his creation and care, "subjected to vanity, not willingly," and by whom this earth is continually evacuated and replenished.

Yours truly.

LETTER VI.

ORTHODOXY APPROACHING UNIVERSALISM.

Popularity cannot save error—Its decay gradual, but sure—What goes steadily to decay to be suspected—Inference, relative to Endless Punishment—Difference between Orthodoxy and Universalism—That difference *diminished*; 1, By the salvation of all infants; 2, By the salvation of children, and this in spite of the lagging creed; 3, By the salvation of heathen—Humanity hitherto nearly all heathen; Heart-revolt; Quotations from Mrs. H. B. Stowe; 4, Relatively few lost; Dr. N. Adams, Dr. L. Beecher, Lee, &c.; 5, Doubtful whether *any* are lost.—Welcome to Orthodoxy—The two Pyramids.—Another route of Orthodoxy towards Universalism—Dilution of Punishment—1, Punishment was in literal fire; Phlegethon directed into Paradise; Fire located; Pictures,—2, The Punishment of the wicked only as severe as *if* in fire; Clarke; Henry; Barnes; Relief Imaginary,—3, Punishment a merely natural consequence; Jehovah in alliance with the Devil; God the author of the *common* law of the universe; Relief still imaginary; How the soul reasons,—4, Punishment consistent with increasing felicity; This modification is *real*—Quotations from Knapp, with remarks upon—Queer!—How to believe in endless punishment, and be Universalists still!—The great gulf dwindled—Significance of Knapp's concessions—Relative relief of Annihilationists and Universalists—The burning mountain sinking.

DEAR BROTHER,—

If the difficulties, affectional, rational and biblical, presented in preceding letters, are more than imaginary, we should expect to see the doctrine that involves them, sinking into decay; for it must then be error. And we know that error, like the human body, has the sentence of death written in itself. No matter though it be "approved in senates, applauded in theatres, and sanctified in pulpits;" no matter though it be cherished as universally as was Judaism in Judea, in the times of Jesus; or Romanism in the times of Luther; still it is doomed to the waste-box of cast-off opinions. A monstrous birth of darkness, it must perish in the light, even though customs, creeds and philosophies provide for it a thousand "cities of refuge."

But the decay of error is generally gradual, and, like the furrows of time, stealthy. And so obnoxious is it to the wasting Providence of Almighty God, that it can know no rejuvenation, more permanent than that which age sometimes experiences, under the hands of the physician and the dentist.

Moreover, as it is the nature of error to decay, so whatever goes steadily into decay, under the increasing light of successive ages, may be justly suspected as not true; but, unlike truth, as possessing the elements of its own ultimate extinction. As, for instance, if the doctrine of endless punishment has been steadily wasting under the auspice of a rising Christian civilization, we have a right to infer that, as error, it will finally fail altogether;—that it is "of men, and will come to nought." So far, I think we are perfectly agreed.

But further, we have intimated that, in view of the difficulties which lie against the doctrine in question, it were natural to *look* for its decay. And now we will show that what we should thus naturally look for, exists in fact — that that doctrine *is* steadily going into decay; or, in other words, that the so-called Orthodox view of human salvation is steadily approaching Universalism, and promises ere long to reach it.

Now the practical difference between Orthodoxy and Universalism is, *the number which, by the former, are deemed lost.* Universalism says *all* will be saved. Orthodoxy says *all* will be saved, *minus* the number of the lost. Any diminution, therefore, of this minus quantity, is an equal diminution of the practical difference between the two systems of faith. For illustration, if x equal the whole human family, and y equal the part of it deemed lost, then we say,

$$\text{Universalism} = x.$$
$$\text{Orthodoxy} = x - y.$$

Now, obviously, if y means a *great* number, then is there a great difference between the two systems of faith. If a *small* number, a small difference. And in just such degree, as the value of y is diminished, do the two systems approach each other, while y has only to be reduced to *zero*, for them to meet and become one.

We now return to show that the doctrine of endless punishment has long been practically going to decay, or, in other words, that Orthodoxy has long been approaching Universalism. And,

1. When the church came out of the middle ages, the endless damnation of infants was fully believed in, and confidently justified by a simple appeal to the sovereignty of Jehovah. To deny it, was to deny that sovereignty, and, of course, a criminal heresy! At length, by assuming baptism as the new birth, relief was partially found in a few drops of water upon the dying infant's temples. A natural outgrowth of "total depravity," and "particular atonement," that doctrine prevailed down to the time of Calvin and later. But it has now nearly or quite faded away. And thus has Orthodoxy taken a long stride towards Universalism. For how numerous are the little ones of earth who tread with tiny feet, the silent chambers of the grave. All these, the church now lays to rest upon the bosom of the Father. To multitudes of these, once excluded, she now throws the gate of heaven widely open, and by so great a number is the value of y diminished, and Orthodoxy brought onward towards Universalism. And, further,

2. It was formerly holden, that most children who survive infancy, but still die at a tender age, are lost. And, taking the penal creed that was,

(or the Orthodox fossil creed that now is,) as the basis of our reasoning, so dreadful a conclusion is unavoidable. For we know that children sin at a very tender age, while it is obvious that they only very rarely experience anything like conversion, (as popularly understood,) while under a dozen years old. And so, nearly all who die from our primary schools, and from the very large class there represented, die into perdition.

So the creed. But creeds, we know, are always lagging far behind the Christian life of a progressive age. Perhaps, therefore, he spake advisedly, who said, it were better that they be changed occasionally.* Unless they are, they are likely to be repudiated, *practically*. For, to the mind on the march of improvement—to the heart swelling with the love of God—creeds are only as the "new-ropes" to Samson. And so it comes to pass, that whether by creed or in spite of it, the pulpits of to-day are preaching these young children into heaven, either directly, or by comforting mourners with the hope of meeting them there! And so here is another large class, now admitted to heaven, which was formerly excluded! So does Orthodoxy approach Universalism; even *so* that the two practically strike hands and walk together, from infancy up to about the age at which Jesus talked with the doc-

*H. W. Beecher. We do not give his words.

tors in the temple. Thus is the value of y in our algebraic illustration, sunk still further down towards *zero*. But further still,

3. It was formerly holden that the heathen of all times and climes were lost. And, according to the popular credal view of probation and punishment, they certainly are. For nothing is plainer than that they die unregenerate. But how is it to-day? Why, so does that doctrine contravene the spirit of the Scriptures and grate upon sensibilities, educated and refined by Christianity, that it is rapidly going the way of all false opinion. The church that was obliged to cast away the dogma of the endless damnation of infants of "two years old and under," — infants in *days*, — is now finding the same necessity for casting away the dogma of the damnation of infants in *knowledge*. And so it comes to pass that comparatively little is said about it, even by professed believers in it, in their very pleadings for the missionary cause. Rather do they, more generally, seek, like Universalists, to move the hearts of their hearers, by portraying the temporal miseries of the poor pagans, children of nature, hastening "after other gods" — rather do they tell us as well they may, of moral pollution, human sacrifice, infanticide, and widow-burning; while the supposed eternal calamity of the fossil creed, is but barely alluded to, passed over with a word.

Up to within less than two thousand years ago, the little oasis of Judea excepted, this was, exclusively, *a heathen world*. The swarming multitudes of old historic and traditionary ages, perishing along the centuries, by disease, famine, pestilence and battle, have sanctified every field and forest and wild nook of earth, with the sprinkling of hostile blood, and left their dust to mingle in all its mountains, plains and valleys. Now of all these, the fossil creed disposes fearfully. But against that disposal, the intelligent Christian heart revolts, and the more *intensly* Christian, the deeper the revolt.* And so it comes to pass, that, if the church of to-day, does not boldly throw open the door of hope and heaven to the ignorant heathen, it forbears to close it against them as formerly — if it does not

*This is well illustrated by Mrs. Stowe's narrative of a conversation between her pure minded and refined "Agnes" and her good-hearted, but coarse and unlettered "Jocunda." The latter may well represent the church as it was, the former the church as it is becoming. In setting forth a colloquy between the two, the authoress, who is doing the most to unsettle and overturn the theology that makes many an "Agnes" shudder, says:—

"Agnes abstractedly stooped and began plucking handfuls of lycopodium, which as growing green and feathery on one side of the marble frieze on which she was sitting; in so doing, a fragment of white marble, which had been overgrown in the luxuriant green, appeared to view. It was that frequent object in the Italian soil, — a portion of an old Roman tomb stone. Agnes bent over, intent on the mystic '*Dis Manibus*,' in old Roman letters.

'Lord bless the child! I've seen thousands of them,' said Joset the heathen down to the account of salvation, it erases them from the account of despair; thus bringing Orthodoxy still farther on towards Universalism—sending the value of y, farther down towards *zero*. So does the doctrine of endless woe, languish rapidly towards nought. And yet further,

4. It is now openly proclaimed by bold advocates of the doctrine in review, that the lost will be relatively few, — bearing only about the proportion to the saved, which the number of the imprisoned, on earth, bears to the number at large. So its late advocate, the Rev. Dr. Adams of Boston. The same I have heard affirmed of Dr. Lyman Beecher,— a

cunda; 'it's some old heathen's grave, that's been in hell these hundred years.'

'In hell?' said Agnes, with a distressful accent.

'Of course,' said Jocunda. 'Where should they be? Serves 'em right, too; they were a vile old set.'

'Oh, Jocunda, it's dreadful to think of, that they should have been in hell all this time.'

'And no nearer the end than when they began,' said Jocunda.

Agnes gave a shivering sigh, and looking up into the golden sky that was pouring such floods of splendor through the orange-trees and jasmines, thought, How could it be that the world could possibly be going on so sweet and fair over such an abyss.

'Oh, Jocunda!' said she, 'it does seem *too* dreadful to believe! How could they help being heathen,—being born so,—and never hearing of the true Church?'

'Sure enough,' said Jocunda, spinning away energetically, 'but that's no business of mine; my business is to save *my* soul, and that's what I came here for.' "

Old Jocundas' are rapidly giving place to young Agnes'.

circumstance, in view of which, we are less surprised at the heart that breathes in the "Minister's Wooing," and at that other great heart, which "leaps at every pulsation sixty degrees beyond the logical limits of its creed." The same view was recently affirmed to me by an orthodox clergyman. It is adopted by Lee in his late work entitled Eschatology. It evidently prevails.

Now, not to stop to show that the Bible teaches the destruction of the masses, just as clearly as it teaches the destruction of so much as one soul, and that, therefore, to prove that one will be lost is to prove that the *masses* will, it is enough that we remark that, here again Orthodoxy makes another stride towards Universalism,—almost reaching it—reducing the value of y almost *down* to *zero*. But finally,

5. Whether any soul will be endlessly miserable, is beginning to be seriously questioned by not a few, deemed orthodox. A few months ago, an able orthodox clergyman affirmed to me that the duration of punishment "was no matter of faith." And the spirit of this remark lies at the bottom of that other remark, so often heard, "*I don't trouble myself about the dead. God will do right by them.*" Surely such a remark would be perfectly idle upon the lips of one who really believed that the Bible positively fixed the doom of the wicked in woe forever.

And thus it is that the hitherto dominant sects, following hard in the wake of Unitarianism, are rapidly entering the deepening twilight of the full day of Universalism. We see them coming with banners all flying! The voice of their music is in our ears! We hail them as brethren, and bid them advance to our heartiest welcome!

Thus singularly is orthodoxy doing what it "would not." Thus is its *y* of distinction from Universalism going down to *zero*. Thus is its heaven constantly enlarging, and its hell diminishing. And to all appearance, the latter must ere long reach the vanishing point. It is a pyramid, built up in darkness, which the church finds ever becoming smaller as she ascends with the ascent of Christian civilization. By and by, she will reach its apex, soar above it, ignore her old barbaric creed, and know a pit of endless woe, no more forever." Not so *heaven*. That is an *inverted* pyramid, broadening as the church ascends, and to continue to broaden, till it shall fill the whole horizon and be lost in clouds of living light.

At the opening of this letter, we remarked that we should naturally look for the decay of any doctrine against which lay the difficulties mentioned in preceding letters. We have now seen the justness of that remark as *practically illustrated* in the decay of the doctrine of endless punishment,— a decay, from which we justly infer its ultimate extinction. An inference which we think future years will also practically illustrate.

But we pass to notice, briefly as possible, another route to the above happy conclusion. Having seen orthodoxy steadily approaching Universal salvation, by its steady *diminution of the number* of the lost, let us now behold its steady movement in the same direction, as indicated by its constant *dilution* of the punishment which the lost are believed to suffer.

1. The church came out of the dark ages believing that the wicked must forever burn literally in "fire and brimstone," so sustained of God, that they should be forever, like the bush on the back side of Sinai, unconsumed. As darkness came brooding over the church, the heathen *Phlegethon* — river of fire — was diverted from *Tartarus* into the *Bible-sheol*, and made to inundate paradise with its burning flood. And, this done, it was seriously speculated, whether the *scene* of endless torments would not be where Geologists look down through fissures in the earth's crust upon its central fires.* But speculations aside, this literal view of endless punishment was formerly holden co-extensively with the Gospel, and proclaimed by both preaching and pictures. Describing the reception

* Rome is said to have located Hell fifteen thousand miles beneath the surface of the earth; that is, seven thousand miles beyond the opposite side.

of "Father Allouez among the Chippawas," in the seventeenth century, Bancroft says: "their admiring throngs who had never seen a European, came to gaze on the white man, and on the pictures which he displayed of *the realms of hell* and of the *last judgment*."

So it was. But not so now. The element of literal penal fire has departed, and with it, so much of the intensity of endless pain as depended upon it. And, whatever other elements of woe remain, the absence of literal fire, it would seem, must leave it greatly reduced. But further,

2. When the light had so deepened upon the church, that the notion of literal penal fire faded from the creed like a phosphorescent hand-writing from a wall, still was she found holding that the pains of the lost would be as excruciating as though in fire. Hence, Clarke, after quoting all the most horrible, from *Milton*, the *Institutes of Menu*, and the *Zend Avesta*, exclaims, "And is this or anything as bad as this, *hell!* Yes, and *worse* than the worst of all that has already been mentioned! * Hence also, Matthew Henry says of the wicked, "the agonies and terrors of the first death will consign them over to the far greater agonies and terrors of eternal death; to die, and be always dying."† Hence, too, Barnes says, "they [the wicked] will

* Com. vol. v., p. 87. † Com.

be doomed to a punishment which will be well represented by their lingering in a sea of fire forever."*

Such was endless punishment, with the fiery element eliminated from it. And its elimination was a step of true progress. For it indicated an awakening of the church's intellect and heart, and under it, for a time, Christian humanity breathed easier. But its rest could not be long. For the people of God soon awoke to the fact that, though the *fires* of perdition had been extinguished, it still held in its bosom other infernal agencies, if possible still more tormenting, and not less violative of the character of the God of the Bible. And thus, finding that the ground of their relief had been only imaginary, their hearts again cried out for the Father. For they felt that, unless man's consciousness is a lie, and God's handwriting upon his heart a forgery, the doctrine of such a doom for the masses must be false. And then, turning to the Scriptures, they found it perfectly safe to make another remove towards Universalism, and made it. This done, they *again* breathe easier.

3. By this second modification of endless woe at the call of Bible-humanity, the *positive* element is taken from it;—it is made to be a mere natural consequence of sin, which the sinner forever suffers, just because he chooses forever to sin. This view is

* Com. on Rev. xx. 15.

plausible, and has brought relief to thousands, and thousands are finding an *indifferent* rest in it to-day. "For," say they, "God does not *inflict* punishment; he merely leaves the sinner to choose sin if he will. The sinner, freely choosing it, must not complain of its consequences; nor need we complain for him."

But even this modification, reached by necessity, must by necessity be abandoned. For it leaves the doctrine of doom no less terrible than it finds it, while it equally compromises the Divine character. For they who hold it, tell us, as they needs must, that, from the wicked dead, God withdraws all means of grace,—thus virtually excluding them from all good influences, and shutting them up to all bad ones. Or, if it does not make Jehovah drive sinners *into* the pit, it makes him so subject them to *only* evil influences, as to render their escape from it impossible;—so that, if there is a personal devil, it is as though Jehovah had struck an alliance with him to guard off penitence from the realms of woe forever.

So it is then, that after all, this notion of endless woe, as a natural consequence of sin, involves, in its last analysis, the essence of all that is appalling in the severest *Edwardian* theology. For, literalize the fiery Scriptures as you will, you cannot make out a case of anguish more extreme than that of an immortal soul doomed, by the withdrawal of all means of grace, to go farther and farther from God, —sink deeper and deeper in despair forever. Nor is it any relief to the loving soul, to know that God's immortal children perish by the common law of his realm, rather than by positive statute. For the two are equally Jehovah's *positive enactments*. All law of sin is of God, — all the pain of transgression, visited upon the transgressor, is penalty. It may be convenient for us to call it sometimes by one name, and sometimes by another, but it is always equally judicial and statutory, in God's sight. So that what has been called the *natural tendency of sin*, is God's will, embodied in legal enactment, no less than was the positive edict by which Cain was a fugitive, Sodom was overthrown, and Annanias and Sapphira died, or, that by which it has been believed sinners will, in the future world, be driven from the judgment seat. And the relief, therefore, which this modification of endless punishments affords, is only seeming. And soon the truly intelligent Christian heart must penetrate through its disguise to its essential horror, by reasoning something in this wise: "If the lost soul retrogress, then, the sensibilities of the victim, gradually blunted, must, eventually, go into perfect decay, and therefore suffering, cease altogether — *not be endless*. Remain stationary, the lost soul cannot, unless miraculously petrified, like the fugitive from Sodom. Whereas, if it progress, its sufferings must increase with the increase of its susceptibility. Any way, therefore, *endless* punishment must set all human language, however burning or freezing, at complete defiance." And thus completely overwhelmed with a conclusion which so belies all human consciousness, and blots the character of God, relief demands another modification; and the heart turning to the Scriptures, finds another warrantable. It is this; that,

4. Endless punishment is not necessarily endless *misery*, but may be only the endless *loss* of a *higher state of felicity*.

Under this modification, the man who sins is, thereby, thrown back, and can never be as happy, at any point of time afterwards, as he would have been, had he never sinned. And *this* modification of endless punishment is *real*, impinging upon the borders of Universalism — nay *is* Universalism; and this, notwithstanding it makes *all* men suffer forever!

Something like the above view would seem to be a necessary *step* in Christian progress towards the Father. And hence it was perhaps, that it suggested itself so vividly to the pioneer theologian, Dr. George Christian Knapp, as expressed in his "Christian theology," translated by President Woods, D. D., and used as a text book in our Orthodox seminaries. Speaking of natural punishments, the Dr. says;

"As every action, morally good, is followed by endless good consequences to him who performs it, so it is with every wrong action. This is founded in the wise constitution of things, which God himself has established. When, therefore, *natural* punishments are spoken of, it is obvious to reason how an eternal duration of them may be affirmed. Indeed, reason cannot conceive it to be otherwise, since there is no promise of God, either in the holy Scriptures or elsewhere, that the natural·evil consequences of sins *once committed*, will ever cease. In order to do this, there must be some incomprehensible miracle performed, and this God has not promised to do. Hence, as far as natural punishments are concerned, their eternal duration may be affirmed both on grounds of Scripture and reason."—*Christian Theology*, Sec. 158.

Here then, we have one law for all; and by that law, all, whether good or bad, both suffer *endless punishment*, and receive *endless reward*! This may seem queer, but (to requote,) "reason cannot conceive it to be otherwise, since there is no promise of God, either in the Scriptures or elsewhere, that the natural evil consequences of sin, *once committed* will ever cease;" while "every action morally good is followed by endless good consequences." And it is just as evident that so called bad men perform some actions, "morally good," as it is that so called good men, perform some actions morally bad. But the doctor, having spoken thus of *natural* punishments, proceeds to speak of those which are termed *positive*, and among other things says:

"With regard to these, we may conceive that they may be removed; indeed, much can be said on grounds of reason, to render this opinion *probable*. To hope that God would remove the positive punishments of sins, in case the sinner, even in the future life, should come to the knowledge of himself, and truly repent, would seem to be agreeable to the divine goodness and justice. That the repentance of the sinner in the future world is absolutely impossible, *is not taught in the Scriptures*."

First, Then, according to the doctor, the belief that the sinner will repent in the future world, is neither unreasonable nor *absolutely* (a valueless word here) unscriptural. And

Second, It is "agreeable to the divine goodness and justice, to hope that in case of his repentance, God would remove the positive punishments of [his] sins." And proceeding to remark upon this supposition the Dr. further says:

"But allowing that positive punishments may be wholly removed from one who may have actually repented, still, the natural evil consequences of sin will not, therefore, of necessity, come to an end. [We have already heard the doctor say they *cannot* without an incomprehensible miracle.] These may, indeed, become more light and tolerable to one who has repented, but even such an one can never be happy in the same degree, as another who has never sinned. Such an one will always stand on a lower point of happiness than others, and there will always be a great gulf fixed between him and them."

Thus does our learned divine show how, without positively violating the Scriptures, the doctrine of endless misery may be so holden as very little to disturb the sensitive benevolent heart. It may only mean the being a little *behind* in climbing the hills of light,—only what *all* suffer! Why, Paul taught long ago, that in the resurrection "one star differeth from another star in glory."

And then, the "*great gulf*," across which it has long been said, the saved will hail their lost friends in torment, comes at last to mean only that in the future world, some, because of their sinful truancy in this, will be forever a little behind the more studious of their class.

Knapp died in eighteen hundred and twenty-five. And considering his position as professor of theology in one of the most learned Orthodox universities in the world, and that Dr. Woods, his translator, let the facts we have quoted pass without notes, we can hardly over estimate the significance of the above concessions. They seem equivalent to saying that Universalism is not *forbidden* by either reason or Scripture. They indicate the great moral difficulty with which their author saw his creed involved, and against which he maintained his adhesion to it. Seeming to have heard the tread of a more heavenly theology, advancing with the advance of Christian culture, he carefully taught how it might be welcomed, without any change in the *language* of the old creed — how all could be Universalists and believe in endless punishment still. And great numbers, profiting from Knapp's shrewd suggestion, having abandoned endless punishment in fact, are still holding to it in name; while others, seeing the folly of attempting to make a Bible doctrine of endless punishment consist with endless felicity, *further* modify their creed by casting that doctrine away, *name and all*. Some of these latter are called Universalists, some Restorationists, and some Unitarians, while others of them are scattered numerously and, perhaps, namelessly among all the congregations and sects of enlightened Christendom. And while they agree with the annihilationist in rejecting endless punishment, the relief they experience, compared with his, is as the flower-garden, compared with the wolf's den — as the rainbow, compared with the cloud it spans — as paradise, compared with paradise burned over — as consistency, compared with absurdity — as heaven, compared with hell! Indeed the relief the latter finds is complete! Our discussion here rests in the joy of it.

To conclude this letter, let us just reflect that we have seen the decay of endless punishment, (forestalled by its absurdities and unscripturalness,) actually taking place; or, that we have seen Orthodoxy rapidly approaching Universalism by two different ways:

1. By a steady diminution of the number of the lost; and

2. By the elimination of the elements of suffering from endless punishment, till it has become consistent with *ever increasing, immortal glory!*

Thus, under the increasing light of heaven, have we watched the subsidence of the burning mountain. Nor, from present appearances, should we deem it could be long, before its volcanic head shall be hidden beneath the level of the plain. And then shall the churches practically see in God, "the everlasting Father," and in Christ "the Prince of an eventually universal peace!" Then shall the notion that any of the Father's immortal offsprings shall lie forever under his wrath, be as foreign to the universal mind, as are now any of the old theological barbarisms which were once popular, which it once was heresy to question, but which now lie deep buried beneath the execrations of an advanced Christian culture. *Amen! Alleluia!*

Yours truly.

LETTER VII.

REACTION.

emarkable admission—Why the more so—*How* reaction—Strong statement of *Lebbeus Brooks*—When shall reaction begin?—No sign of it among the *clergy*, but the contrary—No sign of it among the *laity*—Why the seeming apathy of the laity?—How reaction seems alone possible—"FOOTPRINTS HEAVENWARD" *forever!*

DEAR BROTHER,—

"In the course of the next thirty years Orthodoxy will reach Universalism, provided it shall continue to approach it as it has during the past thirty years." So I said to an able Orthodox clergyman a few months ago, when he admitted the justness of the remark, but thought there would "be a reaction."

Now had the past thirty years been years of darkness — a sort of middle age in miniature — such an admission from such a source were the less surprising. But when it is considered that those years have been years of increasing light, and, consequently, of rapid progress in whatever is ennobling to humanity, then the fact that the currents of theology have set so steadily and strongly in the direction of Universalism, may well startle the Orthodox masses, as we have seen it does the "*New York Observer*;" for it evidently forestalls what the Observer deprecates as a "*catastrophe.*"

Reaction! Does the glorious sun at high morning, retire backwards through his auroral gate? Shall civilization fall back again to brood error beneath the shades of another mediæval night? The conquests which the church has made by thinking, shall she lose by thinking? Certainly if such a reaction is to come, "we see not our signs." The liberal tendency of the age is so set, that, to all appearances, nothing short of a miracle can change or stay it.

And here I may well feel reminded of one of the purest-hearted and clearest-minded Christians* of the age, who, smitten down in his meridian, left behind the following in his sick-bed testimony. I quote it here as clothed with no other or higher authority, than that which attaches to the deduction of pure, calm, discriminating Christian minds, wrapt in holy contemplation, and treading without fear or prejudice, the border lands of eternity. Thus he spake,—

"I have long been thinking that a few years only will suffice to sweep away the the popular theology upon the subject of endless punishment, — that all

* Lebbeus Brooks.

our common schools are but so many volcanoes underneath it — that it must be abandoned, or we must go back to the age of unthinking barbarism." *

So had he long been thinking; and his thoughts were certainly in perfect keeping with the tendencies of the age,—tendencies which are constantly being strengthened by such under currents of strong Christian thought. And it is only because our common schools—the best exponents of Christian civilization,—are multiplying thinkers, that they are so dangerous to false theology. The genius of Christianity will stand by them, as the ancient vestal Virgin by her altar. So shall the world *not* "go back to the age of unthinking barbarism." But, in reference to endless misery, she must either stop thinking, or stop believing. Stop thinking, she cannot; stop believing, she must. But it takes time to stop believing. A train of belief, like a train of cars, cannot be broken up in a moment. But I think the dominant churches, conscious of running out of time, and fearful of being thrown off upon the rocks of infidelity, by a collision with the *up-train* of Scripture and common sense, are gradually putting down the brakes, reducing the speed to a minimum, and will ere long reverse the steam.

But, to return, if we are to have the anticipated reaction, it must begin *somewhere.* May we expect it to begin among the *clergy?* That can hardly be,

* From my journal.

seeing that they, as a body, are everywhere evincing less and less of *hearty* confidence in the decaying dogma. So much is abundantly manifest in their neighborhood intercourse, parochial visiting, and pulpit discourse. We do not set this down, however, as *against* them, but only as a fact. Their true "zeal for the Lord," now more "according to knowledge," may be unabated, and even increasing, notwithstanding. But we can hardly expect the anticipated reaction to begin among them. Where then shall it begin? Among the *laity?* This also seems equally improbable, seeing, that among them also, ("like people like priest,") the doctrine in question is wasting with the advance of intelligence.

It is not very long since I heard an excellent clergyman remark, sadly, that "it is now almost impossible to arouse a church to labor earnestly for a revival." But why so nearly impossible? Is it because the brethren have lost their humanity? because their sympathies have congealed? because they are "given up to hardness of heart?" This can hardly be; seeing that they were never readier, than now, to minister relief to any and all forms of obvious suffering. Nor do we think conscientiousness, and love to God and man, were ever more predominant in their hearts. Why then this deplored apathy—this indisposition to enter zealously into the old forms of endeavor to snatch souls from endless woe? Can it be because they have ceased to regard the command, "Go work to-day in my vineyard?" Evidently not. For never was there more putting forth of intelligent Christian effort, than at this day. Never was man's duty to his God better understood and more practically regarded than now; and never was the spirit of the parable of the good Samaritan more widely shed abroad.

Why then, we again ask, this deplored apathy of the laity? The answer is easy. The laity, *too*, have become skeptical of what was the chief motive to their former zeal and activity in the direction indicated. Time was, when the minister had but to "uncap hell," and the church were in tears of sorrow and pity. But not so now. Now, when, as rarely occurs, the minister preaches an old-fashioned sermon about "wrath to come," the people are little moved, or moved only to admiration of the pathos with which he describes it, and the logic with which he proves it, rather than by any fear of suffering it. And this, not because they have lost the instinct of self-preservation, but simply because they do not believe in the *danger*. And not believing in it, of course they are not moved to rescue their fellow beings from it, but find other more rational, and Scriptural methods of doing them good. And so, among the laity, as among the clergy, we see nothing to indicate the anticipated reaction. And even if we *did*, we see not how it could transpire, in the teeth of the absurdities and Bible-difficulties partly set forth in preceding letters.

Had the essential unbelief in endless punishment, so manifest everywhere throughout the churches, been induced under some *panic*, we might well apprehend reaction from it under some *counter*-panic. But, being only the gradual work of enlightened progressive, Christian thinking, reaction seems out of the question. Or, it would seem capable of taking place, if at all, only through some mighty revolution in things which we are entirely unable to anticipate —only through some sweeping away of the present civilization of Christendom, like that which debased Egypt and the Holy Land, or like that which repeatedly exterminated those old forms of pre-Adamite existence, whose awful record, the geologist deciphers upon the charred tablets of our crusted globe.

But no such thing do we anticipate. Nor do we see how any one can, who understands, either God's image within him, or God's word to him, or the signs of the times around him. Sooner should we expect to go from Christ back to Moses, and thence backward still, *by* the patriarchs, and *through* the six days labor into the chaos of things, when the "Earth was without form and void, and darkness was on the face of the deep."

But no! Christian civilization shall not "go back to the age of unthinking barbarism." The church shall not retrace her "FOOTPRINTS HEAVENWARD." Her cause shall be ever onward towards the grand goal of humanity, divinely fixed in the Universal Brotherhood and Fatherhood. This may be lamented by the bigoted and the ignorant. But a necessity of man's head and heart, a demand of the sacred Scriptures, it cannot be stayed. It is but the grand march of man's eternity,

Nearer, my God, to thee!
Nearer to thee!

Brother, my letters are before you. And now, wishing you "grace, mercy, and peace from God our Father, and the Lord Jesus Christ," I have only to repeat the apostolic injunction, "think on these things," and again subscribe myself,

Yours truly.

ERRATA.

The reader will please mark these, some of which are the following:—

For either, read ether, page 60; for intentions, read intuitions, page 85; for It is, read Is it, page 92; for is the language, read is *not* the language, page 105; for letters, read latter, page 126; for casts, read creates, page 130; for inseparable, read irreparable, page 138; for helpless, read hopeless, page 165; for held, read hold, page 167; for or, read in, page 174; for shook, read shaken, page 144; for tolerated, read tolerable, page 205; for or, read of, page 205; for too, read so, page 219; for are completely, read are *not* completely, page 244; for one, read our, page 250; for graves, read grave, page 373.

www.ingramcontent.com/pod-product-compliance
Lightning Source LLC
LaVergne TN
LVHW020108110826
845151LV00001B/100

9781425543891